THE GIRLFRIEND

GEMMA ROGERS

B
Boldwood

First published in Great Britain in 2026 by Boldwood Books Ltd.

Copyright © Gemma Rogers, 2026

Cover Design by Judge By My Covers

Cover Images: Depositphotos and iStock

The moral right of Gemma Rogers to be identified as the author of this work has been asserted in accordance with the Copyright, Designs and Patents Act 1988.

All rights reserved. No part of this book may be reproduced in any form or by any electronic or mechanical means, including information storage and retrieval systems, without written permission from the author, except for the use of brief quotations in a book review. This book is a work of fiction and, except in the case of historical fact, any resemblance to actual persons, living or dead, is purely coincidental.

Every effort has been made to obtain the necessary permissions with reference to copyright material, both illustrative and quoted. We apologise for any omissions in this respect and will be pleased to make the appropriate acknowledgements in any future edition.

A CIP catalogue record for this book is available from the British Library.

Paperback ISBN 978-1-80600-437-9

Large Print ISBN 978-1-80600-436-2

Hardback ISBN 978-1-80600-435-5

Trade Paperback ISBN 978-1-80635-114-5

Ebook ISBN 978-1-80600-438-6

Kindle ISBN 978-1-80600-439-3

Audio CD ISBN 978-1-80600-430-0

MP3 CD ISBN 978-1-80600-431-7

Digital audio download ISBN 978-1-80600-433-1

This book is printed on certified sustainable paper. Boldwood Books is dedicated to putting sustainability at the heart of our business. For more information please visit https://www.boldwoodbooks.com/about-us/sustainability/

Boldwood Books Ltd, 23 Bowerdean Street, London, SW6 3TN

www.boldwoodbooks.com

For the 'Best Little Gang Ever!!!'
Thank you for keeping me sane.

1

When the email arrived that changed everything, I'd been sitting at my desk for an hour, gazing out of the window at the bus stop opposite the studio, watching drizzle dampen the commuters huddled beneath. It was a dreary Monday in early March, and I needed to finish a commission for a house portrait I'd been working on. The project was an uninspiring two-bedroom mid-terrace and the photo I'd been sent barely had any colour in it, just muted browns and beiges. I wanted to paint a cherry blossom tree in their front garden or brighten the bricks from their dull shade, but that wasn't what the customer had ordered. They'd purchased an A4 replica portrait in watercolour.

I couldn't complain, my business, Edgewater, was flourishing, with new orders arriving every day since a popular influencer had raved about one of my portraits on her Instagram story. She'd sent in a photo of her house – or rather a mansion with pillars by the front door. I hadn't known who she was, too old for her target demographic, but she'd ordered an A3 on canvas – the most expensive commission I offered. Once received, she'd posted it everywhere, exclaiming Abbi Montgomery's portraits were amazing and to check out Edgewater, giving me loads of free exposure to her hundreds of thousands of followers. Orders had flooded in, which meant I could take on less of the freelance design projects I'd been relying on for income over the past two years and concentrate on doing what I loved, creating bespoke portraits of places or buildings that meant something to people.

A sound from my laptop distracted me from the window and I wiggled my mouse to wake the sleeping screen, wishing it was as easy for me to spring to life this morning despite the coffee I'd consumed. The email itself was innocuous, and at first, it looked like spam. The address gogetter@gmail.com didn't raise alarm bells and there was nothing in the subject to indicate what it contained. I assumed it was another potential customer asking for a quote for a wedding venue portrait as those too had been common in recent weeks.

However, when I opened it, scanning the text which jumped out, shouting in uppercase, the small studio I rented seemed to shift and adjust around me. My fingers splayed out across the keyboard, taking on a tremor as blood swam faster in my veins.

> ABBI,
> TELL ANYONE OR CONTACT THE POLICE AND I WILL RELEASE THIS VIDEO TO EVERY SOCIAL MEDIA PLATFORM INSTANTLY.
> I'LL BE IN TOUCH, AND DON'T FORGET, I'M ALWAYS WATCHING.
> YOUR FRIEND

The link was a URL I didn't recognise, one that had likely been shortened. Normally, I would never click on an unknown link in an email, especially from a stranger. It was the first rule of internet safety, phishing was rife, but the email had been addressed to me personally. Even the spelling of my name was correct – an i at the end of Abbi instead of a y.

I hovered my mouse over the link, anxiety leaving a lead weight in my belly. What had I done – or, rather, been recorded doing – that someone could blackmail me for? Either way, it was ominous; the threat of not going to the police had sent my blood pressure skyrocketing.

Steeling myself, I clicked the link, which opened a web page with a photo filling the screen, a still image captured from a video that thankfully didn't play but had an instant impact. My hand flew to my mouth, tears blurring my vision as I took in the scene. It was my boyfriend Rick's bedroom, the walls painted Edgewater blue – a colour so pretty I'd named my new business after it. The shot looked as though it had been taken from the doorway of his en suite bathroom, a full view of the bed and rumpled white sheets, on which I sat astride Rick, naked amidst the throes of passionate sex.

A volcano erupted in my chest. What the hell! Despite my reaction being delayed by the initial shock, I scooted back from the desk as though I'd been stung, gasping for breath.

I stared at the screen in utter horror, as the image of the woman swam before my eyes. Head raised to the ceiling, dark ruby red curls cascading narrow shoulders, the arch of the spine and tiny dimples of a backside which melted onto Rick's thighs, left me in no doubt I was staring at myself.

My face scorched, brain taking over and switching first to denial and then disaster recovery mode. You couldn't see my face, or barely any of Rick for that matter, only his hairy legs and size ten feet, arms outstretched about to snake around my hips to guide me up and down, riding him to climax. The shame rained down upon me like shards of glass.

No one ever could see this photo. But it wasn't just a photo, was it. I steeled myself before clicking uselessly on the image, but it didn't animate. In the email, they'd said it was a video, did that mean they had footage of me and Rick having sex? How long was the video, a ten second clip or the full extent, and when was this? I stared at that screen, trying again to convince myself it wasn't me in the picture despite knowing it was.

Shit, shit, shit! Vomit forced its way up my throat, and I jolted up from the chair, the wheels leaving grooves in the fluffy rug, barely making it to the bin before throwing up the overnight oats I'd eaten for breakfast.

I dashed to the bathroom down the corridor, carrying the bin, almost knocking into Linda who ran a pottery business from the other studio.

'You okay, Abbi?' she called as I dodged her.

I raised a hand, unable to speak for fear I might throw up again and bolted through the door to the sink. Sweat beaded at my hairline, a ghostly reflection staring back from the mirror, a rabbit caught in headlights. I looked away, mortification shining its spotlight over me, and washed out the bin, forcing the sludgy mixture down the plughole.

'Must have been something I ate,' I managed when the door swung open and Linda stood frowning at me. I gave her a weak smile, trying not to cry.

'You don't think you're...' She pointed at my stomach, her eyes glinting.

'No, no, definitely not.' My gut churned at the thought.

Your mother is a whore who was posted all over the internet having sex. I imagined the bullies my unborn child would have to suffer years from now and winced. Who would do this to me, violate me in such a disgusting way? It was abhorrent.

'Sorry, I'm in the middle of something; I better get back to it.' I squeezed through the gap Linda had left between her and the open door, catching disappointment cloud her features at my lack of gossip.

'This came for you.' She pushed the jiffy bag into my hand as I passed, and I muttered my thanks. I didn't have time to deal with her today, there were far more pressing issues, namely what the hell did the sender of the email want in exchange for not sharing the video.

I struggled to catch my breath, the enormity of the situation crushing my lungs like a vice. How on earth had they got it? Had someone snuck into his penthouse and planted a camera, because it couldn't be Rick, not in a million years. He'd never do something so seedy. Even if he wanted to film us, he'd ask permission first and he wouldn't email me a screenshot.

I cringed as soon as I entered the studio, my naked behind still displayed on the laptop for anyone to see if they walked in. Thank goodness Linda hadn't followed me back from the bathroom. I took a photo on my phone in case, for some reason, the link disappeared, and closed the web page, reading the email repeatedly. The dull mid-terrace commission now forgotten, as I searched for some clue to who this was, what they wanted and why they were doing this. It had to be blackmail, there was no other reason, but why hadn't I been given any demands?

If the video or even the picture ended up on the internet, it had the potential to ruin me. It would destroy the business I'd recently established, my good name would be in tatters and I wouldn't be able to leave the house, let alone face my parents.

Oh my God, my parents. Panic consumed me and I forced myself to breathe deeply, in through my nose and out through my mouth, before rummaging in my bag for my phone. Rick had to know; it affected him too. It might only be his legs and feet on display, not massively easy to identify, but I was sure he didn't want to become an overnight sensation either. The photo could ruin both of our lives.

Rick worked as an account director for a wine subscription merchants, receiving impressive bonuses and, to be fair, he did well for himself. He was ten years older than me and earned enough to afford a penthouse apartment near Crawley train station. My own lodgings were shabby by comparison. A one-bedroom flat in a small block, it was the top floor, but by no means penthouse standard, which was why I spent more time at Rick's than I did at home. I'd only had it for a year, moving in two months before I met Rick at a bar in town. It had taken me ages to save the deposit and three months' rent despite my parents' help. I guessed, at twenty-four, the age I'd finally moved out, they were happy to get their life back as my younger brother Ben was already living abroad as a holiday rep in Turkey.

My fingers hovered over Rick's number. He'd left early this morning, driving to Farnborough to meet a potential client and would likely be right in the middle of his meeting now. I'd barely managed to mumble a goodbye, so exhausted I'd passed out on the sofa the night before and Rick had carried me to bed. I dialled, listening to it ring before voicemail kicked in and I hung up.

Glancing back at the laptop, the harsh capital letters seemed to jump out at me from the screen where I'd left the email open. *I'M ALWAYS WATCHING, YOUR FRIEND.* Whoever they were, they were no friend of mine.

Were they watching now? Was there a camera planted somewhere in the studio? I got up, looking through my paints, brushes, the paperwork on my desk, rifling through shelves lined with art books, but had no idea what I was looking for. I spent five minutes examining a tiny round metal item on the floor until I worked out it wasn't a bugging device but a screw cover which had fallen off the desk.

I sighed, a knot woven so tightly in my chest it wouldn't give. There was nothing to do but wait for further instructions because they wanted something in exchange for keeping my sex tape off the internet. What if there were more? What if this was just the beginning? Never mind the multitude of other crimes the perpetrator was committing – breaking and entering, filming someone without their consent at the top of the list potentially with extortion and blackmail to follow – none of those things mattered right now because they had me over a barrel, there was nothing I wouldn't do in exchange for that recording.

2

'Feeling better, love?' Linda poked her head around the door of the studio later, making me jump, coming in to hand me a steaming peppermint tea. She was an attractive, curvy woman with a perfectly round face and consistently red-apple cheeks no matter the temperature. Always wearing tent-like flowing outfits, covered in splatters of clay, I aged her in her early forties, although I'd never asked.

'Yes,' I lied, 'thanks for the tea.' I took it from her and went back to wrapping the completed terraced house watercolour. 'I'm finally finished.'

'Was it a fun one?' Linda asked, hovering to take a look.

'Not really.' I held up the uninspiring photo I'd been sent of the house, and she grimaced, deflating like a punctured balloon.

'Oh.'

'Exactly,' I sighed, 'but I've got a gorgeous one coming up next month, a wedding portrait – the church, that is, not the bride and groom, and it'll be much prettier.' I brushed my wayward fringe out of my eyes and tried to smile, hiding how terrified I was on the inside.

Despite the email, I'd managed to finish the portrait today. A couple of hours ago, it hadn't seemed possible, and I'd considered running away, but the thought of going back to Rick's apartment, where there might be cameras, had kept me firmly in my chair. Thankfully, there hadn't been a lot to do on the commission, just finishing touches, as my hands had taken on a tremor since the email had come in.

'Sorry about earlier.' She pointed at my flat stomach, hidden beneath baggy denim dungarees. 'I shouldn't have said anything.' Linda's chin bloomed the same colour as her cheeks.

'Oh, no worries.' It had been a personal question, but I hadn't given it a second thought, not with what was going on. Linda could be abrupt at times, but I'd come to understand it was part of her personality.

She stared at me, a wistful look in her kohl-rimmed eyes, and for a second I imagined she was the blackmailer.

'I just thought, what beautiful babies you'd make, you and that handsome fella of yours.' Linda giggled and I let the air escape my lungs.

'It's early days for that; we've not been together a year yet. Rick hasn't even asked me to move in,' I replied, the words cloying as they left my lips. I'd said too much, exposing my true feelings while trying to pretend everything was normal. But I was at Rick's practically every night, so maybe he didn't feel as though he needed to make it official. He was almost perfect, kind, thoughtful and funny, but I got the impression he wasn't ready to commit despite him only being a few years away from the big four-oh.

Perhaps that was my own insecurity talking because I perceived him to be out of my league. It didn't help the fact that he was tall with broad shoulders and a peppering of dark chest hair, a washboard stomach and rugby player thighs. He had a handsome face too, with a strong dependable jaw and sharp cheekbones paired with a mischievous grin and steely eyes. When he'd hit on me at the bar, all suited and booted, I'd thought I was dreaming.

'I'm sure it won't be long,' Linda said, jolting me out of my memory. 'Anyway, I'm off out to grab a sandwich, want me to pick you up anything?'

I glanced at the time, it was almost two o'clock, I'd been at it for hours without a break and the fresh air plus some company might calm my nerves, but before I could suggest I tag along, Rick's voice came from the door.

'Well, I was looking for one beautiful lady, but it seems my luck is in, and I've found two!'

We turned our heads in sync to find him leaning against the frame, his charcoal suit bunching at the shoulders, mouth upturned into a playful smile with the glint in his eye that always made me melt.

'Charmer!' Linda said in mock accusation. 'I'll let you two catch up.'

Rick stepped back, allowing Linda to leave before crossing the studio and wrapping his arms around my waist. 'I've missed you.' He planted a kiss on my lips, a mix of chewing gum and a woody aftershave which radiated from his jaw.

'I've missed you too,' I replied as he bent low, nuzzling his chin against the buckle of my dungarees and walking me backwards until I was against my desk. When I woke this morning, Rick was on his way out of the door, a lukewarm cup of tea waiting for me on the bedside table. It was the little things that grew to be big things, and I'd fallen for him hard.

I opened my mouth to tell him about the email, not willing to keep him in the dark, but he lifted the hair away from my neck, his lips brushing the skin beneath. I shut my eyes, wanting to forget everything for one moment and drink in his affection, until he released one of the straps of my dungarees and his desire pressed against my groin.

'Not here, Rick.' I tried to move, but his weight prevented it, still kissing my neck, one hand wrapped in my hair, weakening my resolve.

'Someone might see,' I whispered, torn between wanting to stop in case Linda came back and undressing myself to forget it all.

'That's okay, we can put on a show.' He unclasped his belt buckle and my back stiffened as though a bucket of cold water had been thrown over me, Rick's words jerking me back to that image, of the show we'd unwittingly put on already. Did he know or was I overthinking it?

'Not now.' I pushed him away, and he staggered backwards, wounded at my forcefulness and harsh tone.

'Okay.' He drew his hand through his hair, a short back and sides with a mop of dark waves on top that were curling at the ends.

'I'm sorry,' I sighed, 'I'm not feeling great today.'

'Well, I stopped by to see if you'd had lunch, but I can run and grab you something from the chemist if you need it before I head back to work.' He was so damn nice, and guilt gnawed at my side.

'Just under the weather, that's all. How did your meeting go? You got back fast.'

'I was only with them an hour, but it went great, signed them up for a six-month trial, left them a complimentary bottle that was opened before I'd even left. They're probably drunk by now.' He chuckled. 'Have you eaten?'

I shook my head, even the thought of food made my stomach roll now I'd been plunged back into reality.

'I'll go and grab us something.'

'No don't, I'm going to finish up here soon and head home.'

Rick's eyes dimmed, like a puppy whose favourite toy had been taken away.

'I think I need an early night, my stomach isn't great.' I clutched it like a GCSE drama student; I wouldn't have made a very good actress.

'Oh okay, we can watch that new Netflix thing tomorrow maybe.'

'Sure,' I agreed, faking a smile that made my jaw ache. 'Maybe you can see if your brother is around tonight? Hang out with him?'

Rick shrugged, stepping forward to kiss me on the cheek. 'Are you sure you're okay?'

'I'm fine,' I promised, my insides shrinking. 'Actually, I need to talk to you about something.'

Rick raised an eyebrow, but then his phone rang, penetrating the silence. He frowned at the caller display. 'I'm sorry, I've got to take this.'

'It's fine, go, ring me later.' My words rushed out as though I'd had a reprieve, gut churning at the thought of showing Rick the email. Would he be mad or had he been targeted too? Maybe he had an email waiting for him because it had to be money they were after, and Rick earned way more than I did in commission alone. Plus, he had savings, whereas I was still living month to month.

He nodded, giving my hand a squeeze, and answered the call going out the door. My heart sank a little, but the thought of going back to his place filled me with dread. I was being cowardly; there might be a camera hidden I could find and dispose of. I should have told him about the email, that someone had filmed us. There'd never been any secrets between us, yet this one felt too big to share if he hadn't been threatened too. I'd deal with it by myself, not prepared to risk my relationship with Rick for anything. I hoped he'd call his brother Nathan over; they could go out for a beer and often he crashed at Rick's. Maybe he'd put the camera there? I was clutching at straws, my mind running away with itself because really I had no clue who was behind it.

With Rick gone, I stayed for another hour, tidying up and planning a few of the smaller projects to get done tomorrow, ensuring I had the right colours in stock. Half an hour was spent going through emails, accepting new orders and responding to enquiries. The message from gogetter@gmail.com remained in my inbox, but I didn't dare reply. Googling it brought up no results and every time I saw it, I shuddered. It got infinitely worse when I remembered the package Linda had handed me earlier that I'd chucked in my bag. Retrieving it, I saw there was no branding or indication who it was from, and I knew I wasn't expecting a delivery of art supplies. Praying it was nothing untoward, I tore open the jiffy bag and found it contained a USB stick and a slip of paper with a typed message on it.

**I DON'T THINK YOU WANT MIRANDA AND BILL SEEING THIS DO YOU?
YOUR FRIEND**

I swallowed hard, thrusting the USB into my laptop, eager to see what was on it, why they were using my parents as leverage.

The hairs on my arms stood to attention as it played. If I'd had any doubt the video hadn't been real, it evaporated. It hadn't been some sick artificial intelligence attempt at blackmail, there we were in vivid technicolour. My eyes turned to fishbowls as Rick and I filled the screen, him holding my wrists flat to the mattress while I writhed beneath. This time, I remembered it, the feel of him, the kissing that had started on the sofa before moving to the bedroom. Rick suggesting we embark on some gentle restraining to spice things up.

I was no Paris Hilton or Kim Kardashian, who would be interested in my sex tape? Yet the rock in my stomach grew as my fingers traced the message on the slip of paper. They knew my parents' names, threatening to expose me. My dad was the headteacher of an outstanding Ofsted-rated secondary school, a respected member of the community, it would devastate him. He'd never be able to look at me again and I sure as hell wouldn't be able to meet his eye either.

Knowing someone had a video of me, had watched it and maybe shared it already made me want to curl up and die. Unable to stop the urge to flee, I shoved the contents of the package into my bag, said a hurried goodbye to Linda and left.

Hiking my shoulders up on the short walk to my car, the wind chilled the air and I couldn't shake the notion I was being watched, reminded of the words in the email: DON'T FORGET, I'M ALWAYS WATCHING. Casting furtive glances over my shoulder every few seconds and squinting in the windows of the cars that passed, the sender's presence was everywhere.

'I'm losing my mind,' I muttered, as I popped into the small Tesco Express I passed on the way, knowing I hadn't eaten and had nothing in the fridge at home. That's how often I was at Rick's. Selecting the last pasta bake microwave meal they had, I also grabbed a bottle of Sauvignon Blanc and headed for the checkout. Growing skittish at how close the person behind me stood as we queued, I drew my arms around myself. He was a tall man of around a similar age to me, mid-twenties, whose hot breath ruffled my hair. Could he be the sender? Goosebumps sprang up on my neck and I fought the urge to ditch my basket and run.

Once I'd paid, I gulped in air outside the entrance and hurried to my car parked around the corner, the tall man nowhere to be seen. There were never any spaces outside the studio, no matter what time I arrived. Next door to us was a twenty-four-hour gym I'd become a member of. Their music could sometimes be heard through the wall, but the studio space was cheap. One day I'd live in a house big enough to have my own studio, perhaps one of those purpose-built cabins in powder blue overlooking a magnolia tree in the rear garden. With the way business had been going, it could be a possibility, and I held on to that thought as I climbed in my car and drove through town to the cheap side where my gloomy flat awaited.

The lift was out again, not that I ever used it, the smell of urine was too nauseating, and I climbed the stairs to the top floor. The carpet in the hallway had dust motes gathered along the edges, and from the aroma, it appeared my neighbour Alfie was cooking a curry. I rummaged in my bag for my key and prepared to shoulder barge the door that always stuck. When it finally opened, a pile of post lay on the mat and I bent to collect it. A small, slim box had been pushed through the letter box amongst the junk mail and bills, presumably the vitamins I'd ordered.

Hearing a creak from below, I rushed inside, closing and locking the door, heading straight for the windows to draw the curtains, imagining some bizarre scenario where the tall man from Tesco had followed me home. I peeked through the crack onto the street below, sure I'd see the ominous shadow of a person staring up at me, but no one was there. I remained at my post until my heart rate returned to normal, eventually going back to the kitchen where I'd dumped the mail. I switched on the kettle and leafed through it until I got to the box.

Tearing it open, wrapped in cellophane I found a large heart-shaped biscuit, decorated with red royal icing. I grinned, Rick was such a romantic and often surprised me with little gifts. Then my eyes settled on the text. What I'd initially thought was *Be Mine* piped in flowing icing, on second glance I saw I'd got the message wrong.

You're Mine.

But was it a love note or a warning?

3

Had I not received the email from gogetter@gmail.com, I would have assumed the biscuit was from Rick, but the wording was weird. Rick wasn't possessive, not at all. He never got jealous, even when he'd arrived late on our third date and another guy was trying to buy me a drink. Trust was everything to him and he knew I'd never stray.

I grabbed my phone and sent him a quick text.

> Did you send me a gift?

I watched the screen, waiting for a reply, but none came immediately. Maybe I was being paranoid, I wasn't usually so suspicious, but how could I not be now?

> Not me sweetheart, do I have competition?

Rick's text sent shivers down my spine. If he didn't send the biscuit, who did, and how did they know not only where I worked but also where I lived? Was I being watched?

I wandered around my tiny flat, looking for a camera, paranoia kicking in, but found nothing. Should I leave, go back to my parents' house? Turning up there late at night would invite a whole host of questions and they were already on my back about meeting Rick. I'd shielded him from their interrogations until now, but we'd been together for almost ten months and I knew I wouldn't be able to much longer.

It wasn't that they weren't fantastic parents, my brother and I had a great childhood, but they were always going on about my future and whether art was a sustainable business. They believed I had talent, but the pair were academics and I'd taken a different path. Their expectations were high and I was reluctant to expose Rick to that level of scrutiny in case they scared him off. I hadn't met Rick's parents either, they lived in the Isle of Wight and, reading between the lines, they didn't have a great relationship. He seemed to shut down whenever they were mentioned, so I didn't push it, figuring he'd open up when the time was right.

Finding nothing that looked remotely like a camera, I eventually settled and tried to force the USB and edible gift from my mind. After a cup of tea, I gave the flat a bit of a tidy-up, but the place was still depressing; everything was brown, with little natural light. I'd tried to inject colour with cushions, curtains and some prints for the wall, but it was a far cry from Rick's spacious penthouse with its wall-to-wall windows.

I'd brought home my laptop and sat, logging on to emails, hoping there might be another, one with instructions on what I had to do to get the message and video deleted, because currently I was in limbo, on the edge of a cliff in a gale, not knowing if I was going to tumble into the sea with one strong gust. Line by line, I dissected the capital letters, trying to work out if there was some kind of hidden message, sidelining the guilt because I'd told Rick nothing of the threat. I could respond, ask them what they wanted, but it had to be better to not to engage. Maybe they didn't want anything at all, maybe they just enjoyed the threat of blackmail and would lose interest by my lack of contact.

When early evening approached, I heated the pasta bake in the microwave and poured myself a glass of Sauvignon Blanc. I couldn't eat much, my stomach was still churning. Perhaps a soak in the bath would be what I needed.

Ignoring the spots of mould around the edges where the silicon had worn away, I sank beneath the bubbles, hoping they would dissolve the anxiety and shame at someone recording my most intimate moments. It remained at the forefront of my mind, the image burnt onto my retinas. I should go to the police, but the threat was too real, with one click of a mouse mine, Rick's and my family's reputation would be in pieces. Unable to relax I got out of the bath, the dark cloud following me wishing I could switch my brain off.

The more I drank, the angrier I got at the injustice, even being a little short with Rick later when he called to see how I was and asked what gift I'd received from another male suitor. I didn't want to speak to him; I didn't want to speak to anyone. I wanted to go to bed and wake tomorrow morning to find it had all been a nightmare.

I paced the flat, listening to the Foo Fighters, loud angry rock music which riled me even more until I couldn't help myself, I went back to my laptop and responded. The waiting was killing me, whatever they wanted, money I assumed, for their copy of the video, I could pay it and get my life back.

WHAT DO YOU WANT?

I stabbed at the keys and clicked send, almost dropping my near empty wine glass when a few minutes later someone knocked on the door. It was past ten and immediately the fire in my belly shrivelled to embers. I tiptoed to the door to look through the cloudy spyhole, breathing a sigh of relief to see it was Alfie on the other side.

'Sorry, Abbi, I'm about to hit the sack, would you mind turning the music down?'

I left the door open and dashed to the stereo, switching it off. The deafening music ceased, although my ears still rang. Alfie politely waited at the threshold, his eyes darting around the cramped hallway.

'I'm really sorry, Alfie, I didn't think. It's been a day.' I pulled my bathrobe tighter around me, heat climbing my neck as he looked anywhere but at me.

Alfie was shy, in his mid-thirties and separated. When I'd moved in, his wife was moving out, their argument carried out publicly on the stairwell. It was awkward, to say the least, and once she'd left, I took him over a bottle of red wine, partly to introduce myself, partly a consolation for what had to have been a shitty day. We hadn't chatted much over the months I'd been here, only whenever we bumped into each other in passing, but he'd always been friendly.

'Are you okay?' he asked, finally meeting my eye. His light hair was receding and his face sallow, as though he hadn't seen the sun in a while.

'I'm fine. How are you doing?' I asked gently, always getting the impression he was fragile and on the edge of a nervous breakdown.

'Oh, you know, work, eat, sleep, repeat.'

I laughed, nodding along. 'I can relate. Well, I'm sorry about the music. It won't happen again.'

'No problem, take care.' Alfie turned and walked across the hall to his flat where the door had been left ajar. Maybe I should see if he wanted to go out for a drink or something, he looked like he needed cheering up, but at the same time I didn't want to give him the wrong impression. In truth, I had too much going on to give it much consideration right now.

Back at my laptop, there had been no response from gogetter and I shut it down before brushing my teeth and crawling into bed. The sheets were coarse, cheap compared to the Egyptian cotton Rick bought for his bed, and they itched my skin.

Tomorrow would be a better day. I knew I could get three or four of the smaller projects done and out of the way, mini portraits about the size of a coaster and my first bauble of the year. Extremely organised of one customer considering it was only March, yet I was strangely looking forward to painting sprigs of holly to make it extra Christmassy.

Rick messaged as I plumped my pillow, a photo of him in bed, grimacing at the camera with the caption *Nathan's finally buggered off. Time for bed, but it's cold in here without you!* It made me smile knowing I was missed. Rick couldn't be a part of the scheme to blackmail me, he was like an open book, he kept nothing hidden. In fact, he couldn't even keep what he'd bought me for Christmas a secret, folding three days before, like he would combust if he didn't tell me. I'd opened the diamond earrings that night and we'd had an early Christmas, surrounded by wrapping paper, drinking mulled wine and watching festive movies. It had been bliss.

I considered calling my best friend Jade, but she would likely be in bed already as she worked shifts as a paramedic. I pulled up the duvet, a chill on my back. I'd deliberately kept the heating off, telling myself it was spring, but it seemed the weather hadn't got the memo. I missed Rick's warm body pressed against mine, the cup of tea that would have been waiting for me in the morning. Since being together and staying over there more, I'd grown to hate my flat, with its smelly drains and windows that whistled when it was windy.

I tossed and turned, waiting for sleep that wouldn't come, eventually reaching for my phone to read a few pages of my book on the Kindle app. When the screen unlocked, I saw an email had just arrived on the work account. Usually, I was strict at ensuring a good home, work-life balance, but what if it was from gogetter? Dread weaved its way through my body, rising from my toes, and I bit my lip. I'd never get to sleep if I didn't check. Like tearing a plaster off, it had to be done. I clicked into the app, inhaling sharply as I saw the new email was from gogetter. Maybe it would be what I was waiting for, some instructions on how I could put this nightmare to bed because I couldn't let that video of me get out. The fact the whole thing was being drawn out added to the torture.

Opening the email, I let out a whimper. On my screen was another link, with the words beneath BEAR IN MIND, I'M ALWAYS WATCHING, SWEET DREAMS ABBI... This time, I didn't think twice, clicking the link straight away. Was it going to be the video in full, the same as on the USB stick, mine and Rick's unauthorised sex tape? But it wasn't, it was another screenshot, but a hundred times worse than the one I'd received this morning. I was beside Rick's bed, naked, pulling on one of his T-shirts as I walked towards the camera. It was a full-frontal shot with nothing covering my modesty and I sobbed into my pillow.

You couldn't see my face, the T-shirt obscuring it as I pulled it on, but there was enough of me on display, right down to the tiny panda tattoo on my hip.

Bear in mind... They thought they were being funny, but I was sickened by the joke at my expense.

I looked at the email again, swiping away the image, humiliation washing over me. The thought of anyone seeing it made my toes curl. I was shy, almost conservative with what I wore, rarely showing much skin. Rick had spent the past ten months trying to get me to unleash my inner demon, as he called it, to spice up our sex life. Convincing me to be more adventurous, try new things, different positions and toys, something he got a kick out of. I couldn't bear the thought of anyone witnessing our antics.

I reread the email. *Sweet dreams Abbi*. Did he know I was in bed or was it a coincidence since the message had come in so late?

I threw off the covers and went to the window, glad I was wearing pyjamas, to peek through the curtain at the skyline. My building faced a warehouse, but there were no lights on and no vehicles in the car park either. On the street, the pavement was quiet, but I sensed eyes on me, penetrating every inch of my skin. A solitary figure stood to the left, but I couldn't make out any features or if they were looking in this direction, they were too far away from the street lamp, encased in shadow. It chilled me to the bone and my insides turned to ice.

I could see they were tall – was it the man stood behind me in Tesco, breathing into my hair?

A minute or so later, they walked away, around the corner and out of sight, leaving the street empty. Maybe they'd had a dog I hadn't seen, taking it out for a late walk around the block, because who would want to terrorise me like this? I wracked my brain for someone I'd upset, not deliberately but accidentally, an ex-boyfriend maybe, but no one came to mind. What did they want? I felt the urge to ring Ben; my little brother would know what to do or at least he'd make me feel better about it, but Turkey was two hours ahead and he'd be fast asleep by now. I dismissed the thought, sinking onto the sofa.

It was like I'd been plucked from random, a subject to be mentally and emotionally tortured, because that's what it was. The boulder in my stomach had expanded since this morning, the constant nausea, my body running wild with cortisol. I was exhausted but wired. There would be no sleep tonight, I wouldn't sleep again until I found out what I had to do, but it seemed whoever it was, they were prolonging my angst for their own perverse pleasure. Were they watching me, revelling in my suffering, and how far were they willing to go to get their pound of flesh?

4

When I woke after briefly drifting off at around two in the morning, the sun was only just rising. My head was foggy from exhaustion, ears full of cotton wool, like an out-of-body experience. Surrounded by detritus, my whirlwind search of the flat in the early hours, pulling apart every inch sending dust motes soaring into the air, found nothing. No cameras, no bugs, only a lost earring, an old train ticket from a night out with Jade in London and a bra down the side of the sofa I'd not seen in months.

I couldn't face it – the new day or the mess – and I couldn't face the drive to work either, let alone sitting in the studio to paint or Linda's mindless chatter. All I wanted was to pull the duvet over my head and wallow in self-pity, to hide where no one could find me, where no one would be watching.

It seemed fate had other plans, however, or rather Rick did when he turned up at my door a couple of hours later while I snoozed.

'I bought coffee,' he said, his smile fading when he saw the state of me and the tornado of the flat over my shoulder. 'Are you okay?'

'I feel awful,' I said and this time it wasn't a lie. 'My stomach won't stop churning.'

'Oh no, must be some sort of bug.' He stepped over the threshold, deep rivets between his eyes, trying to find space to tread on the carpet. 'What happened in here?'

'I lost something.' *My sanity.*

His frown deepened as he turned in a full circle, unable to comprehend the state of the place – his place was always so clean, yet still he wasn't judgemental.

'I'd help you clear it up, but I've got a meeting in Slough.'

'That's okay, I probably won't go into the studio today, so I can tackle it later.'

Rick set down our coffees on the worktop, eyeing the heart-shaped *You're Mine* biscuit still in its wrapper by the kettle.

'So, I do have competition then?' His mouth fell into an easy grin, but his eyebrows remained rigidly high.

'It arrived yesterday through the letter box, I thought it was you. I have no idea who it's from.' I tried to drag my fingers through my curls, but they were matted, desperate for a condition, but even that seemed like it would be too much effort.

'Are you sure about that? No secret admirers I don't know about?' He frowned, but his tone was playful.

'None, I promise. They are so secret I don't know about them either. Perhaps it was meant for someone else in this block.' I grabbed the biscuit and chucked it in the bin.

'Or maybe I need to up my game.'

I laughed Rick off as he pulled me towards him and whipped a key out of his trouser pocket.

'Why don't you go over to mine, get into bed and when I get home, I can make you some soup. Let me look after you if you're feeling poorly,' he said, wrapping his arms around my waist and resting his chin on the top of my head. He smelt amazing as always and I was less than fresh, but I held on to him anyway, absorbing his warmth despite looking a state in faded pyjamas and hair like a bird's nest. I usually made more of an effort when I was at his. I would have thought him seeing the real me might make him sprint for the hills, but instead I'd got a key to the penthouse. 'I've got to run, but maybe don't drink the coffee if your stomach is bad. I'll see you later though, yeah?'

I nodded and he bent to give me a kiss on the cheek. I had to come clean and tell him everything, but I didn't want to make him late.

'Loving these pyjamas, very Bridget Jones,' he quipped, giving my behind a playful smack before he made his way to the door.

I gulped the coffee down in one, enjoying the sweetness and hoping the caffeine would get me going, because nothing good was going to come from lying in bed all day. Whoever was watching would get no satisfaction if I didn't react and carried on as normal. On a high from receiving Rick's key, I blocked the emailer, taking back control. Maybe they were empty threats designed to throw my life into chaos and it had worked, but no more.

It took an hour to put the flat back together, but once I'd done that and pushed the hoover around, my mind was calmer. A hot shower and hair wash served its purpose, waking me up. I got dressed and plaited my wet hair, applying minimal make-up so as not to scare Linda, and jumped in the car.

I did my best to push my potential blackmailer from my mind, intending to head to the studio, complete at least two of the smaller commissions and go to Rick's, now I had a key. Without him there, I'd be able to have a good search to try to unearth the secretly planted camera. Last night I'd convinced myself Rick couldn't have anything to do with it, but maybe subconsciously that was why I was putting off telling him what was going on. If I got another email, from a new account, I'd come clean. Rick would of course deny any involvement, reassure me and help figure out what to do.

Locked in the studio, painting the bauble distracted me for a while, until the red of the holly reminded me of the icing on the biscuit I'd received and compelled me to dull it down. Linda had a class in session and I could hear her voice booming instructions above the hum of the pottery wheels. At least she was busy and not interrogating me about my absence this morning.

As soon as I finished two commissions, I packed them and headed out, planning to drop them at the post office on the way to Rick's, along with the bland mid-terrace portrait I should have posted yesterday.

However, when I got to Harper Court after waiting an age in the post office queue, Todd on security couldn't let me into the building because someone had set off the fire alarm and the entire block had been evacuated. Rick's disgruntled neighbours stood out on the street staring upwards, perhaps waiting for smoke to billow from windows, but thankfully none materialised. I sloped back to my car, using the opportunity to give Jade a call, hoping I'd catch her on a break. As expected, it went to voicemail, but she called me back five minutes later.

'Hey, Abs, how's it going?'

'Not bad, busy painting. You?'

'Well, I just removed a piece of Play-Doh from a four-year-old's nose, so yeah, saving lives today.' Jade's default sarcastic tone made me chuckle.

'Who calls an ambulance for that?'

'I know, right! Apparently it was blocking his airways.' She sighed. 'How's Ricky?' Jade loved her nickname for Rick, knowing how much he hated it, more so when she did it in her Bianca from *EastEnders* voice.

'He's fine,' I said, the whole email thing on the tip of my tongue, but the threat of telling anyone loomed large.

'Hey, at least he's not an eats, shoots and leaves.' Jade's panda reference wasn't lost on me, she slipped them in often, a constant reminder of the matching tattoos we'd had done when we'd left college.

We'd met when I'd been asked to volunteer as a patient for Jade, who'd needed a body to work on for her SEACAMB course as part of training to be a paramedic. I'd been loitering in the smoking area at college after my media lesson had finished, canoodling with my then boyfriend. We'd giggled as she'd mimed cutting off my clothes after an RTA as I'd lain rigid on a wad of red tissue paper that was supposed to be blood in the college car park.

We'd been friends ever since, cementing our friendship with wild nights out, a string of awful boyfriends and eventually getting inked with matching tiny panda tattoos my parents lost their shit over.

'He's not one of those,' I replied with a giggle.

'Fancy coming to Octopus bar tonight, there's going to be a group of us?'

'I'm not feeling great, so I'll give it a miss. Thanks though. How's Honking Henry?' Honking Henry was Jade's partner on shift, named as such as whenever he drove the ambulance he used his horn excessively. Plus, when Jade had taken him out for a team debrief after their first shift, he'd got so drunk he threw up. The nickname had stuck and I knew Jade had a soft spot for him, although she was yet to negotiate him into bed.

'He got a new tattoo, a half sleeve, and it's so hot I can't stop staring at his arms when he's driving.'

'At least you've got the defib if you have an episode!'

I loved our chats, and as the conversation continued on the topic of Honking Henry, I relaxed into my seat, forgetting my woes for a few minutes until I saw Todd wave at the residents of Harper Court, gesturing they could go back inside. With the place to myself, it was time to search for the camera.

5

I left my car in Rick's visitor space. His designated space, where the Audi Q4 parked, was empty, so I knew he wasn't back from Slough yet. I greeted Todd as I passed, but he was deep in conversation with a fireman, gesticulating wildly, and didn't hear me.

The lift was crowded, the residents complaining about another false alarm and having to evacuate again. I pressed myself into the corner after pushing P for the Penthouse. It was on the tenth floor and one of two identical apartments, but I had no idea who his neighbour was. Below, the floors were split into four apartments, all lovely, but Rick's open-plan penthouse was all the more luxurious compared to my grotty one-bedroom flat.

He'd told me before that, as kids, him and Nathan didn't have a lot. His parents struggled to make ends meet and Rick's clothes were hand-me-downs from his older cousin. As an adult, he was generous with his money, always paying whenever we went out, but it was obvious he saw it as a status symbol. To him, funding his lavish lifestyle, with the penthouse and the car meant he'd made it; he feared being poor.

Inside, the penthouse was all sleek lines, white and chrome with a splash of blue throughout. Rick's minimalistic furniture and pale wood flooring meant my footsteps echoed as I entered and unease snaked over my skin, despite the overwhelming light. The view out of the wall-to-wall windows never failed to leave me speechless. It was only Crawley, not a particularly amazing skyline, but still, we were in the gods. Rick loved sex by the window, looking out at the world below us. It was one of our adventurous experiments and turned him on, but did little for me. It especially wouldn't now, knowing we had been watched.

It was eerie, being here alone, but I headed straight for the bedroom, where Rick's duvet was folded back in a crisp line to air the bed. Same white sheets as always, but they'd been washed recently, the scent of orchids lingered in the room fighting against Versace Eros. By the door to the en suite were built-in shelves where Rick stored some books and a couple of Funko Pops – The Bride from *Kill Bill* and Vincent Vega from *Pulp Fiction*, the latter I'd bought for him a couple of months ago. He'd admitted he was a massive Quentin Tarantino fan the first time he'd invited me over, and owned steel books of all his films which were lined up beside the figures. I'd got used to being subjected to violent movie marathons where he talked about what an amazing director he was. Rick's penchant for those films were at odds with his gentle demeanour but I'd come to love his quirks despite bloodlust being a continuing theme. They weren't my cup of tea, but I loved his enthusiasm for the 'art' nonetheless.

I rooted around, moving aside the tray in which he kept his watch and cufflinks, searching for anything that could be a camera. It had to be here somewhere. I stood, staring at the bed, visualising my naked form atop Rick from the screenshot, withering inside. It was the right angle, but I couldn't find anything, despite emptying the shelves. If a camera had been there, it wasn't now.

I slowly spun in a circle, exactly as I had done at my flat, eyeing every possible surface, wanting to examine every inch, but the thought of invading Rick's privacy gave me palpitations. I had no right to rummage through his things, especially when he was as much of a victim of this as I was. It was time I told him everything and we could search the penthouse together.

I'd just finished putting everything back when Rick's voice called out from across the penthouse.

'Abbi?'

I jumped, knocking one of the Funko Pops off the shelf, and it bounced onto the carpet at my feet.

'In here.' I scooped it up and turned to see Rick at the bedroom door, carrying a pharmacy bag. He raised an eyebrow, a small smile tilting the corner of his mouth, his blazer draped over his arm. 'Sorry, I was looking at your Funko Pops,' I lied, repositioning The Bride to where she'd been moments before.

'How are you feeling?' He shook the bag. 'I got some stuff for your stomach.'

'Thank you, a little better but still a bit queasy.' I knew the blood had drained from my face as soon as I'd heard Rick shout my name, so I imagined I looked sallow and washed out from that and the lack of sleep.

'Come on then, let's get you on the sofa, I'll make you a peppermint tea. Have you eaten?'

I hadn't given food any thought today, my mind on other things and my empty stomach growled. I shook my head and Rick led me back into the lounge, plonking me on the blue suede sofa and placing a blanket over my curled-up form. He turned on the television, handing me the remote, and walked over to the kitchen to boil the kettle. How did I get so lucky? I'd never met anyone so thoughtful before, always putting me first, and here I was lying to him about what was going on.

'Rick,' I called my voice wobbly, 'I need to tell you something.'

He looked at me from behind the worktop, then carried over the steaming mug and set it on the coffee table, slotting in next to me.

'Me first,' he said with a sheepish grin as he unbuttoned the top button of his shirt and loosened his tie.

'Okay.' I propped myself up on one arm, staring into grey marble eyes.

'That key I gave you, I want you to keep it. Move in with me, Abbi.'

My lips parted and I drew in a long breath. It was finally happening, I'd been longing for him to ask me but dared not get my hopes up.

'Keep the flat if you want for a few months, you know, until you're sure, but I want to wake up with you every morning and I want to go to bed with you every night. It's been ten months, and I should have asked you sooner, but I'm asking now.'

It would have been a big decision for Rick, one he wouldn't have made lightly. He'd told me all about his last serious girlfriend, Heather, who he'd rented a place with before he bought the penthouse. As soon as she'd moved in, she'd become neurotic and possessive, demanding to know where he was all the time. Even once it was over it took months for her to leave, and I was glad she'd moved out of Crawley because Rick said she was all kinds of crazy.

He beamed at me, and I forgot all about Heather, the camera and the email as my heart swelled. I pulled Rick in close, nuzzling his shoulder and kissing his neck.

'Yes, I'll move in,' I whispered into the creases of his skin and he squeezed me tight, pulling back with a huge grin on his face, both of us like Cheshire cats.

'Phew.' He wiped his brow in comedic fashion and I giggled, excited to begin the new chapter of our lives, pushing aside any doubts I'd had about the camera. 'What was it you wanted to tell me?'

I grimaced, the sinking feeling back. 'It was nothing, work stuff, about my accounting software. It can wait.' The moment to come clean had passed; this was a milestone we should be celebrating. I could tell him later, rather than ruin the occasion.

'Not about the biscuit guy then?'

'Definitely not.' I laughed, punching him on the shoulder, wishing he'd forget all about that.

Secretly I'd been hoping he'd ask me to move in months ago, waiting patiently and accepting perhaps Rick wasn't ready for that level of commitment. Things had started slowly, we didn't rush into anything and I didn't force the issue, he was a gentleman who liked to wine and dine me. It wasn't something I was used to, so I respected he wanted his space to see his friends, his brother and play golf. We were never the type of couple who were in each other's pockets, so I was pleased Rick was ready to take the next step in our relationship.

'Well, we can celebrate with a champagne dinner another night, seeing as you're under the weather. Peppermint tea will have to do for today. Let me go and get changed. I've got a couple of emails to respond to, but we'll have an evening on the sofa.'

Rick padded out of the room towards his bedroom and I grinned so hard my cheeks ached, snuggling into the sofa. I couldn't wait to tell Jade the news.

When he returned in faded jeans and a sweatshirt, his feet bare, I had to stop myself from dribbling. He looked like he'd stepped out of a photo shoot and I couldn't tear my eyes away as he grabbed a can of Coke from the fridge before joining me. I couldn't get amorous, having to keep up the pretence of being unwell and forced myself to focus on something else.

'Did you hear about the fire alarm?' I asked, grasping for a change of topic.

'Yeah, I saw Todd on the way in. Seems to be happening a lot lately. All false alarms but they aren't sure why they are going off, they think perhaps it's loose wiring.'

I frowned, that was weird, my mind automatically going to darker places. Was that how someone broke in and planted a camera, were they getting the place evacuated so they could come in undetected?

'This place is secure, right?'

Rick laughed, nearly spilling his can. 'Of course it is, no one gets past Todd without being announced, except maybe you or Nathan.'

I leaned into him and he put an arm around me.

'Now, what should we watch?'

We spent the rest of the afternoon in that spot and Rick even conceded to watching *No Hard Feelings*, a romcom with Jennifer Lawrence. When it finished, he got up to cook himself some pasta, forcing me to have a small bowl, which I picked at.

Everything was perfect until the sun went down and as it got closer to bedtime I became antsy, the doubts I'd pushed aside since accepting Rick's offer to move in suddenly resurfacing. I feigned stomach pains, knowing there was no way I'd be having sex with Rick, even if I had the energy. I couldn't go into his bedroom. Even if there wasn't one there now, a camera had been there before, capturing our lovemaking, our most intimate moments.

There could be a camera anywhere, looking at you right now. Beneath the blanket, the hair on my arms stood to attention.

Rick yawned, stretching his arms high above his body. 'I think I'm ready to hit the sack. You?'

I almost pretended I'd dropped off, in the hopes he might leave me there, but before I could answer, my phone pinged with an email to my work account.

'Another order?' Rick asked, his smile infectious. I used a different sound alert when an email landed in the work account and he'd got used to hearing it a lot recently.

'Let's hope so.' I reached for the phone as Rick cleared the table of our mugs and bowls to stack in the dishwasher. I clicked into the email, bolting upright as the familiar handle popped onto the screen, almost but not quite. This one was from GoGetHer@gmail.com and the blood fizzed in my veins.

'Good one?' Rick asked from the open-plan kitchen, wiping the surfaces and switching off the under-cabinet lights, his nightly routine.

I tried to hide my shaking hands. 'Yeah, I just need to read this, give me a sec.'

He nodded and disappeared into the bedroom. Seconds later, I heard the tap running from his en suite.

When I opened the email, cold immobilising dread hit me like an avalanche.

> ABBI,
> I HAVE A COMMISSION FOR YOU...
> SHAME YOU'RE NOT HOME TONIGHT.
> REMEMBER TELL NO ONE, ESPECIALLY RICK.
> I'LL BE IN TOUCH SOON.
> ALWAYS WATCHING,
> YOUR FRIEND

Beneath the words was a photo of the front door at my flat. A slightly corroded number eight in the centre of a dark wood door which had seen better days and a faded doormat that used to have the word *Welcome* on it.

6

My mouth was so dry, I struggled to swallow. I stared at the screen, pasta rising in my gullet and spilling into my mouth. Chucking the phone, I dashed to the main bathroom and emptied my stomach.

'Jesus, are you okay?' Rick was by my side in a second as I knelt on the tiled floor, wearing only his boxers and a T-shirt, toothpaste still around his mouth from where he'd been cleaning his teeth in the en suite.

'I'm sick,' I uttered, spitting into the bowl as he gently held my hair back until I finished.

'You must have a bug.'

Once I'd recovered, I said I'd sleep on the sofa so I wouldn't pass anything to him, my tears explained away by the vomiting making my eyes water. After supplying a clean T-shirt for me to wear, Rick tucked me in beneath the duvet and pillow taken from the spare bedroom, making sure I had a glass of water and an empty bowl nearby. He stroked my clammy forehead; concern etched on his face.

'Are you sure you don't want to sleep in the spare room?'

I shook my head. 'Carpet,' I explained. At least the hardwood floor would be easier to clean if I happened to be sick again. Fearful I might, as my stomach gurgled with the latest email hanging over me.

'Okay, if you're sure. Sleep well, beautiful, come and get me if you need to.'

As soon as he was gone, I grabbed my phone, reading the email over and over, analysing every word. I hadn't thought the nightmare could get any worse, but whoever the watcher was, they knew so much about me, yet I had no idea who they were. I was being stalked, that email meant they had to know I was here if I wasn't at home, which I guessed also meant they knew where Rick lived too. Why hadn't they told me what they wanted already?

I stared out at the dark sky before getting up to close the blinds, too exposed to be able to relax. All the questions running through my mind put me on edge and I knew I'd be too wired to sleep. Had they known I wasn't at home because they'd knocked on my door or because there was a camera inside my flat I hadn't yet found? Or was there a camera here at Rick's and they were watching me right now?

I turned my phone off and pulled the duvet over my head, it was the only way I could feel safe and not on display like a doll in a shop window. My skin crawled to think someone could be watching me, all the intimate things you did when you were alone, like readjusting your underwear or scratching an itch in an area not polite to do so in public.

I fidgeted for hours, suffocating beneath the duvet, but adamant I wasn't going to give that pervert anything to watch if they'd somehow managed to plant cameras all over Rick's penthouse without his knowledge. Because he couldn't know could he, not if the email explicitly told me not to tell him – but how would they have got in? What if it was Todd, or Nathan? Rick said he had a cleaner twice a week, could it be her? With the sign-off as 'your friend', I even questioned if it could be Jade. I was being paranoid, clutching at straws, but not knowing was driving me crazy. I shifted between tears of self-pity and rage at the person who was doing this to me.

Eventually, the sun began to rise, Rick's blinds shimmering in the morning glow when I dared to peak out from the stifling duvet. From his bedroom came the sound of an alarm rousing him from sleep.

'Happy hump day! How are you feeling?' Rick said, when he pulled the duvet back.

'Like death,' I replied, squinting in the light at his dishevelled hair. At least I didn't have to lie; lack of sleep and anxiety over the email had me at an all-time low.

'What can I get you?'

'Nothing. I'm going to drag myself through the shower in a bit.'

'You're going to the studio?' Rick's eyebrows knitted together in disbelief.

'I have to, I've got a portrait that needs to be sent out by Friday and I haven't started it yet.'

He shuffled to the kitchen in his sliders, yawning as he went.

'Where are you off to today?' I added as an afterthought.

'Coulsdon, then onto Warlingham, but I'll be back if you need a hand moving your stuff over.'

I groaned despite his grin, having forgotten Rick had asked me to move in last night. I barely had the energy to get dressed, let alone pack up my flat.

'Don't worry, you don't have to do it today, we'll wait until the weekend,' he said, but I saw the slump of his shoulders and chewed the inside of my cheek. I'd been too dismissive, ungrateful even.

'It's not that I don't want to, but I still feel rough. I'm not sure I'll manage it.'

He shrugged. 'No big deal. Do you want a coffee?'

I shook my head and glugged water from the glass he'd left me last night, unable to stomach anything else. I'd be running on empty, but it was safer that way. I didn't want to spend the day with my head down the toilet. The rock in my stomach remained, a constant state of heightened anxiety, like the tiniest thing might tip me into a full-on panic attack. I needed to work out what to do about the watcher.

Not even Jade's hungover selfie saying I'd missed out on a good night could improve my mood as I dragged myself through the shower and put on yesterday's clothes. I'd have to go back to the flat and get changed, throw some things into an overnight bag at least. Although how I'd overcome my fear of sleeping at Rick's I didn't know. Maybe it was best to stay at the flat until it was sorted, but now *they* knew where I lived, that didn't sound inviting either. I might be able to relax at the studio, but even there might not be safe, it was where the USB had been delivered.

Rick left earlier than me; I'd just got out of the shower when he said goodbye. I stayed in there to get dressed, keeping the door locked, avoiding Rick's bedroom altogether. I might be paranoid, but there had been a camera there, even if I hadn't been able to locate it yesterday. The skin beneath my eyes had a purple hue, I looked washed out but couldn't be bothered to go back to the flat and get make-up or fresh clothes. Instead, I grabbed a clean yet creased hooded top from Rick's airing cupboard and slung it on with yesterday's jeans and underwear. My hair was a mess from all the tossing and turning, even after I took the plaits out, but it wasn't like I was going to see anybody at the studio other than Linda.

Avoiding the mirror, I collected my things and headed to the car park, raising a hand at Todd as I walked out of the lobby instead of stopping to chat like I'd usually do. Seeing him smile and wave did nothing to alleviate my suspicion. He was lovely, and I'd learnt a lot about him during our brief interactions over the past ten months I'd been seeing Rick. He was nearing sixty, from Ghana originally, married and had recently became a granddad for the second time. I liked him a lot, but someone had been inside Rick's penthouse and it made sense it would be someone with a key.

When I rounded the building to the car park, something fluttering on the windshield of my car caught my eye.

'Not again,' I seethed. When Rick and I first started dating, I'd received a ticket for parking in his visitor's space because he hadn't submitted the registration plate of my car as his guest. Rick had got it revoked, with Todd's help, but it was something I couldn't deal with today on minimal sleep. But as I got closer, I saw it was a red paper heart, secured beneath my windscreen wiper, and not a ticket at all. Somehow my gut told me it wasn't a romantic gesture from Rick and my heart rate spiked as I approached the car.

YOU'RE MINE was scrawled in big black letters on the heart. I ripped it from beneath my wiper, tearing it in two and stuffing it in my pocket, eyes darting around the car park, scanning the vehicles to see if anyone was watching. I wasn't at home last night when the watcher sent me the photo of my front door, so maybe they'd tried here, knowing the old grey Citroen was mine. I was being watched, potentially at home, at Rick's – where else?

The wind whipped my ankles, blowing a stray crisp packet into the air, and I climbed into the car, locking the doors as panic engulfed me, hurrying to start the engine. It took an age for the windscreen to demist, but when it finally did, I sped out of the car park towards the studio, searching for a safe haven.

When I arrived, Linda had a class going, so I drew the blinds and closed the door, shutting out the laughter and loud voices. With the help of black coffee which I hoped wouldn't send my stomach spasming, I got going on the next commission. Usually, I poured my heart and soul into each portrait, spending hours trying to encapsulate every feature as well as the personality of the house or building, but I struggled to get into the groove. The studio and painting in general had always been my sanctuary but even here I felt on tenterhooks.

Linda paid me a visit as soon as her class ended, as usual not bothering to knock. Despite not announcing herself, I was almost glad of the interruption.

'These classes are getting so big, I might have to look at a different studio,' she complained, 'and I'm getting so bored of teaching people how to make bowls.' She had a smudge of brown clay across her forehead and I fought hard not to point it out.

'That's good, isn't it, means business is booming.'

'It is, but this place is so convenient.' She grimaced. 'Are you going to continue your lease? I know it's up soon.' I was taken aback by Linda's abruptness. Although common, I wasn't prepared for it today.

'Are you hoping I move out?' I laughed awkwardly. I'd already decided to renew the six-month lease but hadn't signed the rental agreement yet, the paperwork still sitting in my flat.

'Well, no, but it's a good space. Potentially I could knock through.' She scanned the room, sizing it up, utterly oblivious to my incredulous expression.

Eventually, when her eyes settled back on me, she had the decency to look sheepish.

'Sorry, no, that's not what I mean. I'm just thinking logistically. I don't want you to go.'

'I wasn't planning to,' I muttered, sure I saw a scowl cross her features.

There was an awkward moment of silence before Linda announced she was going to go and grab a sandwich. This time, she didn't offer to get me one or for me to join her.

I swivelled back around in my chair, determined to get lost in my portrait, but her comment niggled me. Did she want me gone so she could have the space, and if so, what lengths would she go to to get rid of me?

7

I tried to get back in the swing, putting my paranoia down to lack of sleep, but it wasn't long before I was interrupted again on Linda's return.

'Found this at the entrance for you.' She passed me another jiffy bag, identical to the one she'd given me on Monday, still chewing on her roll. 'You're popular this week.'

'Thanks.' I put it on the desk, trying to ignore the quickening of my pulse. I hadn't ordered any new paints or brushes.

'Not going to open it?' Linda's eyebrows arched.

Why was she so desperate to see what was inside or was it my reaction she was keen to see? Had she found it on the doormat like she said or was it from her?

I shook my head to dispel the inner voice that seemed to suspect everyone was my stalker.

'Later, I'm right in the middle of something,' I replied curtly, hoping she would get the hint and leave.

'Suit yourself, love.'

I tried to continue, painting an ornate moulding on the cornflower blue front door, but my hand began to tremor and I sighed, putting down the brush and flexing my fingers. My skull pounded and coffee with no sustenance to accompany it had made me jittery. I hadn't got as far as I wanted, but at least I'd started the portrait of the cottage. It was only Wednesday; I could still get it in the post by Friday. Maybe a quick nap was what I needed, and taking advantage of the peace, I lowered my chair, cleared some space on the desk and rested my head on my arms.

* * *

I jolted upright when I woke, the studio dark, and so quiet you could hear a pin drop. No noise filtered from across the hall and I guessed Linda had left. Disorientated, I leaned towards the lamp, knocking the dregs of my coffee onto the floor, swearing when the light didn't come on. Perhaps it was a fuse.

What was the time anyway? Groaning, I stretched my neck and back, sore from being hunched over. Getting to my feet, I stumbled over to the blinds, pulling them open and letting out a high-pitched scream when I found a portly man staring at me through the window.

He waved his hand in an apology, taking a step backwards away from the glass and mouthed, 'Where's the gym?'

I pointed to the right, gesturing it was that way, and bent over, clutching my chest as I sucked in air. He'd given me such a fright in the gloom, I'd nearly peed myself. The gym had neon lights for goodness' sake, unless their power was out too. My phone battery had died but the clock on my wall read gone six o'clock, I'd slept for ages.

In the hallway I tried the light switch, but that didn't work either. Linda's studio was empty, the door locked and my bladder strained for release. Without light, I had no intention of using the facilities. That room was windowless and with my phone dead I had no torch either.

Returning to the studio, I collected my things and locked up, sighing with relief when I got out onto the street. I'd have to remember to email the landlord once I had some power in my phone, at least let him know I was renewing. I sat in the car, gathering myself, realising I'd also brought the jiffy bag out with me too. I'd wait to open it when I got home – if I was going to go home. Should I go to Rick's, would he be expecting me and could I face it? If I was honest, I wasn't going to be the best company, so I drove back to the flat. It was weird, I hadn't received an email before I fell asleep and I didn't know if one was waiting for me, but seeing the jiffy bag in my passenger seat made the blood hum in my ears. Whatever was in it wasn't going to be good.

At least the flat was tidy after yesterday's frantic clean and, drawing the curtains, I tried to ignore the constant sensation of being watched as I stuck the kettle on. I'd searched already, tearing the place apart, and found nothing.

As soon as my phone was plugged in and came to life, I saw I had multiple messages, as well as a voicemail from Rick. He was worried because he couldn't get hold of me but had been stuck in Warlingham for most of the afternoon. He'd suggested in his voicemail he'd be home around six, so he must have got back and discovered I wasn't there. I tapped out a quick text to say I'd fallen asleep at the studio but still felt unwell so wasn't going to come over.

His reply was instant, asking if I was okay, if there was anything he could do, but I didn't have the energy to get into a lengthy conversation. I'd not eaten anything all day and put some packet noodles on the hob to cook. I spent so much time at Rick's, I barely had any fresh food in the flat, although when I got some milk from the fridge for my tea, another microwave meal sat on the shelf. Had I bought two the other day and forgotten? The last few days had been so disorienting I wasn't sure of anything right now.

Halfway through eating, my phone rang, Jade was on the other end.

'Hey, hon, how are you feeling?' Jade was eating too, I could hear her chewing.

I set down my fork, appetite diminished.

'Not too bad, I'm going to have an early night. How are you? Were you on shift today?'

'Yep, finished my fourth in a row, but I've got a day off tomorrow. Will you be at the studio? I can come by and we can grab lunch.'

'Sounds good, you can tell me all about your big night out.' And I could tell her Rick asked me to move in with him.

Jade groaned mid-chew at the reference to her night out, her hangover memories still potent.

My phone beeped and I saw Rick was trying to get through, but ignored it.

'It was a heavy one! Oh, by the way, did you create another Instagram account?'

'No,' I replied, the muscles in my back clenching at her words.

'That's weird, I got a follow request earlier today. Must be a bot, you better report it.'

'I will. Do you remember the handle?'

'Something like Abbi123 or 321, I think. Your picture is on the profile.

Sorry, I assumed you'd created another account or something, like for work. I followed it back.'

'No, I didn't, but I'll check. Like you said, might be a bot. Thanks, hon, I better go, I'll see you tomorrow, okay?' I hung up and opened Instagram. It wasn't an app I used often other than to promote Edgewater as I wasn't into posting pictures of myself, only my portraits. Maybe Jade was right and it was a bot but still my spine tingled with unease.

I found the account quickly, my face staring back at me from their profile picture. It had been taken from one of the photos Jade had tagged me in last summer. She'd been cropped out, but there I was, sipping a Long Island Iced Tea at a bar, grinning into the camera. Could this be the work of the watcher? There were no posts, but whoever it was had managed to get most of my friends to follow them, like Jade, thinking it was me. I scrolled through the list, old friends from college, my cousins, some regular clients and people I used to work with. Rick hadn't been added, his absence glaringly obvious, not that he used Instagram much anyway. I swallowed the saliva which pooled in my mouth and reported the account as fake, hoping that would be the end of it.

Scraping the remaining noodles into the bin, I stretched. Perhaps a hot bath might help soothe my aching back and neck, but first I had to deal with whatever was in the jiffy bag, praying it wasn't another USB stick. It was exhausting being in a constant state of anxiety, always on high alert waiting for the next bombshell to drop. Maybe it was some forgotten order of paintbrushes or sealant for the portraits, because I'd been expecting an email at some point today from the new address, the one I hadn't blocked, but one hadn't materialised. I'd debated whether to block the new one but was reluctant to anger the sender in case it forced their hand and they released the image, or worse the video.

I ripped open the package and dug around in the bag, pulling out an old flip phone with no note or instructions included. What the hell? I held down the power button and waited, the phone coming to life with a loud chime. On first look, there were no contacts, no call history, nothing. Why had someone sent me a phone? The unexpected delivery sent my blood pressure soaring. What did it mean? I didn't have to wait long to find out, it beeped twice announcing a text message had arrived and I read it twice, trying to let the words sink in.

> I WANT YOU TO GET RID OF RICK

It had to be some kind of sick joke, a twisted prank, it couldn't possibly be real. I almost laughed, expecting a knock on the door to find a TV crew with cameras standing outside, the whole thing having been an elaborate hoax. Instead, the flat was eerily silent as the weight of the message sank in.

Get rid? I assumed they meant dump, because I couldn't harm a fly, let alone the man who'd swept me off my feet, the one I wanted to spend the rest of my life with.

I messaged back my answer, one word, clear and to the point.

> NO

It beeped again, almost immediately.

> I THOUGHT YOU'D SAY THAT…

Well, how else was I supposed to respond? I wasn't a child, and I wasn't going to be bullied into ending my relationship.

I deleted the messages. Perhaps I should have asked why because that was what I wanted to know. Why had I, and Rick by association, been targeted? What could I have done to someone to illicit such an attack on my life. I pulled my hair by the roots, winding my fingers into the curls until my plaits were wrecked and my scalp screamed. I had no choice; I'd have to go to the police. What if Rick was in danger, because someone clearly wanted things between us to end. It had to be a scorned ex, but I had no skeletons in my closet. I knew about Heather, and Rick had said she was crazy, but were there others?

I picked up my phone, leaving the flip phone on the kitchen worktop, unsure of whom to dial first: the police or Rick to make sure he was okay. I'd not responded to his last message or answered his call while on the phone to Jade and he hadn't been in touch again. Before I could dial, a pop-up from Instagram appeared on my screen. Abbi321 had tagged me in a post. My chest fluttered, butterflies beating their wings inside my ribcage as my breathing shallowed.

I pressed on the message, taking me straight into the tagged post, and let out a guttural wail at what popped up on the screen.

8

It was a two-second clip played on repeat, me bobbing up and down, naked. Riding Rick while his legs flexed beneath me. My back arched, a mop of red curls twirled down my spine, but it wasn't the same screenshot I'd been sent because at the end, I turned my head to the side. Anyone who knew me would recognise my side profile, lips parted mid-moan. My eyes stung with tears, knuckles white as I gripped the phone trying to stop myself smashing it onto the table. The imposter had tagged my real account @AbbiMont, which meant all my followers would see it.

The thought of so many people seeing my naked behind, of such an intimate act, made the noodles rush straight back up and I vomited the only meal I'd eaten today into the sink. Through blurry eyes, I tried to focus, to untag myself from the video, but I could only report the post, which didn't immediately remove it.

I threw the phone across the room, my chest so tight I could barely breathe. With the walls closing in, I rushed to the door of the flat, pulling it open and falling onto the dirty hallway carpet on my hands and knees. My vision zoomed in and out of focus. I needed air, but the stairs down seemed to move like a carnival ride, so I clambered up and pushed the door to the roof, which was off limits. The rusty padlock, more of a deterrent than a security feature, clanked to the floor and I fell through it.

Crawling on all fours, lungs in a vice, I heaved the solid door to the roof open and staggered out onto the asphalt, the moon peeking out behind another tower block in the distance. Raising my head to the heavens, I gulped in air like I'd been deprived, a free diver finally emerging from beneath the surface.

No, no, no, this couldn't be happening.

My stomach rolled and tipped and I tried to grasp the reality of what was in front of me, a few feet from the edge and a drop to the concrete below.

Would that be better? Better than this?

Humiliation washed over me in a tidal wave. How could I ever look anyone in the eye again? Maybe I should jump because, what about when my parents saw it?

'Abbi?' I'd vaguely heard the door creak behind me, but the sound hadn't registered.

I whirled around and Alfie stood a few feet away; legs splayed with his hands out as though he was approaching a dangerous animal.

'Come away from the edge.'

I hadn't even realised I'd moved so close, the skyline blurry through my tears. I took a step back, turning towards Alfie's outstretched arms and falling into his embrace, sobbing uncontrollably.

'What's happened?' he said, stroking my hair after my legs had given out and we'd sunk to the tarmac.

'I'm ruined,' I hiccupped, unable to regulate my breath.

'How?'

'Someone posted a video of me having sex with my boyfriend online, they've tagged me in it?' I blurted out, without considering that I was revealing my secret to a relative stranger.

Alfie was silent for a moment, letting the gravity of my situation sink in.

'How did they get a video? I mean, no judgement, if that's what you're into—'

'No!' I interrupted. 'Someone planted a camera in his bedroom, I had no idea.'

The silence stretched out between us, while Alfie took his time to come up with a suitable reply. Why did I say anything, I should have kept my mouth shut.

'It can't be that bad, tomorrow's fish and chip paper and all that, people post weird shit all the time.' He fumbled for his phone and I raised my head. 'Let me see if I can help you take it down. How do I find you?' He clicked into the search bar of Instagram and typed Abbi.

'It's @AbbiMont.' I cringed as he brought my account up, it wasn't something I wanted anybody to see but I couldn't refuse his help. However there was no video or evidence of having been tagged in anything as he scrolled through my sporadic posts.

'Try Abbi321.' I straightened my back, urgency in my voice now. Had it been taken down already?

Alfie typed in the handle I gave him.

'Account doesn't exist. Whoever it was, they must have deleted it.'

I let out a snort, holding my hand out to take Alfie's phone.

He was right, the account had disappeared as though it had never existed. My shoulders sagged, the relief all-consuming.

'Shall we get you off this roof?'

Alfie helped me back downstairs, one hand under my arm, the other supporting my waist because my legs were like jelly. We pulled open the door into our joint hallway and found Rick letting himself into my flat. I'd given him a key around a month ago, just in case I ever locked myself out, hoping it might prompt one in return.

'What's going on? I've been trying to get hold of you.' His tone was stern, eyes darting from my face to Alfie's hand at my side, trying to determine if he was a threat.

'She... she had a panic attack,' Alfie stuttered, intimidated by Rick's glare, plus the fact he had hands on his girlfriend.

'I'll take it from here, thanks.' It wasn't a request as Rick pulled me from Alfie's grasp and turned his key to unlock the door. I'd fled the flat without my keys or phone and if Rick hadn't arrived, I would have been stuck outside.

'Thanks, Alfie,' I murmured, looking over my shoulder as I was led in, my eyes trying to convey how grateful I was for his help while the embarrassment of opening up ate at me from inside.

'No problem, take care.' With that, he disappeared inside his flat and closed the door.

'What the hell happened? I've been trying to call you, I thought you were really sick! I've been worried.' He clearly hadn't seen the video in the minutes it had been live.

'I'm fine, I felt faint and needed some air, so I went up to the roof,' I said, trying to pretend I was calm despite the hurricane going on inside. I studied Rick's handsome face, his frown lines and chin jutting out in frustration. Someone wanted us to break up and I couldn't believe the lengths they'd go to, to force me to do it.

'Let me get you some water.' Rick let go of me to fill a glass, grimacing as he tried to wash away the sick in the sink.

While he was distracted, I found my phone in the corner of the lounge where I'd launched it. The screen protector was cracked, but it still worked. I opened Instagram, searching for Abbi321 to check again, but there was no such account and the notification of me being tagged in anything was gone. Had it been posted and deleted soon after or had I imagined the whole thing? No, not possible, I'd almost had a stroke when I saw the video.

I checked my emails, but there was nothing from GoGetHer.

I looked over at Rick and saw he was examining the burner phone, his brows tight together as he looked through it without bothering to ask permission.

'What's this?'

'A phone.' I sighed, unable to hide the sarcasm from my tone.

Rick glared at me as the tension in the air expanded. 'Are you seeing someone else?'

I couldn't help but laugh. 'Of course not.'

'Well, you've been distant, there was the biscuit and now you've got a burner phone. I'm not an idiot.' Rick placed his hands on his hips, expecting an explanation, but I was too exhausted. He carried on, his tone clipped, 'I've asked you to move in, I'm serious about us, Abbi, I've not felt this way before. I'm putting my heart on the line here.'

'I've been sick, I'm still sick, I'm shattered. The phone is old and I have no idea who sent the biscuit. Can we please not do this now, I just want to go to bed.' I went into the bedroom, pulling Rick's hoody over my head and dropping it on the floor with my jeans. I crawled beneath the covers and stuck my phone under the pillow out of sight.

Rick appeared at the door, his face softened as he took in the sorry sight of me curled in the foetal position. I closed my eyes and felt the weight of him on the edge of the bed.

'I'm sorry, I don't want to argue. I was worried. I thought I'd scared you off, moving too fast.'

'I promise I'm just ill, Rick,' I whispered, and it wasn't a lie, I felt like death. The stress of the situation, the sickness and barely having eaten for two days were taking their toll. I wanted to close my eyes and forget it all.

* * *

I woke at dawn, blinking at the window, where for the first night since the original email had arrived I hadn't drawn all the curtains in the flat. Rick snored beside me, still dressed and on top of the covers. My heart swelled, he'd stayed over, wanting to make sure I was all right. I'd been mean last night, not addressing his concerns or trying to reassure him, and guilt ate away at me. I felt better, a little groggy but nothing some food and a coffee wouldn't fix. Sleep hadn't solved my problem; the watcher was still out there and I had no idea what they'd do next, but I couldn't live in fear. I'd tell the police, then I'd tell Rick everything; there would be no more secrets between us.

Snaking an arm around his middle, I shuffled over, pressing my body to his for warmth. He jolted awake, disorientated until he realised where he was.

'Morning, princess,' he croaked, eyes barely open.

'I'm sorry about last night.' I pressed my lips to the side of his neck and squeezed him.

'Are you feeling better?'

'A little. It's early, but I need some food.' I patted my hollow stomach like a drum.

Rick climbed out of bed and headed straight to the kitchen, always looking after me, always putting me first.

'You've got nothing in,' he called. 'I'll run down to the bakers, they should be opening soon.' The clock on my bedside table read 5.55 a.m. and I groaned, rolling onto my back. If only I could stay here all day, eating crisps and doing nothing. I heard the door to the flat shut quietly, Rick being mindful of the neighbours, and I fumbled for my phone under the pillow.

On the home screen was an email alert and I clicked into it. GoGetHer had sent an email late last night, after I'd fallen asleep.

LUCKY ESCAPE, ABBI. I'LL LEAVE IT UP FOR LONGER NEXT TIME.
YOU HAVE YOUR INSTRUCTIONS. TELL NO ONE.
I'LL BE IN TOUCH.
REMEMBER, I'M ALWAYS WATCHING.
YOUR FRIEND

9

I had an immediate rush of tears, a headache knocking at my temples. So last night had been a threat, showing me how easily they could post the footage and ruin my life, before taking it down minutes later. Someone still could have seen it, happened to be on the app at the right time, but overnight I'd had no messages, no outrage from ex-colleagues or family members. No vitriol about what a slut I was.

The watcher still wanted me to get rid of Rick. The idea was preposterous and whoever they were, they clearly didn't know how much he meant to me. It was time to hand things over to the police, delete my accounts and get off social media. If they posted a video of me, at least they wouldn't be able to tag me in it.

There was an option to deactivate my account @AbbiMont and I did, on every single platform I was on. Immediately, a weight lifted, but it didn't solve the problem. If Abbi321 had done the same, deactivated and not permanently deleted, then all the people who had followed their account, thinking it was me, would be able to see anything the watcher posted if they reactivated it. They'd be able to message them too. At least I didn't have to watch my world burn around me.

I left Edgewater, the account I used for my business, alone, checking my settings to make sure no one could tag me. The personal account I was willing to lose, the business one I wasn't, it generated most of my income.

Rick came back from the bakery, and we had breakfast in bed, consuming pastries and coffee, which I was concerned could be too rich for my delicate stomach but wolfed them down anyway. Already feeling lighter knowing I'd deactivated my Instagram account, a small step in taking back control.

'You're wasting away.' Rick laughed, feeding me an extra pastry.

'You won't like it if I get fat,' I retorted, my mouth full.

'I'll love you either way.' He leant over and planted a kiss on my forehead. Inside, my heart ballooned. There was no way I was letting the watcher come between us. Rick was too important, I'd never felt about anyone else the way I felt about him.

I had a flicker of remorse for not being honest with him. Perhaps if I had, it would have put my initial fears at rest. A man like Rick wouldn't have filmed me without me knowing, but the tiniest slither of doubt remained. What would he have gained from it?

He cast his eyes around my bedroom and I waited for him to comment on my lack of furniture. The room was sparse, with only the bed and bedside tables. I had a rail for my clothes but no wardrobe.

'Doesn't look like you're going to have much stuff to move really, in the grand scheme of things.'

'No, but...' I paused. 'It can still wait until the weekend, can't it? I need to catch up at the studio if I want to stay on track.'

'Sure. I was thinking about working from home today, no meetings planned, so I could take you for lunch.' Rick raised his eyebrows hopefully and I pouted.

'That would be lovely, but Jade's going to pop in. Another time?'

'Sure,' he replied, but his smile didn't meet his eyes. He thought I was putting him off, creating distance between us and I couldn't deny the video had shaken me. I didn't want to sleep at Rick's, not in that bed, and the thought of being naked where someone could potentially be watching made me shrivel.

'I'm going to run through the shower.' I scraped the pastry flakes off the duvet into my hand and deposited them onto the window ledge for the birds who nested nearby.

'I'll head off and grab a shower at mine. Will I see you tonight?' Rick asked tentatively.

Usually it would be a given, we'd been living in each other's pockets for months and perhaps he thought I was getting cold feet at the prospect of moving in. He didn't know I'd been hoping he'd ask me for ages. Once I'd been to the police, I'd tell him everything, but I wanted to leave there knowing I had a plan of action, that someone was doing something to make sure the person targeting me was stopped.

'Shall we go out for dinner, to celebrate moving in together?' I suggested. The more time spent out of the penthouse, the better.

He seemed to brighten at that.

'Okay, I'll book somewhere.' Rick gave me a chaste kiss on the lips and left.

Once showered, I washed last night's cups and the bowl I'd left by the sink, opening the window wide to let the stagnant air out and the spring air in. It was going to be warm, so I put on a dress and cardigan, wanting to make myself presentable for the police and for my lunch date with Jade.

As I was locking up, Alfie came out of his flat wearing a suit and tie. Usually, I'd see him in a shirt and trousers for work but never so formal.

'Very dashing,' I said to break the ice after last night.

Alfie's cheeks turned pink. 'Thanks, how are you feeling?'

'Better, thank you. I've deleted my social media accounts and I'm going to the police.'

Alfie's eyes widened and we began a slow descent of the stairs.

'Well, that's good, if they can trace the account.' He sounded doubtful.

'I hope so. Whoever it was contacted me by phone too.' I patted my bag where I'd put the burner phone.

'Hmmmm.' He scratched his chin and I knew he was avoiding telling me that might be untraceable too, but I had to believe they could do something.

'Why you?' Alfie added.

'No idea.' I'd mulled it over and was at a loss. 'But thank you for last night. I was in a right state.'

'It's okay. I was panicking you were going to jump!' he chuckled awkwardly, holding the door to the building open for me, and we stepped into the sunshine.

'I thought about it,' I admitted, only half joking.

'I better go. Have a great day.' He bade me goodbye and walked in the opposite direction to where I'd parked my car.

'You too!' I called to his retreating back. Thank goodness for decent neighbours. As much as I hated my grotty flat, I knew no one over at Rick's building other than Todd. Would the watcher's demands get more sinister when they found out I'd moved in with the man they wanted me to leave?

Knowing I had to put a stop to the harassment, I drove straight to the police station, loitering at the end of the street until it was clear of people and looking over my shoulder before I went in. Trepidation crawled up my spine, and I chewed at my nail. I was going against the rules again; last night I'd told Alfie about the emails and now I was going to the police. I prayed the watcher wouldn't find out.

It took half an hour of waiting in the reception area which smelt of stale alcohol while I grew increasingly impatient to be seen. Eventually, when I was called through to a small office, a middle-aged officer gave me the impression he couldn't really care less about my problem. I explained what had happened, showed him the emails and the text, regaling how I'd had a burner phone delivered to my work and last night I'd been tagged in a video, but it had since been taken down.

'Do you think it's revenge porn?' he asked, taking a loud slurp of a black coffee and setting it back in the ring on the table as he eyeballed me across the desk.

'No, it's a video of me and my current partner. I haven't told him yet, but someone recorded it from inside his apartment, so they had to have gained entry.'

'Are you sure it's not him? He's not recording you without your knowledge?'

'No,' I sighed, 'he's not like that.'

The officer raised his eyebrows, clearly thinking I was an idiot. Doubt slithered like eels beneath my skin, maybe I was. Maybe, I had to confront Rick directly and put my mind at rest.

The officer continued filling out the form, his scrawl barely legible upside down.

'I'll file a report and if anything is posted online, if you see it, report it within the app, let me know and we can try to get it removed. As for the stalking, record any incidents with dates and times. Obviously, if there's any immediate threat to life, then dial 999.' He flipped the form over. 'Do you want me to write a report for breaking and entering? You said a camera was put inside your partner's home – was anything stolen?'

I shook my head, shoulders sinking. I was getting nowhere fast and I could hardly register a crime on Rick's behalf if he didn't even know one had taken place.

The officer stood, indicating it was time to leave, and a surge of adrenaline forced me to my feet.

'That's it?'

'That's all we can do for now. I've taken the phone number used to contact you and I'll look into it, but if they bought a pay-as-you-go SIM, we might not be able to trace it to a person. If I were you, I'd ignore it, block the number, don't engage or respond. Eventually they'll get bored and find someone else to pick on.'

I opened my mouth in disbelief and the officer scratched his chin. His triviality was poorly timed and I didn't bother to respond.

It wasn't random, although why the watcher had chosen me, I had no idea. Maybe Rick was the intended target and I was collateral damage. Could it be an ex-girlfriend of his, someone like Heather, refusing to let go of the past? Or some dodgy dealings at the wine merchants? Had he upset a colleague, someone who was using me to get their revenge and upturn our lives?

Deflated, I trudged out of the station and back to my car, head buzzing like a CB radio playing white noise. The police were supposed to protect, yet I wasn't filled with confidence.

At the studio, I waved at Linda as I passed her workshop, but she only raised her chin in response, her face unusually pale. Had I managed to upset her too? But then I found a letter had been slipped under my door and my breath caught in my throat.

No more, I couldn't deal with any more.

When I opened it, immediately seeing it was from the landlord, my shoulders sagged, but it was a short reprieve. I bit my lip as I read the paragraphs, black inked letters floating in my vision. *Tenancy, agreement, ending.* Rage swirled like a tornado in the pit of my stomach and I marched back to Linda's workshop, bursting through the door.

10

'Did you do this?' I could tell from Linda's sheepish face she knew what I was talking about despite the words that tumbled from her mouth.

'Do what?'

I stepped inside and threw the letter at her. She picked it up, her hands moving slowly as though it might bite, taking her time to read the contents.

'Bit of a coincidence isn't it? You want my studio and now they won't renew my lease?' I spat the words, heavy with sarcasm, the blood steaming in my veins.

'It wasn't like that. Oh, Abbi, I'm sorry.' Linda's eyes dampened, smearing the mascara on her lower lashes, but I was too enraged to care about her pathetic attempt at an apology. The offer on the table from the landlord had expired, a new tenant would take my place and I knew instantly who it was.

'So, you're saying you didn't make them an offer they couldn't refuse to take on my studio as well?' I cracked the knuckles of my left hand one by one as it hung by my side, the vein in my neck pulsing. Why hadn't I signed the agreement when it was sent to me two weeks ago? Why had I left it sitting around, believing I had all the time in the world, only for Linda to swoop in and steal it out from under my nose?

Linda didn't respond, she pressed her lips together and pushed the letter back across the table towards me. I snatched it and stalked from the workshop, a bitter taste left in my mouth. Some friend she'd turned out to be.

Back in the studio, I slammed the door harder than I intended to and sank into my chair. I'd come to love the place and didn't want to leave. It was a good location, close to home with enough space. If I couldn't change my landlord's mind, I'd have to search for somewhere else. It was one problem I didn't need right now and Linda going behind my back was a massive betrayal.

I called my landlord and left him a voicemail before sending a grovelling email, apologising on being late to confirm but I wanted to continue my lease. I didn't know what good it would do; I had no idea what golden handshake Linda had offered to extend her workshop.

Once I'd cooled off, I tried to crack on with the current commission. It was a family cottage called Dilly's for a lady in Devon, but so far I'd only started the door. Maybe immersing myself in the charm of the cobbles and thatched roof would take my mind off things. However, any creativity was thwarted by my fury at Linda's two-faced behaviour and it took three false starts before I finished the cornflower front door.

Halfway through the cobbles, Jade knocked, her friendly gap-toothed smile was exactly what I needed, and I stood to envelop her into a hug.

'Woah, you okay?' she asked as I squeezed her tight, slow to let go.

'Shit day!' I admitted with an exaggerated sigh.

'Well, that sounds like an excuse for a drink. Let's hit the pub.'

'Hair of the dog for you?'

'Nope, I didn't touch a drop yesterday, I was still suffering from the Octopus Bar two-for-one cocktail menu.' Jade laughed, adjusting the waist of her flowing skirt, reminding me of the one she wore when we got our tattoos. I'd pulled down my jeans before climbing on the bed, but she'd considered her clothing choice, wearing a long skirt and exposing one leg without the tattoo artist ever having to see her underwear.

I left my current project on the desk and we headed out to the nearest pub, a five-minute walk away. The Hen and Chicken had a picturesque garden area and we sat with glasses of cider and a bowl of cheesy chips between us, basking in the sun.

'Did you get that Instagram thing sorted?' Jade asked, wrapping a string of melted cheese around a chip before dipping it in ketchup.

I wanted to tell her about the threats and the posted video, but something stopped me. I'd been wracking my brain trying to work out how someone had planted a camera in Rick's penthouse and it had led me to compile a list of people who I knew had been inside. Jade had, a few times, along with Rick's brother Nathan, the cleaner, Todd on security and some of Rick's friends. Any one of them could have hidden a camera inside without Rick's knowledge.

'Hello, earth to Abbi?' Jade patted my arm and I shook the thoughts from my head, mentally scrubbing Jade from my list. She wouldn't do that to me, I trusted her.

'Sorry, yes, I reported the account. They tagged me in some weird video, so I've deactivated everything for the time being, except the Edgewater one.'

'Probably after your passwords; these scammers are getting more clued up by the day.'

I nodded, deciding not to share what the video contained; I wouldn't be able to bear Jade's pity.

'Tell me about your night out with the paramedics,' I said, glad to change the subject, and she launched into a blow-by-blow account of her evening, which involved too many cocktails and her head down the toilet by midnight.

'It was creepy, though, I'm sure someone followed me home. Like they were walking across the street from me but stayed back. I was wasted and ended up going into an off-licence until they disappeared.'

A bead of sweat bloomed at the top of my spine at Jade's words.

'You shouldn't walk home alone, you moron, it's not safe. Why didn't you get a cab?'

'Well, the others were going on to a nightclub and it's only a ten-minute walk, but I will in future, it freaked me out.'

The skin prickled on my bare arms, despite the temperature, maybe I wasn't the only one the watcher was following.

We sat out in the sunshine catching up on each other's gossip. I didn't have much, but told Jade that Rick had asked me to move in. She was pleased for me; he was one of the only boyfriends she approved of. We'd both been out with a few idiots over the years, none of mine noteworthy enough to think they'd had anything to do with the email. I'd seemed to attract immature boys when I was younger. Jade thought I was too nice, too willing to give second chances, whereas she soon kicked a bloke to the kerb if he acted up.

Early afternoon rolled around and I told Jade I'd better get back. At least if I finished the structure of Dilly's cottage, I might be more motivated to paint the garden, which was an array of beautiful colours.

Linda had a class in the workshop but I didn't look in as I passed, still stung from her betrayal. I'd thought we'd been friends, but I guessed Jade was right, I always saw the good in people, which had bitten me on the backside more than once. I had to stop being so trusting.

With the radio on, I got back to painting, finishing the outline of the cottage and relishing the palette of colours Dilly's garden of wildflowers brought with it. It was the sort of place I'd love to stay and maybe that's what I needed, a break on the coast, just me and Rick. He'd messaged to let me know he'd booked a table at Gaucho's in Richmond. Our evening was to be a double date with Nathan and current girlfriend Elena, whom I was yet to meet. When I'd suggested going out for dinner, I'd been thinking more about the local Pizza Express for a few hours out of the penthouse so I could tell Rick about the watcher, but I could hardly back out now. Perhaps a night of socialising would do me good to take my mind off everything, despite the hour on the train it would take to get there.

I worked solidly until five and when I finally finished, with only a few minor touch-ups required tomorrow, Linda had already left. Relieved not to have to endure any awkward conversations with her and pleased with my progress on the cottage, I packed my bag and picked up my phone which had been on charge for the first time in hours. In that moment, everything changed. GoGetHer had sent another email and this one made me sink back into my chair, the room swimming around me.

YOU'VE BEEN CARELESS, SPILLING OUR SECRETS.
WHAT'S HAPPENED IS ON YOU.
GET RID OF RICK. I WON'T ASK AGAIN.
YOUR FRIEND

I sucked air in through my teeth. What had happened? Was Rick all right?

I dialled him immediately as a crushing pain shot upwards through my ribcage. My chest was gripped in panic as the mobile rang and rang, eventually going to voicemail. I left a garbled message demanding he call me back as soon as possible. He was supposed to be working from home, wasn't he? I prayed he was okay. Then my thoughts turned to Jade – what if he'd got to her?

My phone buzzed in my hand and I answered it immediately.

'Hey, babe, everything okay?' Rick's soft voice carried with it a tsunami of relief.

'Where are you?'

'Playing golf, but don't worry, Nathan and I will be round to pick you up at half six in a taxi to take us to the station. I won't be late.' His voice calmed my nerves.

'Okay, have fun, I'll see you later,' I said before hanging up and calling Jade, having a similar conversation, who was in her kitchen banging pans around.

'I'm fine, what's the matter, did you think I'd got run over on the way home?' she asked, laughing at me.

'No, I was just checking in, that's all.'

'God, you're worse than my mother,' she joked. I heard her doorbell ring in the background. 'Gotta go, someone's at the door.'

I twisted a strand of hair around my finger. I needed to get a handle on things, Rick was fine, Jade was fine. What was I going to do, call every single person I knew to make sure they were safe? I gritted my teeth, fingers stabbing my phone like I could reach the watcher on the other end of the email, ignoring the police's advice not to engage. I'd had enough.

GO TO HELL!

I wrote in all caps. They could do their worst, release the video, at least then their reign of terror would be over.

11

I was in no mood to go out and by the time I got home after getting stuck in the rush-hour traffic my mood was sour, yet I knew I'd have to play nice with Rick's brother and girlfriend. It's not that I didn't like him, but Nathan was different to Rick. Where he oozed charm and charisma, always the gentleman, his brother had a penchant for dirty jokes and misogyny.

I let myself into the building and stomped up the stairs, taking out my annoyance on the threadbare carpet.

'Abbi, hi.' A voice came from above, and I saw Alfie looking down at me from our hallway.

'Hey, Alfie,' I said, less than enthusiastically. As I got closer, I saw he had a nasty black eye and a cast on his arm. No longer in his suit, he'd changed into a polo shirt and shorts. 'Jesus, what happened to you?'

'I got mugged this morning at the train station, some bloke in a balaclava.'

I reached the hallway, taking in the bruises on Alfie's face and swollen cheek. 'Jesus Christ, are you okay?'

He shrugged, struggling to meet my eye. 'Yeah, I'm fine. He took my phone, but that was it, said something about being a nosey fucker and ran off.'

I shrivelled, the rock in my stomach was back. Had I inadvertently made Alfie a target?

'Is there anything I can do? Do you need a hand with shopping or...' My voice trailed off.

'No, I'm managing, just popping out for milk and fresh air. Three hours in A&E this morning though, missed my meeting, but be careful, yeah, you never know who's roaming about these days.'

I nodded, pulling out my key and moving towards the flat. WHAT HAPPENED IS ON YOU. The words from the watcher's email bounced around my brain. I turned back to watch Alfie carefully descending the stairs, one step at a time, holding on tightly to the banister. 'Knock if you need anything, okay? I'm going out for a bit, but I'll be back later.'

It struck me once I was inside that what I'd said wasn't true. Rick would expect me to sleep over unless I could come up with an excuse why I couldn't.

My mouth was dry and I drank from the kitchen tap to quench my thirst. I should never have said anything to Alfie, although how the watcher would have known, I had no idea. Did they have a camera on the roof too? What did they have against Rick?

Grabbing a notebook, I scribbled down the time and date of the email and Alfie's assault in case they were connected. If it continued, I'd have to go back to the police with my diary, like they'd suggested, and make them take me seriously.

With zero appetite for socialising or eating, I forced myself to shower and get ready for Rick and Nathan's arrival, slipping on a long black dress and low heels, tying my red curls up.

When they arrived, the pair like excitable puppies, I tried to join in the banter on the taxi ride to the train station. Elena, Nathan's girlfriend, was meeting us at the restaurant as she worked in Kingston at the Rituals store and it was a hassle to come to Crawley and easier to go straight to Richmond. I knew Rick loved that part of London, where the rich people lived, and he dreamed of getting a place on the river, telling me it was only a matter of time. He was going up in the world, he had big ambitions and if anyone was going to succeed, it would be him.

'I got us a table out on the terrace; will you be warm enough?' Rick held my hand as we walked along the towpath, the light from the street lamps bouncing off the gently flowing river.

I nodded, wishing I'd brought a cardigan instead of my light denim jacket. Although it was beautiful weather for March, I hoped there'd be heaters outside for when the temperature dropped later.

'Rick tells me you two lovebirds are moving in together,' Nathan said, and I detected a slight sneer as if he couldn't believe Rick had picked me. The brothers looked similar, both had dark wavy hair, but Nathan's was shorter, and his eyes were bluer than Rick's steely hue. Both tall and athletic, Nathan had a slightly wider jaw and nose from where it had been broken in a fight. He was the more rugged of the pair, younger by eighteen months, and I imagined Rick's mother had had her hands full when they were boys.

'It would seem so,' I said stiffly, but catching Rick's frown, I added, 'Never thought I'd live in a penthouse.' I elevated my tone into something more enthusiastic despite feeling anything but. The watcher's email and Alfie's mugging weighed heavily on my mind.

'What can I say, I fell for her the moment I saw her at the bar, up on tiptoes trying to get served. You would have been there all night if I hadn't intervened.' Rick laughed.

'You are taller!' I shot back with a grin, remembering how charming he'd been, adding my drinks to his order and helping me back to the table with them. Jade's eyes had been out on stalks.

'I'm looking forward to my steak,' Nathan said, changing the subject. He clapped his hands together, rubbing them gleefully, knowing Rick was paying, and I let the brothers chat while I enjoyed the view of the Thames.

We met Elena outside Gaucho's and she was every bit as I'd imagined: blonde, slim and wearing a tight coral dress that hugged her curves. Nathan was punching for sure, but she seemed into him.

I was polite and tried to get into the spirit after Rick shot a couple of perplexed glances my way at how quiet I was. We ordered some drinks and olives, while perusing the menu. The terrace was beautiful with boats drifting by and thankfully there was a heater next to our table.

Nathan, Rick and Elena ordered steaks while I opted for a chicken Milanese salad, despite Nathan's eye roll at my choice.

When the food arrived, Rick's steak was so rare, the red juices oozed from the meat and turned my stomach. I found myself picking at my salad and when Nathan and Elena popped over to the water's edge to smoke, Rick placed his hand on my forearm.

'What's going on? I'm totally getting the vibe you don't want to be here.'

'I think I'm still a bit delicate, you know, from the bug,' I lied, stabbing some lettuce with my fork.

'You wanted to go out for dinner.' Rick dabbed at his mouth with his napkin, giving me a hard stare.

'I know, but I meant just us,' I whispered. 'I'm sorry, I'll try to liven up a bit.' I picked at my salad, annoyed with myself for upsetting Rick. When his brother returned, I asked him about work, knowing he managed a builder's merchant in Croydon.

'Yeah, it's all right, pays the bills and the guys are a good laugh. Going to have to replace the old dorris who works in the office though, she's going blind and keeps cocking up the invoices.' He chuckled and I had to stop myself biting.

'I see your portrait business is going well, Abbi. I follow you on Instagram,' Elena said, smoothing down her dress before helping herself to one of Nathan's leftover chips.

The mention of Instagram sent me off balance.

'It is, thank you, I've been lucky,' I managed.

'It's not luck; her portraits are fantastic,' Rick chipped in, making my cheeks flush with pride.

'You should do a video.' Nathan's comment hit me like a punch in the gut and he winked at me as he necked the last of his Peroni from the bottle. I looked at Rick and Elena who were nodding enthusiastically at his suggestion, but his words had turned my insides to ice.

'That's ridiculous,' I said, feigning a laugh and shaking my head.

'No, it's not, it's good business sense, get yourself on screen, showing off your portraits and, of course, the more skin you show, the better.' Nathan laughed wickedly and the hand holding my wine quivered as I resisted the urge to launch it at him. Was he baiting me?

'Okay, I think that's enough of that,' Rick interjected as I shot daggers at Nathan.

'What? Lighten up, I'm just saying it's a thing. Sex sells, doesn't it, Abbi?'

'I need to use the bathroom,' I said, jumping up so fast, the table wobbled before rushing off to the ladies'. Mortification burned at my neck and my eyes stung with tears. It was him; Nathan had planted the camera. How could he do that to his own brother... or was Rick in on it?

I locked myself in a cubicle, grateful the toilets were empty, and counted in my head as molten lava coursed through my body. I wanted to leave, but Elena had ordered dessert and the bill was yet to be paid. Rick would want to know what was wrong, he already thought I was moody, but I wasn't sure I could get through another minute sitting opposite Nathan's smug face, knowing how he'd done something so perverse. Why say that otherwise?

'Abbi, are you okay?' Elena's voice came from the other side of the cubicle. I'd been so wrapped up in my own thoughts I hadn't even heard her come in.

'I'll be out in a minute.' I even sounded wobbly, but I couldn't blame the wine, I'd only had one glass of the expensive Argentinian Malbec from San Carlos Rick had been excited to try.

I waited for her to leave, not trusting myself to be nice, though it wasn't Elena's fault she'd fallen for a sleazebag like Nathan. Why he'd want to hurt his brother I didn't know. Was it sibling rivalry? Rick was a much higher earner and had done well for himself. He'd bought the penthouse, whereas Nathan was renting a two-bedroom terrace in New Addington with a mould problem and I could tell it got under his skin. Was this about Nathan humiliating Rick? Was I just being used as a pawn in his game?

I left the cubicle and washed my hands, staring into the mirror at my flushed reflection, the contrasting black to the mottling of my skin was not a good look. I took some deep breaths, bracing myself to go back out there and face Nathan. All I had to do was smile and play nice like the good girlfriend I was and get through the evening. But as I was about to leave, my phone pinged with a sound I knew only too well. Another email had arrived.

12

Loitering by the door, I opened the email from GoGetHer.

HE'S NOT A GOOD MAN.

What the hell was that supposed to mean? Why was someone telling me Rick wasn't a good man. I'd known him for ten months and had seen zero evidence of that. If this was Nathan, did he really think I'd believe his empty words? The email sent me spiralling and my head was all over the place, but for the sake of being cordial I pasted a smile on my face and rejoined the table, praying the evening would be over soon.

It wasn't – dessert turned into coffee, followed by a slow stroll back to the train station, where I tried to stifle my yawns. Nathan and Elena wanted to hit the local club, Viva, but I passed on extending our night out. Rick tried to persuade me to stay. Having sunk most of a bottle of wine, he wasn't ready for the night to end.

'Look, you go out with your brother, I'll be fine on the train and I'll jump in a cab from the station back to the flat.'

'No, go back to mine and keep the bed warm,' he pleaded.

'I need to get to the studio early tomorrow; I really need to finish this one piece. I didn't tell you, but it looks like they aren't renewing my lease, so I might have to find somewhere else to paint.'

'Ah, man, that's annoying, but I'll help you, we'll find somewhere perfect.'

It was perfect. But I laughed as Rick swayed on the platform while we waited for the train. He'd persuaded Nathan and Elena to come back to Crawley so he could ensure I got in the taxi safely, then they were going to go on to a bar.

Nathan would also likely crash at Rick's, another reason I wanted to stay at my place. The last time I'd woken up at Rick's and wandered into the kitchen to make coffee when he was there, wearing an oversized T-shirt, he'd eyed me like I was something to eat. Since then, I'd never been comfortable alone with him and if he'd been the one to plant the camera, perhaps my gut had been right.

Thankfully the train journey went quickly, not many revellers out on a Thursday night, even with changing at Clapham Junction to head south, but still Nathan found someone holding a can of Stella to chat to, the pair of them swaying with the movement of the carriage. I cuddled up to Rick, glad to be out of the wind and Elena scrolled through her phone, leaving Nathan to talk to his new friend until we reached Crawley.

'We'll have a quiet one tomorrow, I promise, and we'll move you in over the weekend, okay.' Rick kissed me goodbye and held open the door to the taxi for me to climb inside while Nathan and Elena headed into the Snooty Fox to get a round in.

I pulled out my phone as soon as we were away from the station, the driver thankfully uninterested in making small talk, and sent an email.

I'M BLOCKING YOU. PLEASE DON'T CONTACT ME AGAIN.

Sure, there was the possibility the watcher could email me from a third account but it made me feel good to block him again, like I was taking back control. Rick didn't have a bad bone in his body, and I wasn't going to be drawn into the watcher's lies. I prayed they wouldn't release the video, but if they did, I'd tell the truth, I had no idea I was being filmed, I was the victim in this scenario. But that wouldn't matter if my naked body was splattered across social media.

The taxi driver dropped me off right outside the entrance to my building and drove off. There was no one around, the streets eerily quiet, and I fumbled in my bag for my keys. The nearest streetlight, which was weak at best, flickered, threatening to plunge me further into darkness. The hair on the back of my neck stood to attention and a frigid late-night breeze wrapped itself around my legs. A rustle came from behind me and I spun around, squinting at the bushes across the road. It was probably a fox, but I wasn't going to hang around to find out. My fingers grasped the keys and I unlocked the outer door as quickly as I could, taking the stairs two at a time. Usually, the block had some muffled noise on each floor, even this late – televisions or people talking from the individual flats – the walls were so thin, but it was quiet.

Desperate to be back inside the safety of my four walls, I kept climbing, out of breath when I reached the top. I glanced briefly at Alfie's door – was he in? I guessed he would be, sitting uncomfortably watching television or attempting to sleep with the bulky cast on his arm, poor guy.

My heart rate slowed once I got inside and locked the door, drawing the curtains to shield myself from the street below. Rick was likely propping up the bar with Nathan, the pair of them having moved on to shots by now, and I hoped he didn't have any important meetings tomorrow.

I slid into bed after washing my face and set my phone on charge, the alarm due to go off at seven tomorrow morning, meaning I'd get almost eight blissful hours sleep if I didn't toss and turn.

Just as I'd dozed off, my phone vibrated on the table, likely Rick and some drunken declaration of love, but it was Jade.

'Are you okay?' I said, shuffling upright in bed, blinking away the shadows. Panic pulled me from sleep; there had to be a reason she was calling so late.

'Yeah, I'm fine, but, Abbi...' Her voice trailed off.

'What? What's wrong?'

'I've received a private message from that Instagram account.'

I chewed on my lip as trepidation crept its way up from my toes.

'What did it say?' I couldn't hide the tremor in my voice.

'I'm so sorry, hon, it's a video, of you and Rick, you know... doing it.' Jade's words seemed to float away, as did my entire bedroom.

Breathe, Abbi, breathe.

'Oh God,' I whimpered as tears burned my eyes.

'I've deleted it obviously, but I did send it to you first in case you wanted to see it.' The hand holding the phone shook like it wasn't connect to my body.

'Did you guys film yourselves?' Jade giggled, not quite grasping the gravity of the situation. 'That's kind of kinky, you know!'

If the watcher had sent it to Jade, could he have sent it to everyone, the people who'd followed Abbi321 believing it was my account?

'I'll call you back,' I said, hanging up and opening Instagram, seeing the message notification from Jade. The watcher hadn't posted the video for public consumption, but had they sent it to all my friends and acquaintances? Had they destroyed my reputation with one click, and for what, to get me to break up with Rick?

I clicked on Jade's message and watched through blurry eyes as the image on screen came alive.

It was so much worse than I'd anticipated. It wasn't the same video that had been screenshotted last time, the one they'd made a tiny loop of, my naked back and swivelled head. This was a different night, a different recording, and it looked like engineered porn. I clapped my hand over my mouth, shoulders heaving with sobs as I watched Rick take me from behind as I bent over his bed, still wearing my silk nightie. Mouth open, I groaned towards the camera I'd had no idea was there, but it looked like I'd staged it, like I was performing.

How many people had it been sent to? Had Rick seen it?

Like the compulsion to pick at a scab you know you shouldn't, I searched for Abbi321, who'd earlier posted a pretty doorway with a floral decoration saying how much they'd love to paint it. It was exactly like something I'd post and otherwise there was nothing nefarious that made it look like an imitation account. My face was even on the profile picture. My Edgewater account wasn't a follower of Abbi321, so I hadn't received a message, but as I clicked on the followers of the imitation account I cringed as I scrolled through the list. So many people I knew, had gone to school with or worked with in the past, including my mum's sister, Valerie, who lived in Canada. If she'd been sent the video, she'd be straight on the phone to my mum. An internal scream rang in my ears, drowning out the silence of my bedroom and a gut-wrenching swirl of anxiety grew in my belly.

They'd done it, they'd actually done it. My life was ruined. I'd be better off climbing to the roof and chucking myself off. How on earth would I be able to face anyone again?

I rewatched the video, gazing in horror at the screen, listening to skin slapping against skin, and I threw up in my mouth a little. It would be the end of Rick and I for sure; it would be the end of everything.

I had no messages in my Edgewater account yet, but I expected them to come from people who knew me and were wondering what the hell I was playing at. Unless the watcher responded from the Abbi321 account, pretending to be me? I spiralled, imagining the worst-case scenario, although the worst had already happened.

I reported the account yet again for imitation. Why hadn't it been taken down already?

Jade calling flashed onto the screen and I answered, telling her I was fine but couldn't talk right now and threw my phone under the duvet. Maybe I should call the police, but it was hardly an emergency. I'd be straight down there in the morning, there were laws against revenge porn, blackmail and extortion. This had to come under one of those categories; they had to do something now.

I got out of bed to make a hot drink because there would be no sleep tonight, not now my world had imploded.

13

Miraculously, I did drift off for a few hours, enjoying the blissful few seconds between sleep and consciousness before jolting awake and remembering last night. It was like a cruel version of Groundhog Day, reliving the nightmare again and again. Despite my grief and mortification, the sun still rose and the alarm sounded, indicating it was time to get up. I didn't want to go to the police station, showing anyone that video made feel cheap, like I was trash, but when I checked, the account was still active. Half of me wanted to read the messages I knew Abbi321 would have received, the outrage, horror and embarrassment of every single person who'd opened that video and watched Rick and I having sex. I'd gone past believing it had only been sent to Jade.

While I was getting dressed, the phone call I was dreading came and I was tempted not to answer.

'Abbi, how could you, to Auntie Val – what were you thinking!'

'I know, Mum, I'm sorry. That account isn't mine, it's someone imitating me. I didn't send any videos to anyone.' Although me not being the sender hardly helped my spoiled reputation and Mum's embarrassment.

'I hope your brother hasn't seen it.'

My throat closed, my younger brother Ben, the apple of their eye, but thankfully I hadn't seen him on the list of followers.

'I don't think so, Mum.'

'Well, your father wants you to come over, he wants to talk to you when he gets back from work.'

A lump formed in my throat, the look I knew Dad would give me, utter disbelief and disgust, was already imprinted in my mind. I wasn't sure if I could deal with it today.

'I need to go to the police first; I need them to take the account down.' I avoided promising I would visit, they weren't the greatest with modern technology and trying to explain what had happened would fall on deaf ears. As much love and support they'd given me over the years, they wouldn't understand this. I wasn't sure they'd get over it either.

Less than two minutes later, my phone started blowing up. Text messages and emails, everyone telling me there was a video of me on the internet and Jade trying to make sure I was okay. With every message read, what was left of my dignity dissolved into a puddle on the floor and I was tempted to stay put and wait for it to blow over, but that would be cowardly. I had to face it head on, despite the mortification I felt.

As I was about to leave the flat, dressed in black and wearing a cap, Rick called.

'What the fuck, Abbi? You planted a camera in my bedroom?' he shouted down the phone without offering any form of greeting. Elena had to have been sent the message too, which meant Nathan would have seen us in all our glory. The thought made me sick; I'd never live it down.

'I didn't; someone else must have. It was probably your brother!'

'You expect me to believe that? Do you think I'm stupid? My naked ass has been sent to Elena, Nathan's seen it, it's so messed up.'

I cringed away from the phone, Rick's rage pulsing through the handset. He was incandescent and there was little point trying to prove my innocence, he was too incensed to listen.

'I'm sorry, it's not my account, I'm going to the police.'

But still he raged on. 'Do you know what will happen if it gets out? I'll lose my job, Abbi, for bringing the company into disrepute. Adam got sacked for a bloody tweet. Get it removed. Now!'

He hung up and I burst into tears, my relationship was hanging by a thread, my parents would more than likely disown me and I didn't know who was doing this to me.

* * *

'I can't find the account. It's been removed. You said it was Abbi321 right?'

I sat across the desk from Officer Barrett, the same policeman I saw before. Watching him watch the video was absolute torture, his lip twitched throughout and my face turned crimson.

'Yes, I told you, it's been deleted, or deactivated.' I snatched my phone back. As of an hour ago, Abbi321 no longer existed. 'But it was there. Look this clip has been sent to almost all my friends and followers. This person has imitated me, planted a camera and posted this, surely you must be able to do something? What if they do it again?' I cried, slamming a hand on the table, my frustration boiling over.

'I'll give the details to the South-East Cyber Crime Unit for them to investigate.'

I rubbed my head, fearing I was being fobbed off again.

'Have there been any other incidents, things you have recorded in the diary I suggested?'

'Well, against instructions, I told my neighbour what was going on. Then I had an email which read "what's happened is on you" and I came home to find he'd been beaten up and mugged on the same day. I don't think it's a coincidence.'

'When did this happen? Did he report it to the police?' Officer Barrett scratched his stubble, eyes narrowed.

'It was yesterday and I think so, his name is Alfie, he lives at number seven.'

'Okay, I'll look up the report. I'd also like you to forward all the emails you've received to me, the sender may be difficult to trace if they are using a VPN, but I'll pass them to the cyber unit.'

It was all gobbledegook to me, but I took down Officer Barrett's details, saving them to my phone.

'You need to find whoever this is and make them stop. I feel like I'm constantly being watched, they're ruining my life.' I knew I sounded whiney, but Officer Barrett didn't seem to grasp the hopelessness of the situation I was in.

'And you're sure your boyfriend didn't know about the camera?'

'No,' I sighed, 'he thinks I did it.'

Barrett gave a solitary nod, although clearly not convinced. 'Be careful, this person obviously knows you, intimately.'

No shit! Everyone does now.

I left the police station in a daze, not willing to make the forty-minute drive to my parents' house in Wallington or sit through a lecture. Instead, I headed to the nearest café. Pulling my cap low, I ordered an Americano and gave my name as Lisa. It was ridiculous, I was hardly internet famous, not yet anyway, and no one batted an eyelid, but I wanted to be anyone other than Abbi Montgomery today.

I'd expected Rick to have messaged, maybe apologise for losing his temper earlier, but it seemed I'd had contact from everyone but him.

Most of the texts I'd received were complaints at how inappropriate I'd been sending that video; some, who knew me better, warned me I'd been hacked. At least fifty people had seen me have sex with my boyfriend and the thought made me die inside.

I carried my coffee back to my car, deciding to seek solace at the studio. Thank goodness the commission which had to be posted today only needed a few minor touch-ups. I wouldn't be able to concentrate on anything new. The coaster-sized portraits I'd planned to get done would have to wait until next week, but I didn't want to fall behind. Long waiting times would put customers off and I already had more orders than expected.

When I arrived, I kept my head low, Linda was in full teacher mode. This time, a bunch of school-age students sat behind their pottery wheels. She paused to glare at me as I walked past the windows in the hallway towards my studio. I ignored her, I should be giving her the death stare, not the other way around, but when I reached the door, my heart sank. The word SLUT had been painted in bright red letters diagonally across the wood. Shame oozed out of every pore. No wonder Linda had been giving me evils, it was likely her customers would have seen the slur and unfortunately there was no CCTV in the building or out on the street, except near the gym entrance.

'For fuck's sake.' I gritted my teeth, scratching at the paint with a nail. It looked like it was acrylic and wouldn't have surprised me if Linda had been the culprit.

I unlocked the studio and once inside I looked again for Abbi321 on Instagram, if only to see if Linda was a follower, and had received the video. She followed my Edgewater account, but Abbi321 still didn't exist.

Before I got settled, I took a photo of the offending graffiti then scrubbed at the door with some methylated spirits and thankfully the paint came off easily. The landlord hadn't responded to my messages about the lease, but this would hardly keep me in his favour. I locked the door, closed the blinds and got to work, playing soothing music to take my mind back to Dilly's cottage, zoning in on the photograph I'd been provided to recreate on canvas.

Annoyingly, my phone kept buzzing, but I was too scared to turn it off in case Rick called. He was the only one I wanted to speak to, but he remained stubbornly silent. I'd had multiple messages from Mum. Apparently, Dad had called her from the school where he worked, demanding to know what time I would be arriving. At twenty-four, I was a little old to be reprimanded, but I was sure Dad would delight in telling me how disappointed he was in his daughter. I knew I'd have to face them eventually, but the shame was all-consuming, so I responded to Mum that I had to deal with the situation but would call later.

I finally got Dilly's cottage finished and once dry, I wrapped it up, ready to take to the post office. I'd heard Linda's class finish a while ago, the chatter in the hallway as the students left, but it had been quiet since then. I was cleaning my brushes when someone tried the handle to my studio. The noise alerted me at first and I watched the handle twist and the door shake in its frame. Dropping the paintbrush I was holding, I backed away from the door as it rattled again, then someone hammered on it. I half expected a lynch mob to be outside, protestors against porn or something ridiculous, but Jade's voice carried from the other side.

'Abbi, are you there?'

14

I pulled open the door and practically fell into Jade's arms, letting myself dissolve into tears. Her starched forest green paramedic uniform scratched at my cheek, but I pressed myself against her and she stroked my hair. All the emotional turmoil, the shame and self-pity I'd been holding since last night came rushing out.

'I've been so worried, are you okay? Well, clearly you're not, but it will be all right, Abs, people will forget, and it'll soon be yesterday's news.'

I sniffed, stepping back to wipe my eyes.

'Have you been to the police?'

'Yes, they're passing it to the cyber team, but the damage is done. It went to so many people, Jade. My parents have seen it. Rick is doing his nut.'

'Well, I can't understand why he's blaming you; it's not like you set the camera up... did you?' Jade frowned, her hands on her hips. She looked almost matronly.

'No, I didn't know it was there, he didn't either, someone planted it. I don't know who.'

She snorted. 'Really? Someone broke into Rick's penthouse and planted a camera?' Jade let out a mirthless laugh, shaking her head.

'They had to have.' My voice sounded unsure now.

'I'm sorry, babe, I don't believe that. He had to have known and you need to ask him straight, because it sounds like bullshit to me.' She screwed her face up, incredulous at my naivety. 'Anyway, I've got to go, I'm on a break and Honking Henry is waiting outside in the ambulance. I'll ring you later okay, keep your chin up.'

After dropping her bombshell, Jade left, her short visit sending me reeling. Was I being an idiot? Did Rick know about the camera? It wasn't the first time I'd doubted him, but I'd convinced myself someone had either got in when the building was evacuated during the numerous fire alarms or someone already had access, like Nathan, Todd or the cleaner. After Nathan's comments at dinner, I'd been sure it was him, but had I been blind all along? Rick's over-the-top reaction on the phone this morning was out of character, but had that been a ruse? He was so angry and no doubt hungover after last night, but attack was always the best form of defence and it had been radio silence from him since.

I packed my things and locked up, dropped off the commission at the post office then drove to Rick's. I had to deal with this head on, look him in the eye and ask him straight if he had anything to do with the camera. He had to be working from home again as his car was in his designated space outside the plush building. I waved at Todd as I strode past, who cranked his neck to confirm who I was, hiding beneath the baseball cap, my head low.

The lift to the penthouse took a while, with other residents stopping at almost every floor, giving me time to dig around in my bag for the key Rick had given me. I'd intended to catch him unawares, but if the camera wasn't there before, it would hardly be there now.

I slid the key into the door as quietly as I could, pushing it open, already hearing Rick's deep voice berating someone.

'Just do as I say and it'll be fine. It's not going to come back on us.'

I poked my head around the door and Rick caught my eye. His expression was a picture before he quickly recovered, but he couldn't hide the colour draining from his face.

'Thanks, Gina. I'll be in the office on Monday. Try to have a good weekend.' He put the phone face down on the table and came towards me. 'Abbi, did you get it removed?' His tone was cool, stare accusatory but thankfully calmer than he had been on the phone this morning.

I walked straight past him towards the bedroom, watching him turn and follow me.

'It was a message, Rick, I can't get those removed or unsend them, I wish I could, but the account has gone – for now at least.' My voice was flat, Jade's accusation ringing in my ears. I had to see for myself, but the shelf was the same as when I'd searched it before: books, DVDs and Funko Pops.

'What are you looking for?' He glared from the doorway but didn't attempt to stop me as I pulled out items.

'I'm looking for the camera, Rick – what do you think I'm looking for?'

'I assumed you took it with you when you left.'

His sarcasm irked me. Where had the kind, considerate man I'd come to love gone?

'I didn't film us, Rick, what we had was private,' I snapped back.

'Had?' My choice of words caught his attention and he straightened, arms dropping to his side.

I rubbed the back of my neck, staring at the shelves, hoping they'd give me the answer.

'Someone is doing this to me, Rick, I don't know who to trust.'

'Well, it's not me!'

'How else did someone get a camera in here? Look me in the eye and tell me it wasn't you.'

Rick rushed over, gripping my arms and lowering his head to stare directly into my eyes. 'Babe, loads of people come in and out of here: Todd, Miriam the cleaner, Nathan, Elena, Jade even. It could be anyone.'

'You don't seem outraged.'

'Are you kidding? I've been onto the police as well; I've told Todd no visitors except for you. No one is to be sent up if I'm not here. It's not just you on that video, Abbi. Someone's only got to upload it to YouTube and I can kiss my job goodbye.' He let go of my arms, placing his hands behind the back of his head, and walked around in a circle. 'You have no idea. I've barely slept a wink. Nathan called me after Elena was sent the video and I spent hours on fucking chatbots with Instagram, trying to get it deleted. I'm mortified.'

I sighed. If nothing else, Rick was convincing and I'd been so worried about my own reputation, I'd not given much thought to how Rick might be viewed in the whole scenario.

'I'm sorry, I'm so sorry,' I whispered, tears spilling down my cheeks.

Rick enveloped me into a hug. 'You need to tell me what's going on, I feel like you're keeping things from me.'

'I wanted to tell you last night, but you invited Nathan and I couldn't.'

'So, tell me now.'

Rick made coffee and we sat at the breakfast bar. I told him everything, from the first email on Monday, my visits to the police, the burner phone delivery to the word slut painted on my studio door. He listened without judgement, until I revealed that Alfie had been attacked and I thought it was connected.

'Don't worry about him, he's a weirdo,' Rick said dismissively.

His uncharacteristic slight on my neighbour left a bad taste in my mouth, but perhaps he felt threatened. I remembered the look on his face when Alfie was holding me up after my trip to the roof.

'They want us to break up?' he asked.

'It's ridiculous, I know. I mean, do you think it's Heather, or have you upset someone at work, a business deal or something? Could it be linked to Nathan?'

Rick shook his head slowly, contemplating, but like me he came up with nothing. The pair of us clutching at straws. We'd both been targeted out of nowhere with no rhyme or reason and the watcher had given me nothing to go on other than telling me Rick wasn't a good man.

'Do you know why this person would think you weren't good?'

Rick's eye twitched, but he shook his head again.

Tension gripped my shoulders – could I be sure he was being honest with me or had recent events made me paranoid?

'You know me, Abbi. Have I ever given you reason to believe I'm not a good person?'

I shook my head. It was true; he had never been anything other than lovely towards me. It was why I'd fallen so hard for him, I'd never been treated so well. In the ten months we'd been together, this was the first argument we'd had.

'There you go then.' He placed his hand on top of mine, squeezing it gently before continuing. 'Why don't you give me the phone he sent you, I've got some friends in the IT department – maybe they can help me.'

I chewed on my lip, an unsettling notion bubbling beneath the surface.

'I've left it back at the flat,' I lied.

'We'll get it tomorrow when we pick up your stuff.' He leaned towards me, lifting my cap off my head and placing it on the counter. After what happened, I was surprised he still wanted me to move in. 'I've missed you,' he said, gently kissing my forehead, my cheeks, then my lips. I knew what he meant, he'd missed me physically, and as the thought took hold, his kiss deepened. Initially, my muscles clenched, but I soon relaxed as he entwined his hands in my hair, pulling me closer, tongue probing. The urge to feel his body against mine took over, pressure in my groin building with every sweep of his fingertips across my skin. He got to his feet, gently easing me off the stool to lead me towards the bedroom.

'Not there,' I murmured as he pressed against me, hands running up the back of my T-shirt, grasping the flesh of my back.

We moved to the sofa, rolling around on it, cushions spilling onto the floor, pulling at each other's clothes like a pair of teenagers. The urge for him to be inside me became all-consuming, a need to be in the moment to banish the watcher and the horrors of the past week from my mind. He paused to get some protection from the bathroom, but then the sex was intense and over quickly, a release we both needed. We pulled our clothes back up, giggling, but the spell was broken when Rick's phone began to ring.

'Sorry, I better take that,' he said, doing his jeans up as he crossed the open-plan lounge towards the kitchen.

'Go ahead, I'm going to use the bathroom.' I left the door open, in case I might catch any of the conversation, but as soon as Rick mentioned twelve cases followed by notes of apricot, it was obvious it was a work call. Yet I was sure there were things he wasn't telling me.

15

In the mirror, my cheeks were flushed, lips full and red from kissing, giving colour to my make-up-free face. I shook out my hair, separating the curls after washing my hands and looking inside the cabinet above the sink. A bottle of pills with Rick's name on was on the top shelf, hidden behind some shaving foam. Zopiclone, take one 7.5mg tablet before going to bed. I guessed they were sleeping pills, but I wasn't aware Rick had any trouble sleeping; he hadn't since we'd been together. The prescription label was dated last year, but there would be a lot I'd be learning about Rick once I'd properly moved in.

I heard Rick say goodbye on the phone and closed the cabinet, returning to the lounge.

'Do you want to get a takeaway and have a night in?' I asked.

'I'm sorry, babe, I've got to take some clients out for dinner, I completely forgot to tell you.'

'That's okay, I'll go and start packing,' I replied, snaking my arms around his waist.

'I could do without it, to be honest, especially after last night.'

'You and Nathan hit it hard then?'

'Elena drunk us both under the table. I have no idea where she puts it.' He laughed, the twinkle back in his eyes, and everything was right between us again. 'Listen, don't worry about the video, I know it's easy for me to say, but you could maybe put a post up to say you've been hacked or something. People will forget it soon enough.' He rested his chin on my head, our height difference making it the perfect position.

'That's what Jade said actually: it'll be yesterday's news before you know it.' I nuzzled into his chest, glad we were back on good terms as I mulled Rick's suggestion over. I'd deactivated my personal account and didn't want to put a message on the Edgewater one but decided to write a standard response for all those who'd been in contact with me since receiving the video.

'You've told Jade?' Rick's tone had a hint of incredulity to it.

'She's seen the video; she was one of the recipients of that arsehole's message.'

'What did she say?'

'Just that really; she wanted to make sure I was okay.' I didn't tell Rick she thought he must have planted the camera. I was sure now he couldn't have. 'Well, I'll let you get ready to wow your clients, message me in the morning when you're on your way over and we can load the cars up.' I raised up onto my toes to give Rick a kiss, a weight lifted now everything was out in the open and we could get through it together.

'About ten sound okay?'

'Sure.'

I left the penthouse satisfied Rick had nothing to do with the video, he was just as furious as I was and had already been onto the police. Someone, somewhere had it out for him and perhaps I'd got caught in the crossfire. The watcher had posted the video, it had been sent to my family and friends, I'd been humiliated, but what more could they do? Even if there were more videos of me, one was already out there, the damage had been done. Rick was going to stand by me, whereas this morning I was convinced our relationship was dead in the water.

Considering the day's events, I was relatively calm as I drove home, but deliberately hadn't looked at my phone all day. When I did, over a cup of tea, I wrote out my stock response and sent it to everyone who'd got in touch. It was pretty much an 'I'm so sorry, my account was hacked, it's a long story but I didn't know the video had been taken. I'm sorry to have caused you any embarrassment.' Some responded straight away with sympathy, some were a little more clipped.

My mother had left numerous voicemails demanding to know when I would be coming as Dad was getting irate at my lack of response.

I made the call I knew I had to, to calm Mum down while Dad was at work. He wanted to see me in person to tear a strip off me, but Mum and I agreed it was better to let him cool off and visit over the weekend.

I was halfway through packing my clothes into a suitcase when I began to get peckish. Despite finding more food in the fridge than I was sure I'd bought, I craved alcohol. It was Friday night and if the end of any week required wine, this was one of them. If nothing else, it would drown my mortification of practically everyone I knew seeing my sexual exploits.

Grabbing my keys, I nipped to the local supermarket. It was a short walk down the road, and still wearing dark clothes and a cap, I tried to stay incognito. As expected, no one gave me a second glance. A barbecue chicken pizza and another bottle of Sauvignon Blanc fell into my basket, along with an expensive block of dark chocolate. Rick and I hadn't discussed rent yet, but I guessed I'd be paying similar to what I was now, something we'd have to sort out. Either way, it was perfectly acceptable to treat myself at the end of a shitty week and this one had been my worst ever.

As I was queuing for the self-checkout, my bag vibrated, but when I pulled out my phone, there was no message waiting for me.

With my heart in my mouth I dug around for the burner phone, surprised it hadn't yet run out of battery, recoiling when I saw a message had come through.

> SEE WHAT HAPPENS WHEN YOU DON'T DO AS YOU'RE TOLD. ONCE YOU'VE SEEN WHAT I'VE GOT, YOU'LL WANT TO KILL RICK.

A cough sounded from behind me and I nearly dropped my basket, realising it was a polite nudge to get my attention as I was at the front of the queue.

I scanned my items on autopilot. What did they mean? There was no link on the message – what were they going to show me that was bad enough I'd want to kill Rick? I shuffled from foot to foot, stranded at the checkout while someone verified I was of legal age to purchase the wine. While I waited for a member of staff to notice the flashing beacon above my head, trying to make eye contact with anyone in uniform who could get the thing going again, the burner buzzed for a second time.

> ENJOY YOUR NIGHT IN WITH PIZZA AND WINE.

I spun around, eyeing the queue of blank faces, most looking disgruntled. No one met my gaze and no one looked to me like they were the watcher, but I had no clue who they were. Could it be the lady in her fifties with the shift dress and heels, the workman in his dirty T-shirt and boots or the teenager glued to her phone clutching a bag of Doritos? Whoever it was, they were here, they'd seen me and been close enough to see what was in my basket. An icy finger traced its way down my back, and my tongue glued to the roof of my mouth.

'Sorry to keep you.' A smiling woman pressed a card against the screen, validating my age, and I was able to pay. I stuffed my items into a shopping bag and hurried from the shop, taking long swift strides back to the flat, unable to stop myself looking over my shoulder every few seconds to see if I was being followed. Being watched was unsettling. It kept me on edge all the time.

Back inside, with the door locked, I peeked through the curtains out onto the street below, but it was empty, no figure stood holding binoculars to get a better view and no one crouched behind the bushes.

A wave of exhaustion enveloped me and I changed into my pyjamas after sticking the pizza in the oven, constantly checking my phone waiting for the revelation I'd been promised to appear. Half an hour later, there was still no message and Abbi321 continued to be absent from Instagram. Perhaps it was all smoke and mirrors and the watcher had nothing more to show me. Comforted by that idea, I lay on the sofa with the wine open and only crusts left on my plate, mindlessly watching *The Big Bang Theory* on television.

When I'd lost interest in Sheldon's exploits, I spent some time uploading content to the Edgewater account to keep myself occupied, posting pictures of a few past projects that were already with the customer and a two-week-old photo of me at the easel, paintbrush in hand. I looked happier, enjoying the moment, oblivious about what was to unfold. So much had changed since then.

Intending to head to bed for an early night, if I could get my brain to switch off, I got sidetracked when an email came through from my landlord. A polite but standoffish message giving me the date my lease was originally due to terminate, in two weeks' time, when I'd have to cease using the premises. I put the phone down, grinding my molars in irritation, but another message came through almost immediately.

I stared at the sender's name, my throat tightening: GotHerNow@gmail.com.

I guess he'd been trying to contact me via his previous email accounts, but as I'd blocked him, he'd created a third. There was no text in the email, no instructions, just a singular link. I sat, palms sweaty considering not opening it, living in blissful ignorance because whatever was at the end of that link was going to make everything infinitely worse. Could it be related to the earlier message, proof Rick wasn't a good guy? I hadn't heard from him tonight, but I hadn't expected to, not if he was out with clients.

I chewed my lip, finger hovering over the link, the pizza churning in my stomach, eventually giving in and pressing. The screen filled with a still image, the play button in the middle, but it only took one second to see my entire world had fallen apart.

16

My jaw hit the floor as I let the video play, an eruption of tears streaming down my cheeks. It was another video from Rick's bedroom, the exact same camera angle from the shelf I'd searched today. But it wasn't me standing beside the bed, having my clothes torn from my body in a rush of lust. It wasn't me unbuckling Rick's belt and tracing my fingers south, making him groan and lick his lips. It was my best friend.

Jade's blonde shaggy bob was as distinctive as her panda tattoo and my eyes grew to orbs as I watched the scene play out. The passion between them was like an ice pick to my heart, slicing into everything I knew and loved. In record time, they were naked, rolling around the bed. I let the phone fall from my hand, unable to watch one second more. It was fortunate I'd had the volume turned off so I hadn't had to listen.

I sat, blinking at the television. Sheldon was giving a monologue, but I barely took anything in. My boyfriend and my best friend, how could they? When did it happen? How many times had they had sex? The betrayal was like a visceral pull in my gut, my chest an empty cavern where my heart had been ripped out. How could they have gone behind my back? I was always there for Jade while she rambled on about Honking Henry or moaned about the shifts at work. We'd been friends for what seemed like forever, no one knew me as well as she did. I thought nothing would ever come between us. How could she have done that to me?

And Rick, pretending he was the greatest boyfriend, asking me to move in when he'd been sleeping with my best friend. What a bastard! Was I not enough for him or could he not keep it in his pants? I curled up into a ball, buried my head and screamed into the sofa cushion, eventually collapsing in sobs. My life had come apart at the seams. I thought I'd hit my lowest when the first video was sent around, but what Rick and Jade had done had broken me.

I hugged my knees tightly to my chest, craving comfort, a hug from my mum or a kind word from my dad, but they were so disappointed in me, I couldn't turn to them. My mind spun with what action I should take – should I storm round to Rick's and confront him? Tell the pair of them I never wanted to see them again, block them everywhere and disappear to lick my wounds? It was too painful to think about, yet my brain kept whirring like an out-of-control fairground ride, rocketing from rage to despair. I didn't want to think and I didn't want to feel, so I reached for the wine bottle and drank until I was numb.

* * *

When I woke on the sofa at three in the morning, the television had gone into sleep mode. A dull ache thudded at my temples and my mouth was a birdcage overdue for a clean. Within seconds, it all came flooding back, along with the sharp stab of betrayal that cut so deep I wasn't sure I'd recover.

I fumbled for my phone. Tears falling when I saw both Rick and Jade had text since I'd fallen asleep. I swiped to open their messages. Rick had sent a photo of a kebab around two hours ago from the lift going up to the penthouse, part of him reflected in the mirror, and had clumsily typed *I lov yoi*. Jade had sent a long spiel about Honking Henry, who'd accidentally boob grazed her during a callout which had sent fireworks around her body. I deleted both messages, even the sight of their names had my stomach in knots.

My mind was made up, I was going to go to my parents' and stay for the weekend, dropping the bombshell to Rick and Jade before I left. Neither of them knew my parents' exact address so they wouldn't be able to find me. Creating a bit of distance would do me good, somewhere I could get my mind straight, where I hopefully wouldn't be so alone, because I couldn't bear to be in my own head right now.

I left the sofa and crawled into bed, craving unconsciousness to make the pain go away.

When I woke again, it was light outside and I could hear the bustle of a typical Saturday morning reverberate around the block. The kids beneath were stomping around and the smell of bacon was coming from somewhere. I showered, pausing beneath the running water to have another tearful meltdown, a pity party about losing my boyfriend, my best friend and my studio, before mentally slapping myself and climbing out.

Packing the essentials, I tidied up, partly desperate to leave and get to my parents but also dreading the *talk* I'd have to endure from my dad.

I sat in the car half an hour before Rick was due to arrive, typing a single text in a group I'd created for him, Jade and me. Two simple words I hoped would leave them reeling.

I know.

Then I blocked their numbers so they wouldn't be able to call or text and started the forty-minute drive to Surrey.

I knew they'd let me stay, my parents weren't monsters and they had the space. Ben was out in Turkey, getting ready for the upcoming season, and I contemplated jumping on a plane for a blissful week in the sun, but I'd be running away from my problems.

Isn't that what you're doing now? the irritating voice in my head chipped in.

I still had so many questions; some I wanted answers to, some I wasn't so sure. My heart had been torn in two; I'd been convinced Rick was the one, but how wrong I'd been about him. The video replayed in my mind, over and over, the watcher's message *once you've seen what I've got, you'll want to kill Rick* as background noise. I was waiting for the rage to return from last night, but right now I was consumed with misery at their treachery. I clawed for possible reasons to explain it away; at first, telling myself the video was a fake. When I realised it was real, I came up with excuses; they were drunk, it was before we met and they didn't want to tell me, but the sad truth was they clearly cared so little about my feelings.

When I arrived in Wallington, my eyes red and stinging from crying, I grabbed my suitcase and prepared for the worst, but before I even put my key in the door, it opened and Mum pulled me into a hug. My knees buckled and

I dropped my suitcase, tension leaving my body as I melted into her, squeezing her so tight I feared she might break.

'Oh, Abbi, I've been so worried about you.' She stroked my hair while I sobbed into her shoulder, and when I looked up, my dad stood a few feet behind in the hallway, concern etched onto his face.

'Dad, I'm so sorry, it's all just a mess.'

'It'll be all right, love,' Mum said as Dad patted my shoulder robotically and carried my suitcase up to the spare room without a word. 'Let's get some tea, shall we.'

Mum led me into the kitchen, putting the kettle on and supplying biscuits. My stomach rumbled, last night's wine still sloshing around, and I took a shortbread, hoping the sugar hit would give me a much-needed lift.

'So, Abigail,' my dad said, formal as ever, sliding into his seat at the head of the table and steepling his fingers like he was talking to one of his students, 'what's going on?'

I cried my way through my explanation of the past week, how my life had gone from picture-perfect to a total mess in days. Being harassed online, having two weeks to get out of the studio and the feeling I was constantly being watched had my stress levels at an all-time high. Mum supplied tissues and held my hand as I told them about Rick and Jade's betrayal. Dad's face grew from pink to almost crimson as he listened, his frown deepening with each word.

'Well, it's a crime! And you say the police haven't done anything?'

I shook my head, realising I only had Rick's word he'd even been to see them, and it was clear I could no longer trust him.

'It seems obvious to me it's this Rick's camera and he's filmed you without your knowledge. Abigail, how could you be so naive? Give me his address, I'm going to pay him a visit.' Dad got up from the table and searched for his car keys.

'Bill, stop, that's not going to do any good. It's out there now, Abbi's been to the police, let them investigate. You're a headteacher for Christ's sake, getting locked up for assault isn't going to help anyone.'

Steam was coming out of his ears but he lowered himself back to his seat, shaking his head. The helplessness in his eyes broke me all over again.

'Can I stay for the weekend? I just want to get away, where neither of them will find me.'

'Of course, you need time to process it all. You know you're welcome, it'll be a treat having you here, won't it, Bill?'

Dad grunted in agreement and stalked into the front room, closing the door. Seconds later, the horse racing was on, the commentator's voice blasting through the wall.

'He just needs a bit of time; it was a shock seeing what Val was sent, that's all.' Mum squeezed my arm, offering me a kind smile. The corners of her eyes crinkled, damp with tears, and I knew she was hurting for me. I wished I could make them unsee the video. How could that bastard share something so private.

'I know, Mum, I'm so sorry, I'm mortified. It's not going to affect his job, is it?'

'No, of course not, it'll be fine.'

'Do you think he'll forgive me?'

Mum tutted. 'You silly bean, of course he will. You're his little girl, that's all.'

I prayed I hadn't ruined that image of me for him forever.

I couldn't forgive Rick and Jade for what they'd done, but I'd also never forgive the watcher for sharing the video. I knew one thing, whoever they were, they had to be found and I had to stop them.

17

Mum and I went for a walk around the local park after I'd unpacked, stopping off at the bakery to pick up a sourdough loaf for lunch. It was good to be out in the fresh air, but I wore sunglasses to hide my swollen eyes and puffy face. Mum brought me up to speed on Ben's exploits in Turkey, pulling up the photos he'd sent from his one day off a week. He was living on next to nothing, staying in paid-for apartments, saving to get on the property ladder. I envied the freedom, but it was hard work. Ben had a vibrant and energetic personality, he was much more outgoing than me and during the last season, he'd become well-liked by the holidaymakers, which was why they'd requested he return.

I let Mum waffle on about Ben, trying not to let her obvious favouritism irk me, my mind drifting to Rick and Jade. Hopefully, my message had sent a shockwave and they regretted their actions. Although it broke my heart, I was done with the pair of them because how could I trust them now?

Mum stopped to look in the window of the charity shop and my bag vibrated. I pulled out my own phone first, realising at once, just because I'd blocked Rick and Jade's mobile numbers from texting or calling me, I hadn't blocked them anywhere else.

I scrolled the notifications, both Jade and Rick had made contact via Instagram and email. I revelled in their frustration at my radio silence, both panicking I wasn't responding. Had Rick been round to the flat and let himself in with his key to find it empty? I hoped the pair of them were having as shitty a day as I was; it served them right.

'I'm going to pop inside, I really like that vase. What do you think, for the conservatory?' Mum said, jolting me back to the present.

'Hmmm, it's nice,' I replied, but she was already pushing the door open.

My bag buzzed again, but this time it was the burner phone, that had half a bar of battery remaining.

> I TOLD YOU HE WASN'T A GOOD MAN

I gritted my teeth, because that's what I needed today, an 'I told you so'. I responded, my fingers flying across the keys.

> THANKS FOR THE VIDEO, A TEXT WOULD HAVE SUFFICED! I'VE LEFT HIM, IT'S OVER. PLEASE DON'T CONTACT ME AGAIN.

Mum came out of the shop and frowned at my hands, each one holding a phone.

'Two phones? You're not a drug dealer, are you?' She chuckled, amused at her own joke. I'd failed to mention the burner phone in my rundown to my parents of what had been happening, too consumed by the Rick and Jade betrayal.

'One is for work,' I replied a little curtly, not wanting to get into it. 'Where's the vase?'

'It's got a crack in it.'

We walked home and Mum prepared lunch while I sat and read the paper, something I always did when I visited. Dad was still insistent he had a physical newspaper every day despite news being online. It was the familiar comforts and surroundings that enabled me to relax, to slip into the role of daughter, allowing Mum to take care of me as she did for Dad. I had a rummage in their junk drawer and found a charger that fit the burner phone, seeing as it had been delivered without one, and left it to charge in the kitchen.

I waited as long as I could before reading Jade's and Rick's messages, I'd wanted to delete them, but curiosity got the better of me, and after washing up, I retreated upstairs to the spare room.

Laying on the bed, I opened Jade's first, my eyes widening when I read her message. Apparently, she didn't know what I was talking about and asked what I'd meant when I'd said *I know*? Jaw slack, I opened Rick's, which was more of the same, complete denial in having any idea what my text meant. I bit my teeth together until they hurt. Fury at them gaslighting me filled my veins like petrol and I was going to take a match to it all.

Going back downstairs to retrieve the burner phone, I dashed back to the privacy of the spare room and opened the video. Viewing it again made my toes curl, but there was no doubt about who the people on screen were. How they could possibly deny it was beyond me, but they were covering their arses. They didn't know I had proof. Well, I was going to show them. From the burner phone, I forwarded the video to my personal phone, unblocked their numbers and sent it on the group chat I'd created that morning. I wished I could be there to see their faces when they watched it. Clearly, they had no idea their illicit shag had been recorded.

Dad's words from earlier echoed in my mind about Rick planting the camera and it seemed the most likely possibility now. Was it a thing – did he like recording his sexual exploits? Did he have a bookcase full of tapes, one of every girl he'd ever had in his bedroom? The idea revolted me. We'd been together almost a year, had he recorded us every time? He couldn't be that much of a monster, could he? And if that was the case, how had the watcher got their hands on the videos? Was it someone close to Rick, like Nathan? His words from the meal at Gaucho's reverberated around my ears *'sex sells, Abbi.'* The burner phone beeped, jolting me out of my thoughts.

> WE'RE NOT DONE YET.

The text which arrived from the watcher made me shrink – surely they'd caused enough chaos now. My personal life had been torn apart and I prayed they weren't going to come after my business too. I'd run away, seeking refuge at my parents'; I'd *got rid of Rick* – what more did they want from me?

A few minutes later, my phone exploded with messages from Jade, nothing but apologies, explaining it had only happened the once and was the biggest regret of her life, blah, blah, blah. She didn't specify when it took place, but reading between the lines, it was when Rick and I were together.

Rick's messages came through shortly after, his were similar, apologetic, but he blamed Jade, they'd been drunk and she'd thrown herself at him. It was no excuse.

When I didn't respond, they both kept ringing, but I switched my phone off. I didn't want to speak to either of them. In fact, I wanted to shut the curtains and curl up in bed, where no one could hurt me again.

After a nap, I rose refreshed, sleeping was the only activity I enjoyed because my mind was quiet. I didn't have to think or feel, but when I was awake, the acute ache of sorrow in my chest was a constant reminder.

The rest of the day was uneventful. With my phone switched off and no more contact from the watcher – too worried I'd miss out on an important message to switch the burner phone off – I was able to wallow in peace. Mum made shepherd's pie for dinner, then invited me to watch television with her and Dad as they settled in for the evening, but I retreated upstairs, preferring to be alone, and watched a true crime documentary about a teenager, Lee Boxall, who'd disappeared from the local area back in the eighties.

Sunday brought with it the usual gloom most people felt about the week ahead; mine wasn't to do with work, I loved immersing myself in painting, but I didn't want to go back to Crawley. Even being twenty miles away, my mind was clearer, and I put a plan together for the future, packing up the studio and scoping out alternatives to rent, creating a promotional flyer to door drop whenever I wanted to stretch my legs.

After roast beef for Sunday lunch, Dad finally seemed able to talk calmly about the video, and we had a heart-to-heart. I made him understand I was a victim and hadn't done anything to drag the family name through the mud. As we talked, my parents could sense my unease and offered for me to stay longer.

'I have to go back eventually; I need to keep up with the commissions that have come in and I don't want to fall behind.'

'What will you do when this Rick turns up at your door?' my father asked.

'I won't let him in. I don't want to speak to either of them,' I said. The fact that Rick still had a key weighed heavily on my mind, but I didn't want to add that to my father's worries.

'I still can't believe Jade would do that to you, she always seemed like such a lovely girl.' Mum looked pained and I grimaced. When I'd switched my phone on, there were lots of messages and voicemails, but I'd deleted them all. Nothing they could say would change what they did.

'I know, I can't get my head around it.'

Before I left, Ben made his weekly call and we all sat around the table with the phone on loudspeaker. It was lovely to catch up with my brother, although none of us mentioned why I'd come to stay. He told us the temperatures were warming up already, but he was mostly doing training, learning the dances and the evening shows, preparing for the Easter rush in the coming weeks.

'There's a couple of cheap Airbnbs close to the resort, Abs, if you fancy a weekend away. It would be great to see you.' Ben's voice echoed down the phone and my heart swelled. We'd always got on well, with only three years between us. Other than the usual sibling squabbles, we leant on each other for support.

'Sounds like bliss, Ben, maybe in a few weeks, if I can afford it. I miss you.'

'Miss you too. Honestly, you'll love it, nice little escape. Let me know and I'll see if I can get you a good deal.'

I choked up when we said goodbye, I hadn't realised how much I'd missed not having him around. I'd moved to Crawley for work initially, a part-time entry-level graphic design job which suited the art and design college course I'd found. A change of direction from following in my father's footsteps and training to be a teacher. I'd fallen in love with painting and wanted to do a creative job, at least until Edgewater got off the ground, but by then I'd met Rick and decided to stay. I'd dropped out of the course when I couldn't keep up with orders, so in reality there was nothing left keeping me in Crawley now I was losing the studio too.

It was something to consider. Maybe a fresh start would mean taking a step back and looking for a new direction, another place to live, closer to the people who cared about me. Perhaps, despite their horrific and humiliating methods, the watcher had done me a favour. Imagine if I'd moved in with Rick and never found out about him cheating with Jade? We could have got married, had kids, been ten years down the line. Maybe I'd had a lucky escape after all?

18

I half expected Rick to be at the flat when I got home on Sunday evening, demanding to be given a chance to explain himself. Perhaps he knew there was nothing he could say in his defence, not once the video was out in the open. As I put my key in the door, footsteps jogged up the stairs behind me and I whirled around, but it was Alfie, the bruises around his eye now a muddy yellow. The cast on his arm had been replaced by a splint and I frowned.

'How come the cast is off already, I thought they were on for six weeks?'

Alfie gave me a sheepish smile. 'I cut it off, can't really code one-handed.'

I tutted and shook my head. 'You'll end up taking longer to heal,' I chided.

He shrugged. 'Rick was here this morning, yesterday too, banging on your door. Is everything okay?'

I shook my head again, casting my eyes downward towards the threadbare carpet. 'Turns out he's a cheater. I ended it.'

'Ah, I'm sorry, Abbi,' he said, pointing towards his door and gnawing on his bottom lip. 'Do you want to come in, get a coffee and talk about it?'

'No, you've got enough on your plate. Thank you, though. I'm going to spend the evening looking for a new studio to rent.'

Alfie's eyebrows shot up his forehead. 'Really? I have a friend who's looking to rent out his old workshop in Horley; I can get you the details.'

'Sure, that would be great,' I replied unenthusiastically, unable to match Alfie's buoyancy. 'See you later, Alfie.'

Inside the flat, I locked the door, leaving the key in so Rick wouldn't be able to get in. The flat was as I'd left it, which should have been comforting, but now I found the space depressing. The stark contrast to the warmth of my parents' home and Rick's plush penthouse was a reminder of everything I'd lost. I wasn't materialistic but since Rick had asked me to move in, I'd pictured myself living there. Internally, I scolded myself – yes, it was nice to have the finer things, but I'd worked hard to start my own business and afford the rent on the flat by myself with initial help from my parents. I had my own car and didn't particularly want for anything, and I wasn't going to rely on a man to provide for me.

I mindlessly scrolled websites with studios to rent in front of the television, baulking at how much they'd inflated since I'd searched before. Killing time before I went to bed, I read through listings when suddenly Jade's face flashed up on my screen. She was calling, but I declined and sent it to voicemail. Surely, she would have got the message by now. I had no interest in talking to either of them.

A few minutes later, a text came through on the group chat I'd created with Rick and Jade on Saturday morning, where I'd sent the video. The still frame of Rick between Jade's legs making me twitch.

> Abbi, how could you?

I had no idea what she meant, but a thought weaved its way into my mind unbidden. I opened Instagram, my suspicions right when I saw Abbi321 was back. Their story was a twenty-second clip of the video of Jade and Rick with the words WHORE flashing from red to black. The sound overlaid was 'Maneater' by Nelly Furtardo. I smirked, how apt.

I stared at the screen, the skin flushing on my neck, unable to comprehend the watcher had posted it. Not only that, but tagged them in it too. I couldn't tear my eyes away from the flashing words which thankfully were covering up Rick's behind.

I debated whether to respond to Jade's message but decided radio silence was the best option. I'd told her that account had nothing to do with me, she knew full well I wouldn't send a video of me having sex with my boyfriend to everyone I knew. Why would I want to sabotage my life like that, let alone expose myself as the victim of a cheating boyfriend by sharing it publicly on my Instagram story? Yet a tiny part of me relished in the karma of it.

I got up and retrieved the burner phone from the bottom of the bag, tapping out a text to the watcher.

> HOW DID YOU GET THOSE VIDEOS? WAS IT YOUR CAMERA?

The response was almost instantaneous.

> FINALLY, YOU'RE ASKING THE RIGHT QUESTIONS

I ground my teeth together, it wasn't an answer. They were dropping breadcrumbs and I guessed I'd have to find out myself. What an idiot I'd been, dismissing Rick as having nothing to do with it. If the camera wasn't the watcher's, they must have got hold of the recordings and were using them to publicly shame all of us. I'd swung between believing them to be male, then female, but surely another bloke would clap Rick on the back for his ingenuity. The punishment they seemed to be doling out leant more towards a woman's act of revenge. If so, did it mean Heather was back and had unfinished business with Rick?

I checked Abbi321's followers, some were mutual friends of Jade and I, one was a colleague of hers I'd met on a night out. Linda was also among them, so she had to have been sent the video of me and Rick. The insult painted on my studio door made more sense if it was Linda, although I hadn't thought she would have stooped so low.

Where were these videos coming from? I copied the link and sent it on to Officer Barrett to forward to the Cyber Crime Unit.

Rick wouldn't admit to filming us, not in a million years, and his lack of response to Jade's message spoke volumes. I imagined he was burying his head in the sand, trying to keep a low profile. He hadn't posted anything on social media for over a week, not even when we'd been out to Gaucho's.

I scrolled back through his Instagram posts: gym workouts, golf trips, sitting in a pub beer garden with Nathan until I flicked to one of his Audi Q4, gleaming white and perfectly buffed. He was stood beside the vehicle, beaming with pride. It was before we'd met and he'd garnered forty-six comments. I looked through them, one further down making me laugh.

GarethSinger: Yo Bro, how a market analyst be affording a Q4?

A market analyst? Rick was an account director, unless he'd had one hell of a promotion. I googled Carafe Wines to check the staff profile page but couldn't find him listed amongst the account directors. Did he even work there?

I stared at the burner phone which was stubbornly silent, I wasn't getting any more information tonight and it seemed the watcher's attention had now turned to Jade. I couldn't deny I was thrilled not to be in the limelight and perhaps, although wicked, my treacherous friend was getting what was coming to her.

Yawning, I turned off the television and went to bed. Tomorrow was a new day of a new week, one where I'd look for another premises, closer to my parents, because a change of scene would do me good.

* * *

Linda was waiting for me when I got to the studio, loitering outside the door with a takeaway coffee cup in hand. A peace offering in the form of a caramel macchiato and almond croissant. I didn't have the energy for a fight as I'd spent most of the night having a recurring nightmare of being locked out of my building with no clothes on, everyone laughing and pointing at me in the street. I didn't need to be Sigmund Freud to work out where that had come from.

'Please let me explain. I've spent the weekend feeling awful,' Linda said, her gaze hovering on the faded wood where I'd scrubbed the graffiti, getting rid of her handiwork.

'Sure,' I said, keeping my tone light and unlocking the door to the familiar aroma of methylated spirits. Biting my tongue at adding, *And so you should*.

'I happened to mention during a workshop I was looking for a larger space and this lady, a client, suggested a rental in Haywards Heath, near the station. Another enquired why I needed to move, and I explained I wanted to expand, then he suggested knocking through. Next thing I know, he's drawn me a sketch, talking about how much more revenue I could make increasing the workshops and classes, like he was proper invested. I just got carried away.'

'Sounds like a busybody,' I huffed, knowing how some people got. Sticking their noses in where it wasn't welcome.

'You're right, I don't know why I listened. I'll contact the landlord and rescind my offer...' Linda wittered on, the guilt etched on her rosy face, and I held a hand up to stop her. Was this her way of finding out what had gone on with Rick, the videos she might have seen but thankfully hadn't mentioned? Either it was an apology or prying, I wasn't sure which.

'Linda, it's fine, I think I'm going to find somewhere else anyway.' Her face slackened and she looked crestfallen. 'Not because of the lease,' I added. 'I think it's time I got out of Crawley.'

'Oh!' She opened her mouth to speak, but closed it again.

'I'm not cross, I promise,' I lied. 'Thank you for breakfast.' I assured her as best I could, hoping I could get her back to her own studio so I could make a start on the mini portraits I'd been putting off, but as usual she was terrible at reading the room. Instead of leaving, she pulled out her phone, sticking the screen in my face.

'I created an account, a business one, inspired by you.' She beamed. I'd expected to see a crude logo and some awkward images, but it looked extremely professional, with perfectly curated photos, all colour coordinated.

I raised my eyebrows, taking the phone and scrolling through the four posts Linda had put up so far. 'I'm impressed.' I smiled. 'It looks great.'

'I don't know what I'm doing really, I'm winging it, but your Edgewater one looks so good and it's obviously pulled in business – let's hope this does the same.'

I wasn't sure Linda was winging it, or she'd got someone else to manage the account for her, but it had taken me months to learn about hashtags, lighting and accompanying wording, and that was after I'd perfected taking photos. Maybe she wasn't as much of a beginner as she made out.

'I'm sure it will.'

Eventually, after ten minutes, she left, explaining she had another group of school children in at nine but was happy we'd smoothed things over. I was relieved, even as I closed my door and the blinds, it would make the rest of my time at the studio more pleasant if we could at least be civil. Despite the graffiti, I'd rather have Linda as a friend than an enemy.

I worked like a trojan until lunchtime, not even leaving the studio to go to the bathroom. In those hours, I finished the coaster-sized portraits and checked what I needed to be working on next. It was an unusual commission of a static caravan overlooking Weymouth Beach which I imagined would be hung inside for the owners or their guests to enjoy. In the photograph provided, the Weymouth sky was cloudless with the sand a glistening yellow in the sun at the bottom of the hill.

Before I started, I ran through how many orders had come in, another five since last week and I also did a search for Edgewater on social media. One happy customer had put up a photo of their commission in situ, above the fireplace, and I commented and shared. Usually, I'd be tagged in those posts, but because I didn't want the watcher anywhere near the business, I'd stopped allowing the Edgewater account to be tagged in anything.

Unsurprisingly, both Jade's and Rick's accounts had been deleted or deactivated like mine, but who knew how many people had seen the video before they'd done so. I wasn't a complete monster, I knew how awful it was to have something so private shared publicly, the humiliation they both must be feeling, which was why when a knock came from the studio door and Rick begged me to let him in, I did.

19

Rick looked dreadful, his eyes sallow and bloodshot and he hadn't shaved that morning, which was unheard of. Despite his unforgivable act, it was hard to watch the man I loved sit opposite me, wringing his hands and struggling to meet my eye.

'You need to tell me who's doing this, Abbi. They've suspended me at work pending an investigation. That Instagram account used a fucking hashtag with my company's name in! I might lose my job.'

'Your job as an account manager, right?' I asked.

'Yes, of course as an account manager, what are you on about?' Rick shook his head at me, his eyebrows weaved so close together it was like they were one. He rambled on. 'Jade's in a right mess too – she's been on the phone constantly, crying and screaming at me like it's my fault, but I didn't fucking film her.'

I slowly took it all in, waiting for an apology, but it appeared his infidelity was low on his list of problems.

'I don't know who it is, that's why I went to the police. They've passed it to the Cyber Crime Unit and I'm waiting to hear back.'

'So, this person hasn't contacted you again?'

'No,' I lied, my resolve hardening.

Rick hung his head, rubbing his hands back and forth through his hair, creating static.

The lump in my throat grew with indignation, it looked like I'd have to be the one to bring it up.

'How could you do that to me, Rick, how could you sleep with Jade? I thought you loved me.' My eyes burned, but I refused to cry, I'd shed enough tears over the relationship I'd believed we'd had, for what I'd lost.

'It just happened, it was months ago, we were both drunk and bumped into each other in town. I'm sorry. It didn't mean anything, and I do love you.' He sniffed, wiping his nose on the sleeve of his crumpled T-shirt. 'Please come back and we can fix it.' He said it like an afterthought, staring at me through wet lashes, and I shook my head. His priority was finding out who had planted the camera, or if he was lying and it was his camera all along, who had got access to the footage. My dad had to be right. Jade too, she'd said it had to be his, and I bet that's why she'd been screaming down the phone at him. He'd been filming his conquests without their permission and I had to recover the recordings.

'It's not going to happen, Rick. I can't trust you now, you broke us.' My chin wobbled, but I kept composure, whereas Rick lowered his head between his knees again and his shoulders shook. 'I need to give you your key back, but I've left it at home. I also have some things I need to collect from your apartment.'

When he raised his head to look at me, his red-rimmed eyes almost had me weakening, but I couldn't, I wouldn't. I forced my mind to replay the video of him and Jade – my boyfriend and my best friend going to town while I was at home in bed. The bitter taste in my mouth was hard to swallow.

'I'm going to need my key back too,' I added, but Rick was crying now.

'I fucked it up, I'm so sorry.'

'Go back to the police, Rick. I have no idea who is doing this to us,' I said, making sure I used the term us; it wasn't all about him. 'I can't help you.'

'You must!' Rick yelled, banging his hand on the table and making me jump, his mood switching in seconds. 'You must know – or was it you, Abbi? Did you use the footage to wreck my life, Jade's life too.'

I backed away, but Rick stood, angrier than I'd ever seen him. Spittle flew from his mouth and he clutched my shoulders, pushing me back towards the wall. Despite my initial shock, resentment flared in my chest and I was about to give him a mouthful when Linda burst through the door.

'What the hell is going on?'

Rick let go of me immediately and barged past her out of the studio and down the hallway.

'Are you okay? I heard shouting.' Linda wiped her wet hands on her apron. 'What happened?'

'We broke up,' I replied flatly, 'and he's not taking it well.'

'Oh, love, I'm so sorry.'

'It's fine. He cheated, so it's his own fault.'

Linda grimaced, eyeing me with pity. I couldn't bear it. 'Then you're better off without him.'

* * *

I went for a walk in the fresh air, using the opportunity to contact Officer Barrett about the video I'd forwarded, but he wasn't available. I left a message asking for an update and sat in the local park with a sandwich from a café, nibbling at the edges. The sky was as grey as my mood after Rick's visit. I'd never seen him so riled up, he'd barely raised his voice to me since we'd met, and what was he expecting, that I'd feel sorry for him? Where was he when I was at my lowest, even when the video of us was sent to almost everyone I knew, he was only concerned about himself, his reputation, his job. I'd seen his true colours now.

As I headed back to the studio, my phone rang with a local number I didn't recognise. When I answered, it was Officer Barrett.

'Abbi, I'm returning your call. I've had an update from the Cyber Crime Unit, but it's not great news.'

'Oh?' I said, pausing by a lamppost, kicking at the weeds growing between the concrete cracks of the pavement.

'In terms of the email address, it has since been shut down. The telephone number you've been receiving texts from is a pay-as-you-go SIM, with a fake name registered. I can tell you the person using the phone is in the Crawley area, but that's as much as I've got so far.'

'Can't you trace the IP address or something, from the email?'

'Not if the user uses a VPN.'

'Remind me what that is again.'

'Virtual private network – it's where someone can connect to another server somewhere on the internet, potentially in another country, which allows them to browse the internet using that computer's connection. It's difficult to trace. It hides the IP address.' I tried to grasp what Officer Barrett was saying but barely any of it made sense, the underlying message was that they weren't getting anywhere.

'What about the Instagram account? Abbi321?'

'That's where we've had some success, it's been removed permanently today but again, difficult to trace. You can create an account with fake details. Have you had any more interaction from this person?'

'Only by text, but he posted another video – not of me, but of my boyfriend, I forwarded it to you.'

'Yes, I got it, but it wasn't up for long.'

I sighed, of course it wasn't.

'I'm assuming Rick's been in contact with you?'

'What's his full name?'

'Rick Townsend.'

I heard tapping at the other end, then a moment of silence.

'I've got no report filed for Rick Townsend at all, not about a break-in or internet harassment. What was the guy's name who was assaulted?'

I sank to the kerb, trying to absorb the information, barely registering Officer Barrett's question.

'Abbi, are you still there?' His voice jolted me back to the present.

'Alfie – my neighbour's called Alfie, but I'm not sure what his last name is.'

'Okay, I've been trying to find the report to link them altogether, to start building a case, but I'm coming up with nothing recent for an Alfie either.'

'So, you're saying Rick never filed a report? He never contacted the police at all?'

'I've been unable to find anything under that name,' Officer Barrett said diplomatically.

He must have lied. I'd been played all along.

'Thanks, Officer Barrett. I'll get my neighbour's last name for you, but if you find anything else...'

'I'll be in contact,' he said, hanging up after bidding me a good day.

The realisation Rick hadn't made a report or been to see the police after the supposed break-in told me everything I needed to know. That footage was his and so was the camera. He was protecting himself, the bastard, trying to gaslight me in the process, but I needed proof. I had to get into the penthouse and search for evidence, recordings on DVDs or something, although it could all be on his laptop, in the cloud somewhere, and without a password I was screwed. I still had his key, but all the while Rick was under investigation at work, I couldn't guarantee he'd not be at home.

With the newest commission for the static caravan forgotten, I bypassed the studio and headed straight for my car. The office of Carafe Wines was located in Godstone, less than half an hour away, maybe I'd find some answers there.

Starting the engine of my old Citroen, I headed towards the A22, trying to figure out what I was going to do once I got there. I'd never visited Rick's place of work before; I'd never needed to and I didn't know any of his colleagues either. I wracked my brain at how I was going to play it.

Turning the radio up, I hummed along to Heart FM, hoping inspiration might strike and eventually it did. On Friday when I'd let myself into the penthouse, he was on the phone to someone from work, but what was her name? Tina? No that wasn't it. Gina? Yes, that was right. He'd said he'd see Gina on Monday, and I guessed he'd been in this morning, got called into a meeting about the video when he'd arrived and was immediately suspended, coming straight to see me at the studio afterwards. Maybe Gina worked in human resources, or she was Rick's boss? Either way, she was who I needed to speak to. Perhaps she could tell me if Rick had made any enemies, some office politics he'd got tangled up in or who'd want to target him personally.

20

The village of Godstone was so pretty, lots of green areas and quaint buildings painted white with dark beams. As soon as I entered the high street, I knew Rick's office wasn't going to be some concrete high-rise, but Carafe Wines was not what I was expecting. When Google Maps told me I'd reached my destination, I'd come to a stop in front of a long one-storey building with a thatched roof that looked like it had once been a barn. It backed onto fields and overlooked a duck pond. On the other side of the pond, I could see a small church, its hilly grounds peppered with half-buried headstones. I carried on, pulling into the small gravel car park and climbed out, admiring the beauty and tranquillity of somewhere so picturesque. I'd love to paint it.

If it wasn't for the Carafe Wines sign above the door, I could have sworn I was in the wrong place.

When I entered the small reception area, the lady behind the desk stood to greet me. 'Good afternoon, welcome to Carafe Wines, how may I help you?' Her plummy voice was warm and she wore a striking yellow dress with hot pink lipstick which should have clashed but on her it worked.

'Hello, I was hoping to speak to Gina – is she around?' I asked.

'Let me check for you,' she replied, reaching for the phone. 'Who should I say is asking for her?'

'I'm Abbi Montgomery.'

She gestured towards an orange retro sofa and I sat on the edge, admiring the glossy magazines displayed on the coffee table. Two minutes later, I lifted my head as footsteps approached, frowning as a woman who looked no older than me in slouchy jeans and trainers with a messy blonde bun, stuck her hand out for me to shake.

'I'm Gina,' she said, her South London accent in stark contrast to the receptionist's refined tone.

'Abbi,' I introduced myself, slightly bewildered by the overly firm handshake. She couldn't be Rick's boss, could she?

'How may I help you?'

I got to my feet, looking over her shoulder at the receptionist, who politely averted her gaze.

'It's personal – is there somewhere we might speak privately?' I kept my voice low.

'Sure, do you mind if we pop outside so I can smoke?'

I shook my head and we left via the door I'd just entered and headed back into the car park.

'I know who you are,' she said, pulling a cigarette out of a crumpled box and lighting it.

'You do?'

'You're Rick's girlfriend; he talks about you a lot. I've seen your photo.'

I cringed, hoping it was a photo she'd seen and not my sex tape, which to my fortune hadn't gone viral. Unlike Jade's, which I'd seen reposted a dozen times before it had been removed.

'He's not here, he's been asked to take some leave, apparently. I came in this morning and knew instantly something had happened, but I was off sick on Friday. Everyone was whispering, you know, but no one would tell me until after Rick was sent home, then I saw the... video Carafe had been tagged in.' Gina looked at me apologetically and a flush rose in my neck, despite having nothing to be embarrassed about.

'I'm his ex-girlfriend now,' I said for clarity, grimacing.

'Well, it was a dick move, too many tossers about, I didn't think Rick was one of them, but well, there you go.' She looked into the distance, puffing on the cigarette.

'Will he get the sack, do you think?'

'Who knows, well above my pay grade but they aren't happy. Apparently, the company name was used in a hashtag when the video was posted. It's been taken down now, but was online all weekend. They've had crisis meetings and all sorts about it.'

It appeared both Rick and I had endured shitty weekends, but his was of his own making.

'Is Rick well liked here, does he have any enemies?'

'You think one of us posted it?'

I shook my head and Gina laughed.

'He was saying he didn't know who it was, he was being victimised or sabotaged or something. That it was an online hate crime, but everyone here was well shocked. It's a small team, you know, one big happy family, the owners took it personally.'

'What do you do here?' I asked, trying to gather as much information as I could, desperate not to have wasted my visit.

'I'm a market analyst, like Rick, we work together.'

I coughed, trying not to choke on my own spit. 'I thought he was an account manager?'

She snorted, plumes of smoke firing out of her nose. 'He wished! He spends money like he is, though, big fancy car, nice threads and that, always puts his hand in his pocket when we go to the Fox and Hounds. I thought he was a sound bloke, until now.'

'Me too.' I bit my lip, fighting back tears. It seemed I didn't really know him at all; he'd lied through his teeth about lots of things. 'I know it's a personal question, but what's the salary for a market analyst?'

'We're on thirty-five grand a year, can get more in London of course, but not out in the sticks. I never could work out how he had so much cash, guessed his parents might have been loaded or something.'

I grimaced, knowing that wasn't true.

'You said you were off sick last Friday?' I asked, a light bulb going off in my brain.

'Yeah, some bug doing the rounds.'

'And you never spoke to Rick on the phone?'

'I had my head down the toilet most of the day; I didn't speak to anyone from work.'

So, Rick had lied about his work call when I turned up at the penthouse unannounced. Who had he been talking to?

Gina dropped her cigarette and ground it into the gravel with her trainer, looking at me expectantly.

'Thanks for your time, Gina, I appreciate it.'

'Men like that don't deserve second chances, don't give him one, eh?' With that, she turned and walked back to the office.

I sat by the duck pond for a while, watching a mother round up her goslings as I let Gina's words sink in. Rick had been on the phone to someone, he'd said something about it not coming back on us, whoever 'us' were. I guessed the next thing I had to do was go to Rick's and search the penthouse properly. If he'd made recordings of me and Jade, who else had been an unwitting victim?

Pulling the burner phone from my bag, I composed a message, having to know I was on the right track.

> RICK RECORDED US DIDN'T HE?

The phone was stubbornly silent, and I guessed maybe I wasn't a priority any more. We were a bit of fun, entangled in their quest for revenge and now I'd left Rick, the game was over for them, but it wasn't for me. Nothing like a video you didn't know you'd starred in being sent to your family and friends to develop a thirst for vengeance. And yes, perhaps I did want to get my own back, but I couldn't work out who I was angrier with. Rick might have filmed us, but he hadn't been the one to humiliate us publicly, that had been the watcher. Maybe the films were for Rick's own perverse enjoyment, to savour when he was alone.

I opened Instagram, searching for Abbi321 and other alternative names, but there was no account pretending to be me with my photo as their profile picture. Rick's account was gone, and Carafe Wines had posted a press statement purporting to have nothing to do with the pornographic video where their company name had been used as a hashtag. I wasn't sure Rick would be able to come back from that, but maybe it served him right. I'd had a few more messages from people who'd only just opened their surprise video from Abbi321, and I sent them my stock response, cheeks flaming. Would the humiliation ever end?

The burner phone buzzed, announcing a message had been received.

> I TOLD YOU HE WASN'T A GOOD MAN AND THAT'S NOT ALL OF IT.

Their message made me nervous – was there more I didn't know? Perhaps it was time to confront Rick and demand the truth, because what else did he have to lose? He'd lost his girlfriend and potentially his job although he'd so far escaped any criminal charges.

As I was walking back to the car, my phone rang from a number I didn't recognise. I let it ring and answered it at the last minute, in case something had happened with my parents.

'Hello?'

'Abbi, it's Claire, Jade's mum.'

'Oh hello, how are you?' Shocked to hear her voice, I stumbled over my words fearing I was about to get a mouthful.

'I'm fine, love, but have you heard from Jade? I'm a bit worried as I haven't been able to get hold of her for a couple of days.'

I closed my eyes, a pit opening in my stomach. Claire obviously didn't know what Jade was going through. It didn't sound like she'd seen the video her daughter had been a part of, which was merciful. Like me, I guessed Jade had shut down, barricaded herself in her flat and switched off her phone.

'No, I haven't, but I'll give her a ring.' My jaw clenched, knowing I couldn't lie to Jade's mum. All the nights I'd spent around there before I got settled in the flat, the dinners and lifts home she'd given us from the pub.

'Thanks, love. I've been banging on her door, but she's not answering, I'm getting worried.'

The pit expanded to a cavern and my throat became tight. *Jesus, Jade, you better not have done anything stupid.*

'I'll let you know as soon as I've spoken to her.'

'Is anything going on with her at the moment?'

'Not that I know of,' I lied. 'I'll head there now and call you later, Claire, I promise.'

Rushing back to the car, I jumped in, speeding out of the pretty village of Godstone and towards Crawley as fast as my car would carry me.

21

'Jade, it's Abbi, open up.' I banged on the door, the image of Claire doing the same thing earlier on today fresh in my mind.

I pressed my ear to the wood, trying to listen for any signs of life coming from the other side. Was she out working or at home and not answering? I pulled out my phone and called her, putting my ear back against the door to see if I could hear it ring, but the call went straight to voicemail. It was either switched off or had run out of battery.

I hammered again, calling for Jade until one of her neighbours opened the door and looked out.

'I don't think she's in,' the woman said sarcastically. Jade's flat was in a similar block to mine, although she rented with another paramedic. She'd told me before the pair of them were on opposite shifts, so it was practically like living alone.

'Have you seen her? I really need to speak to her?'

'She's a paramedic, right? She went to work this morning; I passed her on the way back from the shop.'

Every muscle that had been wound so tight uncoiled and I nearly melted onto the landing carpet. 'Thank God,' I said, slumping against the frame.

'Here she is.' The woman pointed to a head bobbing up the stairs towards us, but it wasn't Jade, not unless she'd dyed her hair pink.

'No, the other one,' I said. 'Never mind.' I rushed to the stairwell to accost

Jade's flatmate before she'd even reached her own front door. 'I'm worried about Jade, she's not answering her phone or the door, her mum's been trying to get hold of her, do you know if she's inside?' My words tumbled out in a rush.

The woman with the pink hair, who'd I'd not even bothered to introduce myself to couldn't hide the panic that flashed on her face. Her pace quickened and in three long strides she was at the door, key in hand, calling Jade's name.

'She hasn't been out of her room since she got home from work yesterday,' said she was sick but wouldn't open up to speak to me.'

My pulse which had been gradually escalating kicked up a gear as Jade's flatmate opened the door and headed straight to Jade's bedroom. I followed behind, the neighbour who was now invested in the drama peeking in from the front door we'd left wide open behind us.

'It's locked,' she said, trying to turn the handle. 'Jade, open up, it's Becca.'

We waited a beat, but no sound came. Signs of life, we needed signs of life. Becca banged again and shouldered the door, which shook in its frame.

'It's not like her,' she huffed. When throwing her weight against it didn't work, Becca kicked beneath the handle in her heavy boots until the wood split. She burst through the door, and I searched through the gloom for Jade as musty air leaked out.

Her curtains were closed and there was a lump beneath the covers that looked too small to be my best friend. *She's out, she must have gone out.*

I tried to stay calm, but panic held me in a chokehold as I told myself my best friend was okay.

Becca rushed to the bed and pulled back the covers. Jade lay curled up, like a cat in front of the fire, expressionless, her eyes closed and dried vomit on her chin.

'No, Jade, no!' I cried as Becca rolled her over, checking for breathing. She was amazing, yelling instructions while performing CPR, but I stood, paralysed, unable to help. Jade's skin had a greyish tinge, like she was dead already. No, she couldn't be. The ground was collapsing under me, I was falling, tumbling.

'Call an ambulance!' Becca screamed at me in between supplying Jade with air, breathing life back into her as I fought back hysteria.

I fumbled for my phone, mentally back in the room with the chaos surrounding me seeming in slow motion.

'I'm through.' The woman behind me, Jade's neighbour, had her phone to her ear, already connected to the emergency services, giving them the address.

'She's breathing,' Becca panted, pushing back her pink fringe, 'and she's got a pulse.'

Tears erupted as relief flooded the room. Jade was rolled into the recovery position, her eyelids fluttering as Becca tried to rouse her, in limbo between consciousness and unconsciousness. It was then I noticed the bottle of vodka and discarded pills on the carpet.

'Thank God she threw up.'

'Thank God you came back when you did!' I replied, clutching my hand to my chest, trying to keep my pounding heart inside.

A few minutes later, more paramedics arrived, taking command of the room as soon as they entered. Becca's face was pale, as though she was trying to process what had happened, the life she'd undoubtedly saved. What would have happened if Becca had come home and not checked on Jade?

'Are you going to the hospital?' Becca asked as they strapped Jade to a gurney and wheeled her towards the lift.

'Yes,' I said immediately, 'I'll ring her mum en route.' I was dreading making the call I couldn't avoid.

I'd never been in an ambulance before, let alone one with flashing lights and sirens. It was far too loud to make a phone call, and I felt in the way as Jade was worked on in the back. Despite not being critical, she was in serious danger. Her blood pressure was too low, and she was administered fluids, the paramedic telling me it was likely she'd have her stomach pumped at the hospital once they'd determined how many of the pills she'd taken.

I felt for the team, who both knew Jade, their faces full of anguish at treating one of their own. The paramedic in the back, Tim, knew she'd been having a rough time, the pair of them had been on shift all weekend, and he admitted some of the unit had been less than kind after the video went viral.

My heart broke for Jade, having to suffer the sneers in the rec room, the whispers behind her back, everyone knowing her business and potentially sharing it with their friends. At least I didn't have that, my humiliation was via direct message, not posted into the public domain where anyone could get their hands on it. I was angry at Rick and Jade's betrayal, but I didn't want this.

When we got to the hospital, Tim wheeled Jade into Resus and I waited outside, sinking onto a low wall opposite the entrance, away from the smokers congregating outside in their patient gowns. Reluctantly, I dialled Claire, and the phone barely rang before it was answered, so I knew she was waiting for my call.

'Claire, it's Abbi,' I said to Jade's mother, chin wobbling along with my voice as fresh tears came.

'Abbi, what is it?' Claire's voice was desperate, and it faltered as I sniffed down the phone.

'You need to come to the hospital, East Surrey. Jade's here, we think she's taken some pills, she's unconscious.'

'Oh my God.' I could hear movement, the snatching up of keys and footsteps on the line. 'Is she okay?'

'I don't know,' I sobbed. 'Just get here, I'm waiting outside for you.'

'I'll be right there,' she said, and I heard the beep of her car unlocking and the turn of an ignition before she hung up.

My shoulders shook with gut-wrenching sobs as I prayed Jade would be okay. If the watcher hadn't posted the video, none of this would have happened. It was all their fault. They could have sent it to me privately to expose them, why were they so intent on public humiliation. Had the hate she'd received online and at work driven Jade to overdose or the guilt for sleeping with her best friend's boyfriend? My skin burned as I punched the keys to the burner phone.

YOU BASTARD. JADE TRIED TO KILL HERSELF!

The reply came quickly, and I had to stop myself from launching the phone into the path of a passing car.

RICK DID THIS. ARE YOU MAD YET?

Damn right I was mad, I was incandescent. If anything happened to Jade, I'd hunt the watcher down and destroy them.

I debated whether to go inside and get an update, to make sure Jade had pulled through, but I remained sat on the wall, chewing my nails to the quick until Claire tapped me on the shoulder.

'Where is she, where's my baby?'

'Resus,' I said, jumping to my feet, trying to keep up with Claire, who jogged towards the entrance. Jade was an only child and the centre of Claire's world; I couldn't imagine the devastation she'd feel if something happened to her.

We were at the desk in minutes, a frantic Claire asking about the condition of her daughter, where she was and if she could she see her. I stood behind, like a spare part, choked with emotion. Guilt clawed at me, it was my fault her daughter was here, but how could I tell her mum about the video – Jade would be mortified.

'Suspected overdosed? Why would she?' Claire raised her voice, anguish pouring out of her as she spoke to the nurse overseeing the ward. Trying to take in the information that her beloved daughter had consumed a concoction of pills and vodka alone in her room with the curtains drawn.

'I don't know, Mrs Parsons. Perhaps her friend might have some idea?'

They both looked towards me expectantly, but I shook my head, unable to speak.

22

I stayed at the hospital for a while, reluctant to leave Claire alone, but made my excuses when Jade's dad arrived. Jade was conscious and groggy, but I hadn't been in to see her, explaining to Claire I didn't want to clog up the ward. She'd looked at me quizzically, perhaps believing I couldn't bear to see my best friend in that state. It was true, I couldn't, especially after all that had happened. The main thing was she was going to be all right. What she chose to tell her parents about her suicide attempt was her decision to make, not mine.

I got in the car and headed for home, emotionally wrung out. So much had happened in a small space of time, but, if anything, it spurred me on to find the watcher and perhaps to do that I had to either make Rick tell me the truth or find out what he was hiding.

At the last minute, I took a detour to the penthouse, not sure if Rick would even be home until I saw his car parked in his space.

Todd nodded at me as I passed, adding, 'I don't think he's in good spirits today, Miss Abbi.'

The weight of Rick's hands on my shoulders from his loss of control in the studio earlier caused a crackle of apprehension to ripple my skin. Was he still angry? Was I about to walk into the hornet's nest?

'What makes you say that?' I asked, pausing mid stride.

'Didn't speak when he left this morning, came back a while later laden with bottles – beer, I assume. Ignored me completely. Haven't seen him since. Seems him and his brother must be having a party of sorts up there.'

'Thanks for the warning,' I replied. My cheeks burned because initially I suspected Todd could have planted the camera – what had I been thinking?

It was Nathan who opened the door. I didn't use my key, especially as I'd told Rick that morning I'd left it at home.

'Hey, Abs,' he said, his lip curling up into a smarmy smile as his eyes cast over me.

I swallowed, forcing a genial look, knowing full well the letch standing in front of me had seen me practically naked and was picturing it now. How many times had he watched the video? He might have been the one to set the camera up, he could be the watcher, torturing his brother. Who knew how deep their sibling rivalry went.

'How is he?' I asked.

'Not great, he's hammered, been drinking all afternoon. If you're here to babysit, I'll head off.'

I snorted. The last thing Rick would be receiving from me was a babysitting service. Did Nathan think I'd be tucking his brother into bed for the night, stroking his brow as he wallowed in self-pity, reeling from the mess he'd created?

'Rick, Abbi's here,' Nathan called over his shoulder, pulling open the door and letting me inside. His eyes burnt into my behind as he followed, the smack of his lips as he licked them. Being around Rick's brother always made me feel like I needed a wash. He'd been the one I knew I'd have to watch, but it turned out the pair of them were as perverted as each other.

The penthouse was a tip. It looked like Rick had thrown a tantrum, papers scattered everywhere, a barely eaten sandwich in the kitchen and half the fridge contents discarded on the counter. I found my ex-boyfriend slumped on the sofa, changed into grubby jogging bottoms and a T-shirt. He was surrounded by crushed cans of Stella but perhaps him being inebriated was a good thing.

'You came.' Rick gave me a weak smile, which I returned, knowing I'd have to play the game. His eyes were hopeful, yet I experienced a stab in my heart at his expression.

Nathan was already shrugging on his jacket and grabbing his keys and phone off the table. 'I'm off, bruv. I'll ring you tomorrow, yeah?' Nathan didn't wait for a response and saw himself out while Rick struggled into an upright position. He looked pathetic and in an instant my pity subsided, it took all my willpower not to pummel him into the sofa, the stupid, lying, cheating bastard.

'Jade's in hospital, she took an overdose,' I said, folding my arms and standing over him.

Rick blinked, trying to process the information before his hands covered his face, shame emanating off him. 'Oh God.'

'Yeah, so you need to tell me where the recordings are. We need to delete everything so there's nothing to post, because someone has got their hands on them.'

'I told you; it's not me. Why don't you believe me?' Rick whined.

Because you lied about your job, you lied about screwing Jade and you're lying to me now.

I gritted my teeth, trying to swallow my frustration, but I had to play this right.

'If another video is posted, if Carafe are tagged, then your job is gone.'

'It's gone already, they'll get rid of me, I know they will. I'm fucked,' he slurred.

Oh, poor you Rick, Jade's lying in a hospital bed right now and it's all your fault.

'Tell me what you did, Rick, tell the truth. You've been videoing us for months, haven't you, how many women have you recorded without them knowing?'

He waved his hand dismissively without answering, reaching for another beer. I counted the cans; it would be his tenth. Where had the man I'd fallen in love with gone, had he been pretending to be kind and generous, because the one in front of me was cold and bitter. He clearly wasn't going to tell me the truth, so I had to try another tack.

'Fine, fuck it. It wasn't you,' I said dramatically, heading for the freezer, where a bottle of vodka was stashed.

Rick looked at me quizzically as I grabbed two shot glasses, his frown slowly transforming into a gummy smile.

'Our lives are ruined anyway. If you want to get wrecked, let's get wrecked.' I walked Rick's shot over to him and he knocked it back as I tipped mine into a pint of water I assumed Nathan had poured for him.

'Yeah!' He pumped the air with his fist, wiping his mouth on his sleeve. 'That's the spirit.'

I grimaced at the victorious expression on his face.

'Are you going to stay over?' The seductive wink he tried reeked of desperation and I tried not to laugh at his audacity.

'Steady on, lover boy. I haven't forgiven you yet.'

Like I ever would, but I could let him believe I might.

'I'm sorry about Jade, she threw herself at me,' he scowled like a child who'd been refused an ice cream.

'That's no excuse,' I muttered, not believing a word of it.

I turned away to put some music on, whacking the volume up, and made a show of dancing around the kitchen, refilling the shots and pouring mine down the sink when Rick wasn't watching.

'You're my girl.' Rick pointed at me from the sofa, swaying and hiccupping. It was working, he could barely string a sentence together, eventually trying to stand and falling flat on his face.

'I think you've had enough, don't you?' I had a rush of dopamine from how wasted Rick was. This might actually buy me some time. 'Come on,' I said, hoisting him up and helping him to the bedroom.

I plonked him onto the bed and began undressing him. He raised an eyebrow, dribble forming on his lips, but thankfully I knew it was all he'd be able to raise. In minutes, he was snoring, lying naked on top of the covers.

'Let's see how you like it,' I muttered, retrieving my phone and taking photos of Rick with his less than impressive flaccid penis on display. I didn't intend to do anything with the pictures, but it was good to know I had them, in case I needed them.

I unlocked his phone, using his sleeping face and systematically went through it, but it held no videos or suspicious texts. Then I remembered the call with Gina on Friday, the one she hadn't received, and scrolled through his call log. Just before the time I'd arrived, Rick had taken a call from Nathan, not Gina. Why did he lie?

My mind drifted back to what I'd overheard. *'It's not going to come back on us.'* What wasn't, the recordings? Were the two of them in it together?

Under the guise of tidying up, I methodically went through the penthouse, room by room. Some of the papers discarded from his bag were bank statements, ridiculous amounts of money arriving in his account, hundreds of small transactions on a weekly basis but not from corporations, just random accounts. Was he investing or seeking investments? Money laundering perhaps? I also found his contract with Carafe Wines, which I guessed he'd dug out to find out if his suspension breached it. On the contract, it clearly stated he was a market analyst, so who was he wining and dining, or playing golf with if not clients, or had he been in the office the whole time? So much of what Rick had told me was a lie, I could no longer trust anything he said.

I found his mortgage statement, where he'd spent the past year overpaying as much as he could on the penthouse. Looking through more paperwork, the Audi Q4 I'd assumed was on lease or hire purchase, he owned outright. Something didn't add up and Gina's voice popped into my head, where was Rick getting his money from? A renewed sense of worry clung to my skin like sweat, he wasn't selling the recordings of us, was he? Vomit climbed my throat, but I forced it back down, clamping my lips together. Rick wouldn't do that, would he, he wouldn't sink so low?

I trawled through every room as the snores got louder and louder, but no matter where I looked, I found no evidence of a camera or any discs, and my spare key was nowhere to be seen. He'd either disposed of the recordings, or everything was stored on his laptop, which seemed to stare at me smugly from the breakfast bar.

I tried multiple times to guess his password but had no success, eventually slamming the lid closed as my thoughts turned back to Jade, hoping by now she was stable enough to be moved out of Resus and onto a ward. I had to make sure any videos of us were gone for good and with that in mind I left Rick drooling onto his pillow, stuffed his laptop in a carrier bag with the rest of my belongings and headed for the only person who might be able to help.

23

I knocked politely on Alfie's door, running on pure fumes. The day's events had exhausted me, but I couldn't rest until I'd tried everything possible to get into Rick's laptop. He would surely be out for the count for hours, allowing me to take the laptop back without him being any the wiser it had gone.

I knocked again, getting impatient, and eventually Alfie came to the door.

'Sorry, I was in the toilet,' he said before realising it was me. 'Oh hi, Abbi, everything okay?' His bruises were fading but still visible behind his now pink face.

'Were you expecting someone?' I looked behind me down the stairwell, but it was empty.

'Only Uber Eats,' he chuckled, patting his stomach. 'I can't be arsed to cook today, it was one hell of a shitshow at work.' Alfie was still wearing his shirt, although it was unbuttoned at the collar. Reddish hair crept from the top of his chest up to his neck and he had one sleeve rolled up to accommodate his splint.

My stomach growled loudly, and I blushed, I hadn't eaten all day, not even the almond croissant Linda had bought me for breakfast.

'You can join me if you like?' Colour spread from Alfie's face to his ears until they glowed pink.

'I was wondering if you could help me with something,' I said, raising the carrier bag that was making my arm ache.

'Sure, come in.'

'You mentioned coding before – does that mean you work in IT?' I asked, stepping inside the door, eyes taking in Alfie's flat that was vastly different to mine. The colour scheme of mine was as beige as a kid's dinner despite the pops of colour I'd tried to introduce, whereas his was stark white with black furniture. Not only that, but it was extremely tidy, almost anally so.

'Well, I'm a software engineer, so yes, I technically work in IT.'

I pulled the laptop out of the bag and placed it gently on Alfie's small dining table.

'This yours?' He frowned, hand rubbing at non-existent stubble.

'It's Rick's,' I said, chewing my bottom lip. 'I'm convinced he's got recordings on there – you know, private ones.' My face turned crimson. 'Like the kind I mentioned when we were on the roof.' I swallowed down my mortification as Alfie shifted from foot to foot, waiting for me to continue. 'I searched his flat and there's nothing there – no discs or anything – so perhaps it's all digitally stored on here.'

'Does he know you've got it?'

I shook my head and Alfie stared at me, the silence stretching out between us until we both jumped at a loud knock on the door. My breath caught, was it Rick? Had he woken up and come searching for his stolen laptop?

'Uber Eats, sir,' came a muffled voice from the other side of the door and we visibly relaxed. Alfie's eyes met mine and we both laughed, the tension evaporating.

Five minutes later, we were sat opposite each other at the table for two and I watched as Alfie spooned rice into a bowl for me, sharing his dinner despite my objections.

'I always over-order, then I've got leftovers,' he said, grinning. 'We'll eat, and I'll have a crack at the password, might be able to run a programme, I'll see.' He clapped his hands together like it was gameplay for him. He didn't realise the power he held. If I could get my hands on the footage, I could go to the police with evidence. I had no idea what the charge would be but was certain it was illegal to film people without their consent. Having said that, stealing and breaking into Rick's computer was also illegal and I'd have to lie about how I'd got hold of the videos if we were successful.

Alfie devoured his bowl of beef in black bean sauce and egg fried rice in minutes, telling me about the different programming languages used in coding. I tried to follow, but it was beyond me.

'I'm sorry, I'm not technically minded,' I admitted with a shake of the head.

'Most creative people aren't, to be honest, but if you gave me a brush, I could probably manage a basic paint by numbers, but that's it.' He gave a hearty laugh and pushed the bag of prawn crackers towards me. I took one out of politeness, eating quickly, keen to find out whether we could get into the laptop or not.

Alfie's small flat reeked of Chinese takeaway and stale air. I wanted to open a window but didn't want to appear rude. It was the most time I'd ever spent with my neighbour, and it was becoming painfully obvious we didn't have much in common, but he seemed like a nice enough guy. I needed as many friends as I could get right now.

'Have you been seeing anyone?' I asked, recalling our first proper encounter on the day I'd moved in. When I'd taken over a bottle of wine on the same day his wife moved out, leaving as I'd arrived, carrying boxes up the stairs, the pair of them having a loud slanging match.

Alfie frowned, getting up to take our bowls to the kitchen and disposing of them in the sink.

'Sorry, I didn't mean to pry,' I added, my neck itching with heat. I'd overstepped the mark.

'No, not at all,' he said quickly. 'I haven't, as it goes, haven't really had the time. Plus, it's all apps and swiping right these days, isn't it. I'm not sure it's for me.'

I watched as he moved awkwardly around the kitchen, almost unsure in his own space, perhaps it was my presence or what I'd said.

'I know what you mean, it doesn't appeal to me either.' I sighed, hoping my solidarity would excuse my intrusion into his personal life. Currently, he knew a lot more about me than I did about him.

'Right, let's have a look at this laptop then, shall we.' Alfie wiped the table and poured us both a glass of red wine. He retrieved his glasses and lifted the lid, switching the machine on, typing instructions in set-up mode. Intrigued, I got to my feet and looked over his shoulder as he worked, typing in what looked like code or commands. I'd come to the right place. 'This is his personal laptop right, not a work one?' Alfie asked, lifting his fingers from the keys as though they'd just delivered an electric shock.

'Personal, I'm sure. The sticker gives it away.' I pointed to the small yet iconic image from *Reservoir Dogs*, the actors walking together, the song 'Little Green Bag' playing in my head whenever I saw it. I imagined Rick would have had to hand his work laptop in the moment he was suspended.

'Okay, good. So, from what I can see, Rick's got it locked down pretty tight. I can tell you it's five lower case letters, but that's about it so far.'

'Well, that's good, right?' I said, enthused by how fast Alfie was working.

'Not really, it means there's over eleven million possible combinations.'

My jaw dropped.

'Let's try another way.' Alfie rebooted the machine, and got up from his seat, gesturing for me to sit. 'You know him best, what do you think it could be?'

I laughed feebly. 'I've already tried; I have no idea.'

'Not even now you know it's five letters?'

I shook my head but entered a couple of guesses. I tried *rugby*, knowing how much he loved the sport, then rickt for his last name, forwards and backwards. I tried *death* and *proof*, my least favourite Quentin Tarantino movie, then *brown* for *Jackie Brown*. Each time, it denied me access. Finally, I typed *porno* into the laptop, but that didn't work either.

'Okay,' Alfie said, blushing again at my last entry, pulling the laptop towards him and taking over the keyboard. After ten minutes of random guesses, we still weren't any closer to unlocking Rick's laptop. Outside had grown dark, Alfie's flat looked over a small park where the swings moved with the wind. The streetlamps outside buzzed and he switched on the light above our head, which was too harsh, making his skin look almost translucent. 'The only other way is if I remove the hard drive and put it in another machine, but I don't have the right model here. I could get one from work tomorrow?' he said hopefully, but I was already on my feet.

'I'm sorry, Alfie, but I've got to take this back tonight, otherwise he'll know it's missing.' I picked up the laptop and slid it back into the carrier bag. 'Thank you, though, I really appreciate your help, and dinner too. Next time, it's my treat.'

'No worries, any time.' The look on Alfie's face gave me pause, he looked eager and hopeful.

I headed for the door, looking forward to going back to my flat, if only to use the bathroom before I needed to get back over to Rick's. Hopefully he'd still be in his drunken stupor and wouldn't have realised his laptop had left the building. Alfie had some unopened post on a small side table by the door, where a wonky bowl held his keys.

'By the way, when I spoke to the police, they were trying to build a case against the person who'd posted that video, they asked me for your last name so they could link the report of your mugging.'

Alfie stared at me, his face blank. 'They think the mugging is linked to the person harassing you?'

'Well, I told them it might be. It's a bit of a coincidence you were the only one I talked to about the video and the next morning you're mugged on your way to work, *and* I get an email to say they know I didn't keep my mouth shut.'

Alfie blinked repeatedly. My gaze travelled from his eye, which was healing nicely to the splint on his arm, one of the Velcro straps hanging loose.

'How is your arm now?'

'Turns out it was only a hairline fracture,' he said, giving it a rub. 'I'm almost healed.'

'That's great.' I smiled as he opened the door, noticing the perspiration forming at his receding hairline.

'So, what is your last name?' I asked, chuckling as if I'd forgotten he hadn't already told me.

'Stokes,' he coughed, patting his chest. 'See you later, Abbi.'

'Bye, Alfie.' I watched as the door closed and turned my back as I sensed him looking through the peephole. Goosebumps flared on the base of my neck as I hurried to unlock my flat. The name on the letter by Alfie's front door was Stockton, not Stokes.

24

I rushed inside my flat to use the bathroom. It had been hours since I'd last been, and as I sat on the toilet emptying my bladder, I tried to work out why Alfie would lie to me about his last name. Was he trying to cover up something? Had he been in trouble with the police or would googling him lead to me finding out about some scandal?

As soon as I got back to my phone which I'd dumped by the door, I typed both names into Google, but nothing relevant came up. Like Rick, had he not made an official report about his mugging?

I couldn't deny it weirded me out a little, but I reminded myself Alfie had been nothing but nice to me – in fact, he'd been a hero in my time of need, twice now. We hadn't been able to get into Rick's laptop, but he'd tried and at least now I knew it was five lowercase letters. Perhaps I'd be able to crack it myself if I had more time. The only problem was that meant staying close to Rick, which was something I didn't want to do. He repulsed me now; he'd lied to my face, cheated and broken my heart, there was no coming back from that, but could I pretend I was considering giving him a second chance?

My mind was scrambled, I had too much to think about, too much to consider, the lease of my studio ending being one thing. I had two weeks to pack up and despite Linda's offer to withdraw her proposal to the landlord, a new start somewhere else would be welcome. I had to dig out the flat paperwork and see how much notice I'd need to give to move on, but that could wait until tomorrow. Now I had to drive back to Rick's and return the laptop, glad I'd only had half a glass of red wine.

I called Claire first on the way, to get an update on Jade, who told me she was stable and currently out for the count. Then I called Mum; wanting to respond to the text she'd sent checking I was okay. She was shocked when I told her about Jade, how she'd succumbed to her demons over the posted video publicly revealing her sleeping with her best friend's boyfriend. I told her it had been a hell of a day, but Jade was in the best possible hands, and I hoped she'd be all right. Before we said goodbye, I asked her to keep an eye out for rental opportunities nearby as I was considering moving closer to them.

'Oh, Abigail, that's great! We'd love to see you more.'

Perhaps I was a substitute for her number one son but then I had a stab of guilt at the thought.

'Has Rick been in touch?' she asked.

'He came to the studio this morning,' I replied. Feeling like it was a million years ago already.

'I hope you told him where to go!'

I laughed. 'Of course I did.' Not mentioning I'd been back to visit him later.

'Good, because leopards don't change their spots,' Mum said with utter conviction.

She wasn't wrong.

We said our goodbyes and Mum made me promise I'd keep in touch.

My chest tingled when I got to Rick's, concerned that Nathan might be back, but the visitor parking space was empty. I greeted Todd as he was packing up to finish his shift, handing over to Frank, who did nights, strutting through the reception area as though Rick was expecting me and heading straight up to the penthouse. I guessed he hadn't struck me off his approved visitor list yet.

Creeping through the front door and easing it shut, I could hear Rick snoring from the bedroom as soon as I entered. Unable to resist having a look, I peeked my head inside. He'd rolled over onto his side, still naked with no covering and mouth wide open. I snapped another photo on my phone, an idea springing to mind.

I'd learnt a lot at my first graphic design post before I'd created Edgewater, namely the software and skills needed to layer images. How to use Photoshop to its full potential and create fake images that looked real. It might come in handy if I needed a little leverage.

Before I left, I took one of the bank statements Rick had discarded and helped myself to two bottles of Carafe Wines' chianti from his stash, managing to catch Todd on the way out the foyer.

'A gift for you, Todd,' I said with a big smile. Partly a silent apology for my suspicions and partly to ensure I kept him on side.

'Why, thank you, Miss Abbi, that's a lovely gesture. The missus will be delighted,' he said with a grin as we walked to the car park. 'How is the lord of the manor?'

'Not particularly noble tonight, I'm afraid. I'm leaving him to it.'

'I don't blame you. Have a lovely evening.'

'You too, Todd.'

I headed home, my petrol tank almost empty. I was exhausted by the day's events and looking forward to crawling into bed, but my mind was too wired to sleep.

Back at the flat, I read through all the watcher's emails, scanning the screenshots again, maybe I was missing something. At the top of the image, when I enlarged it, I saw a tiny slice of what looked like the bar from a search engine. Was the screen grab taken from an internet site? I sat bolt upright, any thoughts of sleep evaporated. Had I been posted on the internet?

I grabbed my laptop, opened Google, inputting my name, then Rick's, followed by amateur porn, which led me down a wormhole of websites I had no interest visiting. I looked back at the screenshot, scrutinising every inch for clues, but it was no use, I couldn't see enough of the text to determine the web address. I had to get into Rick's laptop – or maybe there was a way using the bank statements I'd taken from the penthouse. I got out of bed to retrieve them, each payment was for around thirty-seven pounds and there were pages and pages of them, but there was no way to trace who had sent the funds, the names were random letters and numbers and when I googled them it led to nothing.

Frustrated, I crawled back into bed and tried to sleep, but my mind was working overtime. In the end, I got up again, this time to get the burner phone, which was down to its last bar of battery.

> TELL ME HOW TO FIND THOSE VIDEOS

I sent the message, as all the leads I'd followed had come up with nothing. I had no choice but to keep Rick believing there was a chance for a reconciliation because I needed to make sure no more videos would make their way to the internet or social media.

Eventually, I fell asleep, waking to my alarm, which I hadn't even remembered setting, unenthused about going to the studio. I had to start the caravan commission today to stay on schedule but snoozed the alarm for a few minutes. When I rolled over to get out of bed, a glass of water was on my bedside table. Had I put that there last night? I didn't remember doing it and it wasn't as if I was hungover, the only alcohol I'd had was half a glass of red wine at Alfie's. Maybe I was so tired I'd been on autopilot and forgotten.

A strong coffee and hot shower were what I needed, and I felt more human by the time I was dressed and ready to leave for work. When I got in my car to head to the garage to fill up, the petrol gauge had moved, the tank now half full. I frowned at the display. I knew I hadn't gone to a garage last night, too eager to get home. Someone had stolen my old Citroen, taken it for a joyride and kindly filled it up with petrol before returning it? Either that or I had a defunct gauge.

I looked around the car, in the back seats and glovebox, but nothing was out of place. It was so random. Was the watcher now committing random acts of kindness, demonstrating they could get into my car with ease? I almost laughed with how ludicrous it was, then, like a jolt of electricity, it struck me – was that who'd left the water by my bed? I shuddered at the thought, skin swarming with a thousand ants. A stranger, in my flat, whilst I was sleeping, watching me. How had they got in? Stupidly, I hadn't left my key in the door last night, knowing Rick was passed out and there was no way he'd be coming around to let himself in.

I started the engine; throat so dry, I could barely swallow. My feet wouldn't connect with the pedals until I adjusted my seat. Someone had been in my car. I drove to the studio paranoid a bomb was going to go off, or my car would catch fire, but it drove better than ever. Still, the thought of the watcher being inside my car and flat had adrenaline firing around my body. The invasion of privacy alone horrified me; were there no lines they weren't willing to cross? Visions of a shadowy figure at the end of my bed, watching me sleep, daring to touch me, made my flesh turn to ice. I had to tell Officer Barrett.

When I got to work, a bouquet of flowers was waiting for me outside the door to my studio, bright red roses. Within seconds, Linda had materialised with a stupid grin on her face.

'Beautiful flowers!'

'Hmmm,' I grumbled, sticking them under my arm to unlock the door. I was not in the mood for Linda buzzing around like an annoying wasp at a summer picnic.

Linda hovered for a while after showing me a new reel she'd created, but I gave her minimum engagement and eventually she slunk back to her workshop. I didn't have the patience today; too much weird stuff was going on and I was frustrated at hitting a dead end with Rick's laptop.

I shut the door and started on the static caravan, getting lost in the long blades of grass and bumble bees searching for pollen. When I took a break to use the bathroom, I checked my Edgewater emails, finding two commission requests had been withdrawn. One email was polite, citing a change of financial circumstances, the other called me a dirty whore.

I sat and stared at my phone open-mouthed, eyes welling up. It was so easy to spout hate hidden behind a keyboard without seeing the person you'd attacked. I hadn't thought anyone, other than the people Abbi321 friended on Instagram, had been sent the video of me and Rick, certainly not any of my customers, but, perhaps like Jade's, the video had been passed along. Had I gone viral too?

25

With a weight in my chest, I returned to the studio and did a Google search for Edgewater but found nothing related to my business, not until I trawled back through comments on Instagram. Someone had put an angry emoji where I'd shared the commission a customer had posted on their account, the one of their piece above the fireplace. When I clicked on the customer's post and read the comments, I found the culprit.

> Beware this woman, not a legit business, it's a cover for porn!

Indignation burned my gullet. Should I respond? The voice in my head told me not to. It was rule number one, never engage, but still, this person YOLO264, whoever they were, had lost me two customers.

I searched through YOLO264's posts, but there was nothing that told me who they were, only that they had a chocolate Labrador called Milo. My thoughts turned to Jade and how bad the online abuse and the hate from her coworkers must have been for her to even consider ending her life, or perhaps it was those closer to home that had pushed her over the edge. I checked the time, visiting hours were at two and I needed to speak to her, hear her side of the story, perhaps she could shed some light on how we'd been filmed.

I got back to the caravan portrait, immersing myself for a couple of hours, surprised I hadn't yet heard from Rick, checking if his flowers had arrived.

When I looked for a card, there was none. Perhaps he was still wallowing, maybe he remembered nothing of our interaction yesterday, he had been wasted.

When it got closer to two, I called Claire and left a voicemail to say I'd be stopping by at the hospital and jumped in the car.

At first, I had a pang of guilt on arrival that I'd bought no gift with me, but when I got to the ward, it was replaced by a searing flash of anger as I saw Rick by Jade's bed. Legs spread wide and slouched in the guest chair, he looked like he was sulking and I guessed he must have remembered what I'd told him about Jade's overdose. Jealousy enveloped me like a shroud, and I turned to walk away, but he'd already spotted me.

'Abbi, I was just checking Jade was okay,' he called, giving chase down the corridor, but witnessing the two of them together after what I'd seen in that video made me seethe. It all came flooding back, his hands all over her, the ecstasy on their faces, I couldn't bear the pinpricks of betrayal, sharp as needles.

'I'll wait outside until you're finished.' My voice spikey.

'You came, last night,' he said as if finding it hard to believe now in the cold light of day. 'It means a lot. I know full well you didn't have to look in on me, I appreciate it.' Rick reached out to touch my arm, but I shrank away from him. 'Maybe, you know, in time...' he said, and I bit the inside of my cheek, visualising smashing his laptop to pieces or beating him to death with the roses he'd bought.

'What you both did...' I choked out the words.

'I'll make it up to you, I promise. I love you, Abs, it's only ever been you.'

Yeah, but it hasn't, has it?

His begging was pitiful, and I wanted to tell him to go to hell, but I had to play the long game. He'd set up that camera, he'd filmed me and Jade, there might be others, and what had he done with the footage, because the watcher had got it from somewhere and, from the screenshot, it looked like the internet.

A light bulb went off in my brain, a straightforward Google search had led me nowhere, but maybe the videos weren't on the internet as such, maybe they were on the dark web. I narrowed my eyes at Rick; did he know about all that stuff? Could he be into something like that, without me having a clue for all these months?

'You go and see Jade. She's pissed at me anyway, but she's okay, that's the main thing.'

I shook my head, despairing. How had I been in love with the twat standing in front of me? 'Are you really surprised, Rick? *Someone*,' I said sarcastically, air quoting with my fingers, 'filmed her having sex with you and posted it on social media.'

'I told you; it wasn't me. I swear to you, on my brother's life.'

I snorted. Nathan clearly didn't mean much to him and maybe that was something I should consider – how much did Rick's brother know and were they in it together? Did he know about my video because it had been sent to Elena or because he was Abbi321?

'Listen, why don't you come over later, I'll cook, and we can talk.'

I crossed my arms, the nerve of him galled me.

'You can drop my key back if you want, but let's at least have a conversation about it. Remember, I'll probably lose my job too, I didn't do this to myself. Why would I want to ruin everything we had?' His slate eyes pleaded with me to consider his proposal.

'Maybe,' I said through gritted teeth, still trying to contain my temper as porters and nurses hustled around us.

'Okay,' he relented, 'hopefully, I'll see you later.'

I waited a couple of minutes to compose myself before heading back to the ward. Jade was pale and clammy, her usually wild bob was glued flat to her head and tucked behind her ears. Vomit stained her hospital gown, and she fingered the identity bracelet, pulling it taut against her wrist. It was obvious mine and Rick's visit had made her uncomfortable.

'Abbi, I'm so sorry about Rick,' she whispered, eyes spilling over.

I'd had enough apologies to last a lifetime, they changed nothing. Neither of them could take back what they'd done, and we couldn't all pretend our lives hadn't been blown up with their actions.

'How are you feeling?' I asked stiffly, pulling up a chair. My back was rigid; I didn't want to be there with such mixed emotions.

'Shit,' Jade managed a weak smile, 'but they said I should be able to go home today. Mum's got an appointment at the doctor's tomorrow; she wants me on antidepressants.'

'Did you tell her why you did it?'

Jade shook her head and stared hard at the flimsy sheet covering her legs.

'Why did you?' My words came out in a whisper. It was hard to hate someone you'd loved so deeply for so long. Jade had been my closest friend, my confidante, the person I turned to in a crisis.

Eventually, she looked at me. 'Work was awful, everyone was sharing it. I had notes in my locker, someone even printed a still image out and stuck it on the windscreen of the ambulance Henry and I had to use. He wouldn't speak to me, embarrassed I guess, and I couldn't bear the disappointment on his face. It didn't stop at home either, my Instagram blew up with messages, death threats and links to porn sites. It had been reposted so many times.' Jade sobbed, burying her face in her hands. 'I thought it was you,' she continued once she'd composed herself, 'that you were behind a hate campaign, because I'd done the worst thing I could do to my best friend.'

'I didn't,' I said, welling up myself at Jade's outpouring of emotion, devastated our friendship could never be the same again. It was like grief, mourning what we'd had, what Rick and I could have had if they'd never slept together. 'Why, Jade?' It came out like a whine, but I had to confront her, to get the truth.

'I don't want to make excuses, I was drunk, we bumped into each other at the Octopus Bar, had a laugh, he convinced us to do shots. I'm not even sure how I ended up back at his. I just remember him kissing me, telling me Honking Henry must be mad not to see how beautiful I was.'

I swallowed the bile that rose up in my throat.

'The next morning, I left before he woke up. I was mortified, and we never spoke about it again. We both pretended it hadn't happened, and I thought perhaps it hadn't, maybe it had all been a bad dream, until the video.'

'Did you know you were being filmed?'

'No, I had no idea that bastard had filmed it. He's still denying it, of course.'

'Who was Rick with at the Octopus Bar?'

'His slimy brother, who was chatting up some girl who had to have been barely eighteen.' The girl couldn't have been Elena then. What if Rick was telling the truth and knew nothing about the recordings? What if Nathan was behind the camera – he had access to the penthouse. I twirled my hair, it needed a treatment, dry at the ends.

The silence stretched out between us and Jade returned to pulling at her identity bracelet.

'Can you ever forgive me?' Her small voice cut deep into my heart.

'I don't know,' I answered honestly. Right now, it was too raw, too new. Maybe in years to come I'd say she'd done me a favour, because if it hadn't been Jade Rick slept with, it would have been someone else. He could have been cheating all the way through our relationship for all I knew. I'd trusted the wrong people, but it wouldn't happen again.

'Thank you, for coming to the flat. You saved me.' Tears streamed from Jade's eyes, full of regret.

'Your mum sent me, but don't do that to her again, eh,' I replied gently.

'Abbi!' Claire was jubilant as she swiped back the curtain, beaming at me, and I hoped she hadn't overheard.

'Hi, Claire, I was just going.' I stood, catching Jade's chin wobble as I did.

'Oh, you don't have to go on my account. Jade was desperate for some proper food, so I nipped to McDonald's.' She held a brown paper bag, dark at the bottom with grease and rolled at the top to keep the heat in. The smell was seeping out, turning my stomach.

'I need to get back to work. Take care, Jade.'

'Bye, Abbi.' I could tell she was trying to hold it together for the sake of her mum. Those two words were heavy; there was no plans made to see each other again. It could be goodbye forever, but I guessed that was up to me.

When I got back to the car, I bawled, hollowed out, my well empty. I'd forced myself the past week to function amid heartbreak and betrayal, but coming face to face with Jade and Rick together had finished me off. I was still no closer to finding the recordings, and I was truly alone in my plight.

26

You've got to get a grip, Abbi! I scolded myself, sitting crying in my car wasn't going to get me the justice I deserved. I'd done nothing wrong, yet I'd been exposed and vilified on social media by a man who was supposed to love me, and a stranger. It seemed perfect timing when Ben sent me a message, letting me know he was here if I needed him. Mum had obviously told him what had been going on in my life and him reaching out meant a lot, despite there being not much he could do from Turkey. I appreciated the gesture and responded to say thanks, and it worked both ways.

The heavens opened, sloshing water onto my windscreen and hammering on the roof. I watched as people dashed across the road, rushing for shelter beneath the overhanging entrance of the accident and emergency department. Distracted from my misery for a moment and buoyed by Ben's message, I looked through my contacts, sure I had Nathan's number somewhere. Perhaps I could needle the truth out of him and tapped out a message.

> I'm worried about Rick – can we meet?

Hopefully that would do the trick. Nathan would be working, but maybe he could get away; he managed the builder's merchants, after all. It would take me around forty minutes to drive there and as I considered my route, my phone buzzed with a response.

> Sounds good, I'm actually on my way up to Crawley to see him. Want to meet up first?

I responded I would, glad I wouldn't have to drive to Croydon, and arranged to meet him at The Black Swan, a pub on the edge of town right by the motorway, somewhere I hoped we wouldn't bump into anybody we knew.

When I got there, the downpour had stopped and Nathan was pulling up in his sporty Ford Focus with added spoiler and enormous exhaust. I assumed when men hit their thirties they grew out of that stuff, but not Nathan.

'Abbi,' he said, snaking an arm around my waist and leaning in to kiss my cheek in the middle of the car park. I tried my hardest not to pull away, to wipe his disgusting saliva off my face, instead smiling sweetly and gesturing for us to head inside.

We sat in a booth at the back with our drinks. Nathan had on scruffy shorts, desert boots, and a T-shirt with a hole at the neck, having come straight from work. I didn't look much better, having spent minimal effort getting ready this morning, but that didn't stop Nathan eyeballing me across the table.

'Rick said you stayed for a bit last night, put him to bed and tidied up, it was nice of you,' Nathan said, wiping the condensation from his half-pint glass with his stubby thumb.

'After the suspension at work, he was in a bit of a state.'

'Yeah, I tried to talk him around, but he wouldn't listen, determined to get shit-faced and block it all out.'

'Did you know about him and Jade?' I asked, chewing on my lip, the skin ragged where I'd been doing it so much.

'Nah,' Nathan replied, clearly lying, 'what can I say, he can't handle his booze, he's never been able to, makes stupid decisions when he's had too many. Our dad was the same.' Before I could react, Nathan reached across the table and grasped my hand. 'But he loves you, Abbi, he does, on my life.'

I squirmed in my seat, my hand growing hot. Nathan's touch repulsed me, but I couldn't let that show.

'Was it him, did he plant the cameras, has he been filming us all this time?'

'Of course not. I mean who's going to want to watch him fuck.' Nathan fell about laughing, finally releasing my hand, which I drew beneath the table. 'Watch him fuck, see what I did there...' Nathan thought it was hilarious. What was he on about?

He downed the rest of his lager, still chuckling, and jumped up to get another half. I'd not touched a drop of my drink and forced down a mouthful. Nathan had left his phone behind and I lightly tapped the screen, seeing Instagram notifications waiting for him. Messages sent from handles I didn't recognise. Before the screen timed out, I was sure I saw a name beginning with A? Could it have been Abbi?

I bit the bullet and asked the question I was dreading as soon as Nathan returned, relieved his phone had gone dark.

'Is Rick into weird stuff – porn and that?' My cheeks burned with the humiliation, but the glint in Nathan's eye was hard to miss.

'Porn?' he said so loudly people three tables apart turned to stare; I wanted the world to swallow me whole. 'He's a bloke, Abbi, we're all into porn. If you're not, there's got to be something wrong with you. It's the biggest money maker there is.'

I frowned. 'What do you mean by that?'

'Well, there's so much out there, whatever fetish you're into – feet, animals, corpses – it's all on offer, at a price.'

I baulked. 'Please don't tell me Rick's got some weird fetish.'

'You should know better than me!' he snorted and I rolled my eyes, waiting for him to continue. 'Listen, not that I'm aware of, but sex, yeah of course, everyone watches porn. In fact, I'm surprised after that video you've not been approached to star in a film.' He chuckled and rage burned in my belly.

'Enjoy it, did you?' I sneered.

He lowered his voice, leaning towards me. 'Can't say I didn't imagine what it would feel like. You know, if you ever fancy having a go with a younger model, just shout.'

I wrinkled my nose, internally heaving at the thought.

'I'll be sure to do that,' I replied sarcastically. Had he filmed us or was he the watcher? Jealous of Rick's flair with the ladies, tormenting Jade and I by sharing the video?

'And don't worry, you're way hotter than Jade.'

I clenched my jaw, trying my best not to give Nathan a piece of my mind or cover him in what was left of my drink. What Elena saw in him, I didn't know.

'So, are you two going to make it up then, seems a shame to chuck it away for one silly mistake.'

I snorted at Nathan's question – one silly mistake, I sure there were many more I wasn't aware of, but I tempered my reaction. I was here for one thing: information.

'I don't know, how can I trust him now. Someone planted that camera, your brother swears blind it wasn't him, but I'm not an idiot, Nathan. If it wasn't Rick, then who?'

'I dunno, could be Todd, he has keys to everyone's place, or the cleaner.'

'Or you?' I said, my eyes locking onto his.

He leaned back in his chair, raising his hands. 'It wasn't me.' There it was again, that glint in his eyes. I didn't trust Nathan as far as I could throw him. He had to be involved somehow.

'Well, the police are looking into it now. I'm sure it won't be long before they might want to speak to you too.'

Nathan shrugged, trying to look nonchalant, but I wasn't fooled.

'Right,' he said, necking his second half of lager, 'I'll have a piss, then we'll head to Rick's, shall we? See how the daft bugger is.'

I agreed and he left the table, taking his phone with him this time. I had no desire to see Rick, but I was on a mission to find any recordings and as desperate as I was to get back to the solitude of my own flat, it wasn't going to help with that.

I left my barely touched drink and walked out with Nathan to the car park.

'I've got to drop a commission into the post office, so I'll see you there,' I lied, before watching as Nathan took off, the loud exhaust echoing around the car park.

I drove slowly to Rick's, Nathan had already arrived and claimed the one visitor space, so I parked in a staff one, hoping the bottle of wine I'd presented Todd with might allow me some leeway. He was all smiles when I entered, standing up to greet me from behind the desk.

'Miss Abbi, thank you so much for the bottle of wine, it was absolutely delicious and got me some brownie points with the wife.'

'You're most welcome, Todd, and there's more where that came from, just don't tell Rick,' I said, raising a finger to my lips and winking.

Todd gave me a salute, the lines around his eyes crinkling.

'Actually, could you do me a favour, it's a bit cheeky, but there'll be another bottle of wine in it for you.'

'Anything.'

'Well, firstly I've parked in a staff spot as Rick's brother is visiting.'

Todd grimaced; he liked Nathan about as much as I did.

'That's fine, no problem. What else?'

I checked my watch. 'At, say, quarter to five-ish, could you ring up to Rick and ask him to come down and check his car, say some kids were playing in the car park or something.'

'Prey tell, Miss Abbi, why do you want Rick out of the apartment?'

I sighed, perhaps honesty was going to be the best policy here, hoping I could count on Todd's fatherly protectiveness kicking in.

'Because…' I paused, the truth getting stuck in my throat. 'I think he has a video of me on his laptop. He's got a camera up there somewhere and he's filmed me without me knowing.' Todd's eyebrows shot up and I didn't need to spill any further grisly details as he already looked affronted, but I added, 'It's not one I want him to share, so I want to delete it.'

'Of course, leave it to me.'

'Thank you, Todd, another bottle of red coming right up.' I reached over and patted his hand before making my way to the lift.

27

Nathan answered the door with a loud 'there she is!' pulling me inside. Rick appeared a minute later, looking slightly less dishevelled than earlier, but he still hadn't shaved. Patchy stubble made his olive skin look darker and his curls, usually slicked back, were almost as wild as mine.

'I'm so pleased you came over for dinner, I've made moussaka.'

I smiled tightly, having forgotten his invitation and what he would be reading into my appearance.

'I can't stay for too long,' I said.

'It's all right, I'll eat what she can't manage,' Nathan piped up and Rick glared at him.

'I was thinking perhaps Abbi and I could have some time alone.'

'I've come all this way and Elena is busy tonight, I'll eat with you, and I'll meet Dave and the boys down the pub later, everyone's a winner.'

Rick sighed at Nathan not getting the hint and I put my bag on the kitchen side.

Rick's laptop was on the breakfast bar, open, and as I moved past it to get a glass out of the cupboard, I stroked the keypad, bringing it to life. It hadn't locked and I could see Rick was working on a report for work. My luck was in.

I glanced at the time, Todd was going to call in about ten minutes, so I loitered in the kitchen.

'Have you heard from Carafe?' I turned my back to fill my glass at the sink.

'They've asked me to do a couple of bits from home, so that's good news, looks like I might get saved after all.'

Nathan slapped Rick on the shoulder and slumped onto the sofa, putting his boots on the coffee table. 'Great news, bruv, told you it would all blow over.'

'Get your boots off,' Rick snapped. Tensions seemed high between the two of them and Nathan rolled his eyes but did as he was asked.

Rick joined me in the kitchen, my heart sinking. Every few seconds I'd been brushing my finger over the keypad to make sure it didn't lock. Rick turned the oven on, then, when he thought I wasn't looking, checked the bin for the cooking instructions. I knew he hadn't made it himself but wasn't about to call him out on yet another lie.

At five forty-four, the phone rang, and Rick picked it up, frowning as he listened.

'Really? Okay, I'll be right down.' Grabbing his keys, he turned to Nathan. 'Todd thinks some little shits have been at my car!' Knowing he wouldn't be able to resist the urge to check on his prized Audi, Rick headed straight for the door.

I held my breath waiting for Nathan to move from the sofa, but he didn't budge, flicking through the television channels with the remote instead. Rick was already summoning the lift and my frustration mounted.

'What if they're tooled up – don't you think you should help him out?' I said, sounding like I was in some dodgy television drama, but Nathan got up with a sigh and trotted after his brother.

As soon as the door closed, I brought the laptop to life again and minimised the report Rick was working on. A quick look through Windows Explorer revealed nothing but work documents and one chapter of a novel written three years ago. Reading the first line made me cackle with laughter, a literary genius he was not. I opened Microsoft Edge and looked at Rick's bookmarked internet sites, my lip curling as Pornhub was third from the top after Google and Spotify. I was tempted to search through Pornhub in case my video had somehow found its way on there, but it dawned on me his internet history might be a better place to search.

Glancing at the time on the laptop, Rick and Nathan had already been gone five minutes and would soon be back, so I opened Chrome and clicked on the top right-hand corner, scrolling down to internet history. It looked as though Rick had been looking at Sky Sports, news and stock market information before shopping for rugby shirts. I moved the cursor further down when a ping came from beyond the front door, Nathan's voice, although muffled, was distinct, heading out of the lift.

Shit, they're back.

As I was about to close the tab something caught my eye.

Watchmefuck.com.

There was no time to click onto the website, so I shut down both internet pages and reinstated the report, moving swiftly to the sink to refill my water as the pair of them walked in.

'Told you it was kids messing about,' Nathan griped, flopping back onto the sofa.

'Car okay?' I asked, watching as Rick slung his keys on the counter, my door key absent from the bunch.

'Yeah, not a scratch on it. Good of Todd to let me know, though.'

'Why don't I take him down a bottle of wine later, I'm sure he'd appreciate it. Keep him sweet and he'll look out for you.'

'Great idea, babe,' Rick said, then looked at me apologetically for his faux pas. With me being here, he found it all too easy to revert back to normal, when I was the opposite, especially now I'd found potential evidence of his involvement in this. What was that website? I had to see if I was on it. But for now, I'd have to suffer dinner with him and his brother before I could make my excuses and leave.

The moussaka was dry and overcooked, but I ate as quickly as I could, forgoing Rick's offer of wine and sticking to water. As I was helping load the dishwasher, Rick told Nathan to go so we could talk, and I knew I'd be trapped for a little longer.

Rick poured his heart out on the sofa, each word going in one of my ears and out the other. I wasn't interested that his parents' marriage used to be an unhappy one, that his mum cheated when him and Nathan were just boys, leaving the family home for a while so his dad struggled to pay the rent by himself. That he'd never forgiven his mum, and their relationship was strained, which was why he rarely visited. Those might be the reasons Rick was the way he was, but it didn't excuse his behaviour.

I told him I needed time to think. I didn't trust anything he said any more. All the denials, the pleas for forgiveness meant nothing. My only goal was to find those recordings, discover the truth and make sure he'd never have the opportunity to do it again.

By the time I'd got out of the penthouse with another bottle of wine for Todd, it was almost eight – too late now for me to run to the DIY store and pick up a chain for my door.

I raced home, stopping for a quick chat with Alfie when we passed on the stairs. He had a date apparently and I wished him luck, glad me sharing a takeaway with him the other night hadn't been misconstrued for something it wasn't. He was still waiting to hear back from his mate with the workshop, he'd said, but would let me know as soon as it was free to view. Bumping into Alfie reminded me to email Officer Barrett with both of Alfie's last names – the one from the mail I'd seen, and the one Alfie had given me. I didn't know what the story was there, or why they were different, but going on my gut, I was sure he was a good guy.

I got changed into pyjamas and fastened my curls into a bun, settling on the sofa with my laptop, making my email to Officer Barrett the first port of call. Mum had flooded my inbox with listings for potential studios in Wallington and surrounding areas and it warmed my heart that she'd been thinking of me. Putting them aside to go through later, I opened an internet browser, entering the name of the website I'd seen on Rick's computer, cringing as I typed it in. What was I about to see on watchmefuck.com? Dreading what would flash up when it loaded, I stalled at the first hurdle because it was a membership only website and I had no log-in. At least I didn't have to teach myself how to access the dark web because it popped up straight away.

On the information page, it stated it cost fifty dollars to obtain a lifetime membership, which included some videos for free, others – the interactive streams and lives ones were pay per view – an extra eighty dollars a pop, in addition to the membership. What on earth did interactive mean? I had visions of webcams and people joining in like some kind of mass online orgy, and the moussaka threatened to make a reappearance. Reluctant to create an account for myself for fear of exposure, the only person I could ask to help was my brother. I squirmed at the conversation we'd have to have but there were no other males in my life I trusted implicitly, not anymore. I messaged Ben, asking him to call me when he was free. Turkey was two hours ahead, so technically he should have finished for the night, but there was a possibility he was out.

Frustrated at the lack of progress, I tried to switch off and watch some television, keeping an ear out if Alfie returned. He might be able to help, although I would be embarrassed asking him to sign up to a porn site for research purposes. We weren't that close. Rick texted wishing me goodnight, saying how lovely it was to spend time with me, and he hoped I'd consider getting back together. I deleted it without replying. A bunch of roses, which I'd discarded on the kitchen side, wasn't going to make up for what he'd done. The web was closing in, although, if the site was based in the US, could he be involved or was it just another porn site he'd been looking at? Nathan's sentence from when we were at the pub echoed in my mind: 'who'd want to watch him fuck... see what I did there.' I hadn't picked up on it at the time but that followed by his smug laughter meant it had to be relevant. It had to be the site he was referring to.

If I was on there, maybe Jade was too? Was she back home now? I hadn't heard from her – not that I expected to, she was likely giving me space in the aftermath of what had happened, something I wished Rick would do. I needed to put some hours in at the studio tomorrow, try to get ahead with the commissions, but when I checked my emails, no orders had come in today. I was getting around one or two smaller ones a day now which had slowed since the Instagram influencer had promoted the portrait I'd sent her. I knew the bubble would burst and it would even out eventually, but how much of it was down to the lies being spread about me online? How many customers had YOLO264 put off?

I guessed I should be grateful I still had a business to run, but it stung nonetheless and I had to find another studio to work out of because my flat was too small. It was all so overwhelming I couldn't bring myself to look through the listings Mum had sent, despite having about a week and a half before the lease was up. I added it to the list of things I needed to worry about and fell asleep on the sofa, phone in hand, waiting for my little brother to call me back.

28

Ben rang at four minutes past six, pulling me from sleep. I'd been having a nightmare: someone was watching me through my window, hovering outside despite being four floors up. What with the website, I'd forgotten to secure the door and my first thought was if someone had been inside while I'd been asleep. Surely I would have heard them from the sofa. As I answered the ringing phone, I untangled myself from the blanket I'd pulled over me before nodding off.

'Yo, Abs, what's up?' Ben sounded way too buoyant for this time in the morning, whereas I struggled to form a sentence.

'Morning.' I rubbed the sleep from my eyes and listened to the sound of Ben walking, the low thrum of traffic in the background. 'Are you on your way to work?' I asked.

'Yep, about to hit the breakfast buffet – and after last night I need it.'

'Was it a heavy one?'

'You could say that. Sorry I missed your message, I was, ahem, busy.'

I laughed, knowing he was likely getting up to things he shouldn't with a female staff member. 'Well, be careful little brother, I'm not ready to be an auntie yet.'

'God no! Believe me, I'm not ready either. How are you doing, Mum told me what happened – well, she gave me the light version.'

I sat upright, steeling myself for Ben's reaction before giving him a brief rundown of what had gone on with Rick. He didn't sound shocked, just mildly disgusted and pissed off on my behalf. I told him I was trying to trace the video and wanted to become a member of a porn site, using his email address and credit card because I didn't want my name to be flagged up. I left out the stalking and someone having been inside my flat and the car, it would only spook him, and I intended to rectify that today with a deadbolt.

'That all sounds well and good, for me anyway,' he chuckled drily, 'but you do realise we have the same last name.'

'Your credit card will have Benjamin Andrew Montgomery on it, it's a pretty common last name, Ben. I'll transfer you the money. You get a free membership to perv as much as you want.'

'What, at videos of my sister! Gross!'

'No, of course not! I'm hoping I'm not going to be on there, but if I am, I'll be taking action to get them removed immediately!' I hadn't contemplated what I'd do if I found myself on the site, knowing I'd been watched by untold amounts of people, scrub myself with bleach probably.

'Okay, fine,' I heard shuffling the other end, 'have you got a pen?'

I jumped up to write down Ben's email address and password, as well as his credit card details.

'You owe me, okay,' he said, 'and don't read my emails either.'

'I have no interest in spying on you,' I replied, contemplating whether I'd find something to knock him off Mum's pedestal, but I wasn't going to pry. Ben was entitled to his privacy, and I knew what it was like to have it stolen. 'Thank you, I mean it. If I could have asked someone else, I would have, but I don't really have any male friends I can approach about something like this.'

'All right, sis, I get it. I gotta go, let me know what you dig up and give Rick a kick in the balls for me.' Ben hung up and I made myself a coffee before booting up the laptop.

Annoyingly once I'd applied for a membership and paid the fifty dollars, which I assumed had to mean it was a site in the US, I had to wait for log-in details to be sent to Ben's email address. They still hadn't arrived by the time I'd showered and got ready for work, so I took the laptop with me to the studio, bumping into Alfie, who was leaving at the same time.

'How did the date go last night?' I asked, noticing his eye was almost healed and he was no longer wearing the splint.

'Not bad, she's into period dramas and horror films – how's that for an oxymoron.'

'Variety is the spice of life.'

Alfie held the door to our building open for me, and we walked out onto the pavement. 'Did you manage to get into Rick's computer?'

'Sort of, I found a website in his internet history. Something his brother said made it stand out, but it needs a membership. I've signed up and once I get the details, I can see if I'm on there. Obviously, I'm praying I'm not.' I blushed, talking about the publication of my sex tape with a relative stranger, but Alfie didn't bat an eyelid.

'If you need any help, then shout. I better go; I'm going to be late for my train.' Alfie waved goodbye and jogged towards the station as I got in my car, glad to see everything where I'd left it, hoping some painting would take my mind off waiting for the membership to be approved.

When I arrived at the studio, Linda was holding a class, but as soon as it finished, she appeared at my door to say hello.

'That looks amazing,' she said, looking over my shoulder at the outline of the static caravan, an off-white with beige trim.

'Thanks,' I said, putting down my brush. 'How are things?' I wasn't particularly interested in conversation with Linda, but with such a short time left at the studio, there was little point in holding a grudge.

'Good, thank you, classes are fully booked and I'm thinking of offering an evening class. How about you?'

'Yeah, okay,' I said unconvincingly, not wanting to bring up the elephant in the room.

'Have you, umm, found anywhere?' She didn't mean to get my back up, but my hackles rose anyway.

'Not yet, but I will. I emailed the landlord about extending the lease, but he hasn't got back to me,' I lied, wanting to keep Linda wondering if she was getting the studio or not. Her eager expression turned stony. 'But I'm also considering moving back to Surrey if there's nothing left keeping me here.' My tone was stand-offish, but I couldn't help it. I loved my little studio, and she'd whipped it away when I'd taken my eye off the ball.

Linda squirmed in the doorway and the silence stretched out between us.

'Have you heard from Rick?' she asked, changing the subject.

'Unfortunately, yes. He's a bit like a bad smell I can't get rid of.'

Linda forced a laugh. 'I thought so, I've seen him hanging around now and then, like he's keeping watch.'

Linda's words struck a chord, but I dismissed them – Rick couldn't be the watcher, he'd hardly sabotage his own career and relationship, would he?

'You okay, you seemed to drift off?'

'Just tired, I better crack on,' I said, hoping Linda would take the hint and leave. We weren't friends and I wasn't going to be keeping in touch.

I checked my emails before I resumed painting, getting a jolt of excitement when I found Ben's log-in details had been sent over. Jumping up to lock the door to ensure Linda couldn't see in, I opened the laptop and navigated to the website via the link in the email, not caring I was using the building's Wi-Fi. I was going to be leaving soon anyway.

The menu page was a load of thumbnails, women on screen frozen, some naked, some barely dressed. The images were stills of previously recorded streams, couples having sex in all sorts of positions and settings. It looked amateurish; home movies uploaded for a voyeur's enjoyment.

I clicked on 'categories' to see what would be listed, but an error message came onto the screen.

Cannot be viewed from your location.

What location? The building? Did I need to be on 5G and not Wi-Fi?

I clicked back and the menu page loaded, but when I clicked on a random video, the same error message came up. I couldn't navigate away from the opening page. My knee jiggled beneath the table, frustration mounting. I'd paid fifty dollars, or whatever the conversion was in British pounds, yet I still couldn't access the website. Was I being duped out of money, was the membership fee a scam?

I clicked back to the landing page, scrolling down the thumbnail images until I gasped. Jade was there, a frozen shot from the clip I'd been sent with Rick's bedroom visible in the background. Jade grinning in the light of the bedside lamp, her shaggy bob looking wild and unkempt in the throes of passion. I clamped a hand over my mouth and clicked on the image, jaw tightening as the same stupid error message appeared.

If Jade was on there, did that mean I was too? I went back again, scrolling further. At least fifty videos were on the menu page, let alone what would be in the categories. Panic built in my chest and my lungs tightened. I needed air and closed the lid of the laptop, rushing outside to suck in oxygen like a marooned fish. This couldn't be happening. How many people had watched Jade and Rick, paid for the privilege to do so? How could I tell her in her fragile state that she was on a website, an unsuspecting porn star – and what if I was too?

My hollow stomach fizzed, Nathan had practically given me the name of the website. He'd found it amusing, knowing something I didn't. I was sure he had to be involved, as was Rick. I recalled how much he enjoyed sex by the windows in his penthouse, looking out at the world below us. He wanted to be watched, admired and lusted after. How had I not seen it before? I knew in that instant he'd filmed us, Jade too, no matter how much he denied it. He'd allowed his videos to be publicly posted on this website, but someone knew what he'd done and tried to warn me.

The watcher, as creepy as they were, was trying to help. Could they be a member of watchmefuck.com and somehow realised Jade, and me, if I was on there too, had no idea we were being filmed?

29

I walked around the block, head spinning. Were there other women on there too, wives and mothers who had no idea they'd been filmed during sex. I had to get into that damn site, but how? The only person I could ask was Alfie, but it would have to wait until later.

As I walked through the park where I sometimes sat with my lunch, Mum called. She'd been pottering around the garden, enjoying her retirement and was excited to hear what I thought of the listings she'd sent, having found another on a local Facebook group. I thanked her but told her I hadn't got to them yet, changing the subject and filling her in on some of my conversation with Ben this morning. That he was hungover, but on his way to work.

'That brother of yours,' she quipped, but I could hear her beaming down the phone. 'Have there been any more videos posted?' she added warily, as though testing the water.

'No, thank God, and I think I'm getting closer to finding out who did it.' It wasn't technically true, but if I could find the source, as in who was responsible for filming, I'd be cutting the snake off at its head.

'That's great. Be sure to go to the police with whatever you find out. Honestly, you're practically doing their job for them.' Mum sounded irritated at the lack of support I'd received and I understood how she felt. Officer Barrett hadn't replied to me and it seemed I'd have to chase him.

I couldn't imagine the police were invested anyway, not with something so small but if I could get onto the amateur porn website, there might be more to find.

I grabbed a sandwich and a coffee from the deli across the park and returned to the studio. With headphones on and the blinds closed, I was able to forget about the lurid things I'd seen that morning and let the canvas guide me. Whenever I painted, I truly relaxed, thoughts floated through my brain but didn't settle, while calming music poured into my ears. Other than the stiff back and neck from bad posture, it was a lovely couple of hours, and my unsettled mood melted away.

By the time I emerged, Linda had gone, but her workshop door had been left open. With all the lights off and the pottery stations cleaned, it was ominous, the large room full of shadows, echoing my footsteps on the concrete floor. Looking over my shoulder in case Linda was going to materialise out of nowhere, I edged towards the table at the front of the room, where she directed her classes, curiosity getting the better of me. The room smelt damp, but each wheel had been cleaned ready for tomorrow's lessons.

I weaved between the stations, drawing my fingers across each table, which came away dusty with dried clay. When I reached Linda's table which was clear on one side and full of paperwork, lesson plans and budgeting spreadsheets on the other, something caught my eye. My last name, Montgomery, was printed on a piece of paper covered by Linda's random notes and scribbles. I slid it out, reading in the light which was receding through the window out onto the street. It was my lease, the paperwork confirming the date at which it was due to be terminated. Why did Linda have a copy? It was addressed to me, the same letter I'd received and put aside, believing the landlord would at least contact me before relinquishing my studio to someone else. I'd not jumped on it fast enough, leaving Linda to swoop in with her big plans for extending her pottery business.

Miffed at the intrusion of my privacy, I tore the letter in two, it was mine anyway and Linda had no right to have it, however she came by it. Had the landlord given her a copy, and if so what for, to prove how much I was paying, or was it to show Linda the date I'd been sent the letter which I'd forgotten to respond to? The sooner I was away from this place, the better. I craved solitude, away from nosy busybodies who thought they had a right to know things about me.

I left the door ajar and hurried out of the entrance to my car, keen to swing by the DIY store before it closed. Dad had bought me a small drill, and I was sure I'd be able to fit a deadbolt myself. I stopped by the supermarket after picking up the deadbolt, needing to pick something up for dinner. Checking my phone as I waited in the queue, Rick had sent various messages throughout the day, asking how I was and when I'd like to meet up again. He clearly didn't understand the concept of giving me time to think like I'd requested. I ignored the messages, giving in to the overwhelming loneliness at going back to an empty flat. I missed Jade, I missed Rick too and considered driving back to my parents, to be in familiar surroundings with people I loved, but I had to get onto that website, which meant I needed Alfie's help.

Back at the flat, I unloaded the shopping, microwaved a lasagne and ate mindlessly before having a go at fitting the deadbolt. It was slightly wonky, but it worked, and I knew I'd feel safer in the flat alone because of it. I'd already knocked at Alfie's on the way in but had no response, so I used the time waiting for him to get back to get some washing done before looking through the rental listings Mum had sent me. One lock-up unit looked as though it could be a good fit, only fifteen minutes from my parents' house on foot through a new estate and with dedicated parking. The rent was more than I was paying currently, but that was to be expected as it was closer to London. The outside wasn't much to look at, but it was worth considering.

Getting impatient, I tried Alfie again, but there was still no answer, so I ran a bath, letting the hot water soak away my stress. Outside I could hear kids playing football in one of the neighbouring gardens, relentlessly hammering their ball against a fence. I laid back and closed my eyes, running more hot water into the tub. When I opened them, the room was filled with steam, and I turned the tap off with my toe. My bathroom was small and functional, black and white tiles on the floor and the only furniture was a mirrored cabinet above the sink. The glass had steamed up, condensation running through the outline of a large heart.

I bolted up, water sloshing onto the floor. Had Rick done that when he was here? It seemed like the sort of juvenile thing he'd do. Or was it the watcher, reminding me they could get in and out when they wanted? Well, not any more! I scowled at the mirror, my irritation giving way to the creeping sensation I wasn't alone. The warmth of the bath water couldn't stop my skin erupting with goosebumps. The football had ceased being kicked against the fence, yet the silence wasn't peaceful. Naked in the tub, I was too vulnerable.

Annoyed my peace had been ruined, I got out and wiped the mirrored cabinet with my towel, scrubbing out the heart, hoping it would be out of sight and out of mind. It was weird. Only last week there had been a glass of water on my bedside table I didn't remember putting there the night before. Was that when it started or was it the extra food in the fridge? Wearing my bathrobe, I searched the small flat, which only took a couple of minutes, but no one was hiding, waiting to pounce.

The burner phone in my handbag had finally run out of battery, but I didn't bother charging it. The watcher had accomplished what they'd intended, I'd split up with Rick, all evidence pointing to my now ex-boyfriend being the person who'd planted the camera. They'd made their point, posting the videos, getting my attention and now if they had any sense, they'd crawl under a rock before I found out their identity and reported them to the police.

A knock at the door made me jump and I switched on the lamp in the lounge. Outside, dusk had arrived and the thought of an unannounced visit from Rick wasn't appealing. I waited, hoping the caller would go away, relieved I'd fitted the deadbolt, until a persistent knock came again.

'Abbi, it's me,' came Alfie's gentle voice through the door and I rushed to open it, realising as his gaze travelled down, I was still in my flimsy bathrobe.

'Alfie, hi. Oh God, I'm sorry,' I said, swiftly adjusting the robe to make sure I was properly covered, blushing like mad at my nakedness beneath.

'Sorry, I didn't mean to disturb. I saw on my camera you knocked a couple of times, I've just got back.'

The word which sent an icy trail down my spine: camera. I'd had enough of those to last a lifetime and when had Alfie got one, I hadn't seen it and why did he need it?

'Yes, yes, I did actually. I was wondering if I could ask for your help with something again?' I said, pushing my questions aside and trying to compose myself.

A warm smile lit up Alfie's pink face. 'I'm all yours.'

30

I invited Alfie in, excusing myself while I hurried to my bedroom and threw on jeans and a sweatshirt.

'Can I make you a tea?' I asked when I returned and found Alfie examining the stack of books I had in the lounge, drawing a finger across the creased spines before picking up a glass paperweight in the shape of a Panda next to a photo of the pair of us. Both birthday gifts from Jade which now hurt to look at.

'That would be lovely.'

'Was it another date?' I asked, waiting for the kettle to boil.

'Sorry?' Alfie's brow creased.

'Tonight? I thought you might have had a second date, after the first one went so well. The girl into period dramas and horror movies.'

'No, I was working late, unfortunately, and there was a leaving do I had to show my face at.'

I nodded, waiting until I was at the table with our mugs before I explained to Alfie what I needed help with. 'I've found a website, it's a bit... well, graphic. It's a porn website and Jade's video is on there.'

'Christ!' Alfie said, rubbing his face with a freckled hand. His pale complexion seemed to glow whenever he blushed, which seemed to be all the time.

'It needs a membership, which I've got, via my brother, but it said something about not being in the right area to be able to view the content and I didn't understand.'

'Okay, show me.'

I opened my laptop and logged on, letting him take control of the mouse, watching Alfie's eyes narrow as he took in the landing page, the risqué thumbnail images I'd scrutinised searching for my face this morning. It was beyond awkward, the pair of us squirming like we weren't two acquaintances about to watch porn together. I chewed the inside of my cheek and Alfie scrolled down, finding the video of Jade and clicking for it to begin. The same error message appeared on screen and Alfie nodded as though he'd been expecting it.

'As I thought, you need a VPN to watch.'

'Why?' I asked, remembering Officer Barrett's explanation of a virtual private network hiding the IP address of the person visiting the website.

'I believe perhaps the website has been set up so only those in particular countries can view it – the US maybe.'

'Does that mean it's a US site?'

'Not necessarily. Come over to mine, I've got a VPN set up, we can view it from there. Bring your laptop with you.'

I looked at the time, it was after nine, but I guessed it wouldn't take too long. Leaving our mugs of tea behind, I took my laptop, keys and phone and followed Alfie across the hall to his flat, the question I wanted to ask on my lips, why did he have a VPN?

Inside, Alfie's flat smelt of stale air and cologne, dishes were stacked in the sink ready for washing and it was obvious he hadn't been expecting company. He cleared his throat as if reading my mind.

'Excuse the mess.' Alfie pulled out a chair for me and retrieved his laptop from his satchel.

In less than two minutes, the website was up and running. I'd logged in and my mouse hovered above Jade's video, reluctant to click.

'How about I leave you to it,' he said, in tune with my thoughts again. It was going to be excruciating enough without having him watch the reason my relationship disintegrated over my shoulder. 'Do you want me to put a free VPN on your laptop, it'll only take five minutes?'

'Sure, thank you,' I said, patting his arm.

A minute later, he was back placing a tumbler of brown liquid over ice beside me. I still hadn't clicked.

'Bourbon,' he explained. 'Dutch courage.'

I smiled weakly, taking a sip, flames scorching my throat.

Alfie left the room, taking my laptop and heading for what I assumed was his bedroom, leaving me to face the misery alone.

I clicked on the image of Jade's face and the video loaded immediately, the bar along the bottom showing me the whole thing was over twenty minutes long, a vast difference from the short clip I'd seen. It showed everything, Rick pulling her towards the bed, taking her in his arms and kissing her roughly. Then it became more frenzied, he tugged her clothes from her body and Jade unbuckled his belt as tears rolled down my face. My throat closed as I forced myself to watch Rick push her onto the bed, kissing her panda tattoo before settling between her legs.

I shuddered in my seat, choking on my own spit that pooled in my mouth. I skipped a few minutes, brief flashes of Rick manoeuvring Jade into a multitude of positions as though he was performing in the sexual Olympics. But was that it? Was he performing, knowing a camera was there?

When the chest palpitations came, I knew I'd seen enough and skimmed through other videos of people I didn't know. Nameless faces exposing themselves and their kinks on camera, searching for myself in a sea of fornication.

I stopped on one video, knocking back the bourbon as I prepared to play it. Rick's face was in the thumbnail, but no woman. I waited to watch myself appear on screen, but a petite brunette stumbled into shot, clearly intoxicated, before straddling Rick and gyrating. His fingers dug into the flesh of her behind, leaving marks. There were others too, at least ten women all filmed in Rick's bedroom, and I squinted at the screen, looking past their naked bodies to the surroundings. When was this? The bedside tables were empty, with the exception of Rick's phone charger and a bottle of lube – urgh, he was such an arsehole.

I nearly vomited when in another video a woman who appeared to be unconscious didn't even flinch when he ejaculated over her face. Sick to my stomach, I couldn't tear my eyes away from the depravity on screen. His contempt for these women made Jade's video appear like he'd treated her like a princess. Rick clawed at them, manoeuvring them like rag dolls solely for his own gratification or for those watching. He revolted me.

'Permission to enter?' Alfie's head popped out from the room he'd disappeared into. I'd been sitting here for almost forty minutes watching video after video, my insides hollowing out with each one. Rick and Jade had torn my heart out and having to stomach watching it again had been pure torture. It was a pain I never wanted to relive, but despite the circumstances, the nauseating content I was having to view, I was glad I wasn't alone.

I waved Alfie in, swiping away my tears. 'I can't find my video on here, but there are others, lots of them, other women, some look wasted.' I clicked on another, watched as Rick pushed a girl onto her knees before he eased her head down onto his erect penis. I swallowed the bitter tang away. He made me sick.

'There – did you see that?' Alfie said. Setting down my laptop on the table, he pointed at the screen, 'Rewind it back.'

I did as he asked, missing whatever it was a second time too.

Alfie took control, pausing at the right moment. 'He's looking at the camera, Abbi; he knows it's there.'

I stared as the video played longer, horrified when I saw a topless Nathan come into shot. My throat constricted as bile threatened to surface, the pair of them were in it together. I gritted my teeth, utterly disgusted at their despicable behaviour and what was playing out on the screen. The bastards shared everything, even women.

'Holy shit. Do you think she even knows what's going on?' Tears filled my eyes as I watched the pair of them take advantage of the intoxicated girl in the worst possible ways. She didn't look sober enough to consent.

Alfie's hand covered his mouth as we were both mesmerised by what was unfolding, it looked like a crime being committed.

I started going through the categories, clicking any videos which looked like they'd taken place in Rick's bedroom.

One category was called Water Sports. I knew vaguely what that was, weirdos urinating on each other for sexual gratification. My stomach churned as I spotted Rick's blue subway tiled bathroom, the large walk in-shower. I leaned back in my seat, watching sex take place in the shower, folding my arms across my chest as my cheeks burnt.

'There,' I said.

Alfie cleared his throat and leaned in to see what I was pointing at. 'What am I looking at?'

'That's my shower gel.' Outrage fired in my belly, muscles clenched I bit my lip drawing blood. 'He's been doing this while we've been together.'

Alfie stepped away, returning a few minutes later with another shot of bourbon.

'I'm so sorry, Abbi,' he said, resting a warm hand on my shoulder. His touch should have been comforting, but I wanted to shrug him off. Everything about men repulsed me right now, Rick and Nathan especially, they were animals.

Alfie must have sensed my muscles clenching as he didn't let his hand linger.

I rubbed at my arms, there was a chill in the air as I clicked through more videos, almost desensitised to what I was seeing on screen. Barely any of the women seemed sober.

'I'm not convinced all these women know what's going on. There's loads of videos uploaded, people I don't know, but Rick's got enough of his own on the site. My God, he's profiting from this!' The penny finally dropping. He must be being paid per video, which was why there were so many he'd participated in uploaded. This was where the income stream had been coming from, all those deposits I'd seen on his bank statements. How had it gone unnoticed? Had Todd seen these reams of women coming and going to the penthouse?

'What are the live streams?' Alfie asked, leaning across me to navigate to the menu section on the left-hand side of the screen.

'I don't know, but I remember when I signed up, they cost extra, like a pay-per-view kind of thing.'

'Jesus, you can watch people live?' I wasn't sure if Alfie's disdain was real, but he appeared genuine. 'There's one planned for tomorrow night.'

'I need to call the police, they need to see this and arrest Rick, I can't believe all the women he's filmed consented.'

'What if Rick is on the live stream? You could catch him red-handed, or the police could.'

I considered Alfie's suggestion for a moment.

'Think about it, if you call the police now, yes there's evidence, but he could deny it, say all the women consented to being filmed.'

'Jade didn't!' I butted in, but maybe Alfie had a point.

It was late, my call to the police could wait one more day, couldn't it? At least I'd be able to warn Jade. If I could get hold of Officer Barrett, maybe I could convince him to drop in on Rick around the time the live stream was due to happen, in case he was the star of the show.

I stood, collecting my laptop, keys and phone and thanked Alfie for his help. He walked me to the door, a commiseratory smile on his face.

'At least you know, come tomorrow, they'll be looking into Rick and the website. Oh, and I've put the VPN on there, it's a green shield on your desktop. So, if you need to go back on there or show the police, you can. Log-in is AbbiMont, password Panda.'

'Thanks, you've been amazing. I guess, come tomorrow, at least it'll be shut down,' I sighed, turning back towards him once he'd opened the door, 'although another one will pop up in its place.'

'You didn't find your video on there?'

'No, thank goodness. Let's just say after the past couple of weeks, I can't wait to get out of Crawley.'

'You're leaving?' Alfie's chest deflated, he looked crestfallen, and I experienced a tiny pang of guilt.

'Well, you know about the studio,' I said, fiddling with my keys awkwardly. 'I've got to be out in just over a week.'

'But my friend has the perfect spot,' Alfie slipped in, but I carried on.

'And I've split up with my boyfriend, because he slept with my best friend. I've got nothing to keep me here.'

'Take a look at the place before you decide, I'll chase him up. You'll love it and living here isn't so bad, is it? At least you have good neighbours.' Alfie grinned, eyebrows raised waiting for a response.

I laughed despite how wretched I felt. 'I do, and okay, I'll come and see it,' I replied to placate him. Alfie had been nothing but kind to me when I had no one else to lean on. I could take a look at the place, but it would have to be something truly spectacular to be worth sticking around for. Crawley held too many bad memories for me now, the place tainted by Rick and Nathan's depravity. I was sure I wouldn't see it as anything else than where the pair of had weaved their web of deceit, all in the name of greed.

31

I locked up, sliding the deadbolt across, and fell into bed utterly drained, too exhausted to let the hatred for Rick consume me, but now I was finally on my own, the gravity of what I'd seen tonight hit. Rick had been cheating, not only with Jade, but with other women too. More than cheating, abusing them, committing criminal acts of violation. He'd filmed them to upload as content on a members-only internet porn site. The man I'd loved was a disgusting pig who should be locked up. More than that, he deserved to be ridiculed and gawped at, by strangers online, to lose his dignity like Jade and I had lost ours.

How could I have been so blind. But, in my defence, he'd concealed it well. I would never have said he was capable; he must have two separate personalities: the sweet and charming boyfriend and the money-obsessed misogynist who saw women as commodities. Rick was no better than a pimp and we'd been clueless, sucked into his warped business venture, profiting from intimate moments that never should have been shared. My mind spun at when he even had the time – or were the client dinners, golf trips and being out with the lads cover for him finding women to pick up and bring home? I'd been stupid enough to believe he was where he told me, when all the time he was making content for the website.

Who ran it, was it Rick, or maybe Nathan, because he was on there too? It must be how Rick made his money because he didn't make it as a market analyst. He'd lied about everything – who he was, what he did and how much he loved me. I truly believed he was the one and I'd been taken in like a fool. Bitterness scratched at my skin like hives. I needed him to feel an ounce of the mortification and shame he'd forced me and Jade to experience. Yes, she'd been complicit, albeit drunk, but he'd groomed her, plied her with drink and she hadn't known it had been filmed. She was as much of a victim as all of us.

I got out of bed and charged the burner phone. When it switched on, a message came through that had to have been sent whilst the battery was dead, although I didn't know when.

> DO YOU HATE HIM YET?

The text blurred my vision as revulsion poured through me like lava. Yes, I hated him, with every fibre of my being.

I stabbed at the keys, composing my reply.

> I WANT YOU TO DESTROY HIM

Once the message had been sent, I took the SIM out of the phone, cut it in two and flushed it down the toilet before going back to bed.

Sleep was slow to grace me with its presence; endless questions spun in my head, but I knew I wouldn't be able to get the answers. Maybe Officer Barrett might have more luck. I imagined the conversation I'd have with him tomorrow morning and whether he would take any convincing to act on what I'd told him.

* * *

After a night spent tossing and turning, flitting between misery and white-hot rage, I managed to get a few hours' sleep, tempted to turn off my alarm and stay in bed. Instead, I got up on autopilot to make coffee and stand beneath a hot shower, hoping it would snap me into focus. My laptop was still on the table, drained of battery where I'd left it on all night, so I plugged it in, leaving it to charge.

Once dressed, I messaged Jade, unsure whether she was back at the flat she shared or whether her mum had forced her to recuperate at home. I told her I wanted to pop round as I had something I needed to tell her, and I didn't have to wait long for a response.

Apparently, Jade had been at her mum's since she was discharged from the hospital but was intending to return to the flat this morning and would meet me there around ten. I couldn't deny I was relieved Claire wouldn't be hovering, not knowing how much Jade had told her since her overdose. Our meeting would be awkward enough as it was and would likely cause Jade distress, so I had to tread carefully.

I was in no mood to paint, so there was little point in heading to the studio. Instead, I logged on to watchmefuck.com, where the countdown for the live stream was on the landing page. It was set to start at 10 p.m. I looked through more videos, searching for my face or Rick's but found nothing. As a member, I now had rights to upload my own content, which would be screened and verified before it was published on the site. If only I had something embarrassing on Rick to submit, although if he ran the website, which potentially either him or Nathan did, it would never see the light of day.

One of the last categories I clicked on was one called Interactive. It only had one video and from what I gathered, it was the last live stream and had been online for a week. Intrigued, I clicked on it and rather than the video alone filling the screen, it had a chat box to the right-hand side. The video began and a half-naked man appeared on screen whom I quickly recognised as Nathan. As much as I despised him, his body benefited from the physical nature of his job. He was tanned and chiselled, larger than his brother in every way. The girl in the video, when she appeared, was not Elena and it hadn't taken place in Rick's flat either.

I'd never been inside Nathan's home in New Addington, so it might have been there, judging from the grotty-looking bedroom, but as I was looking for clues, I became distracted by the chat box, which began to fill with messages.

User69: Get her on all fours.

DrunkisBest: Smack that ass!

Nathan grinned at the camera, which I assumed to be a webcam because he looked like he was reading. The naked girl, like some of the others, seemed a little out of it, but she was laughing and playing along.

GirlsGirlsGirls: Choke her, she likes it.

Fanny4Fun: Tie her up.

I watched as Nathan followed some of the commands, positioning the girl on all fours and slapping her behind, licking his lips and grinning. The comments in the chat box got more and more degrading, making me sick. The girl was a puppet, and the watchers of the live stream were actively taking part, sitting at home behind their laptops jerking off as they instructed Nathan what to do.

'Jesus Christ,' I muttered. It was horrendous, but I couldn't tear my eyes away. This girl had to know she was being filmed, but did she know how much she was being exploited, that men were making money out of her?

There was no way I could let the next live stream go ahead. It was too much, too sordid and I wasn't about to see another nameless girl be taken advantage of.

I closed the laptop and put it in my bag. Jade needed to see this, what she'd unwittingly become a part of.

One question remained, why had Rick not shared my video, what made me so special when he clearly didn't give a shit about women? They were merely things, props for him to use and abuse. I knew there was so much about this that was illegal, and my contacting Officer Barrett became more urgent, but I had to speak to Jade first.

As I was getting ready to leave, my phone started blowing up, my insides immediately churning at the notifications popping up on the screen. Had something else been posted about me? I almost couldn't bring myself to look. The phone going crazy was making my throat constrict, transporting me back to that nightmare where dread engulfed my body and didn't leave for days. No more, I couldn't take it. I'd be unable to bear it happening again, I wasn't mentally strong enough to endure it.

Steeling myself, I opened a message from Jade which had a link and several wide-eyed emojis. Oh God, whatever it was couldn't be good. I clicked and the Instagram app launched. My hands shook as the image appeared on screen until I saw it wasn't me at all. Abbi456 had created an account, posting and tagging Rick in the photo I'd taken of him sleeping in his bed. In addition to my ex-boyfriend drunk and lying naked on top of the sheets, eyes closed, and mouth open mid-snore, another man, equally undressed stood beside the bed, holding what I guessed was his erect penis and pointing it towards Rick's open mouth. Both men's equipment had been hidden behind a sticker, but it was obvious what was going on.

I gawped at the screen, it looked real, but I knew it not to be true. I'd been there, in his bedroom, it was my photo. But to anyone else, it appeared like something else entirely. Rick didn't look as though he was sleeping but was about to perform oral sex on his male companion. I clamped my hand to my mouth, unsure whether to laugh or cry.

How on earth had the watcher got hold of the image? How had it been stolen from my camera roll?

The photo of Rick on Instagram had already been shared fifty times, but I knew the new Abbi account would be deleted soon so it couldn't be traced. There was no text written on the post but lots of hashtags, mostly porn related and stuff Rick sometimes searched, his interests like rugby and golf, knowing him well enough to try to spread the post as far and wide as possible in his circle. Carafe Wines had also been mentioned again. If they were considering rescinding Rick's suspension and having him return to work, no doubt that would be off the table now.

My text to the watcher last night bloomed fresh in my mind.

I WANT YOU TO DESTROY HIM

If anything would, it was this.

Some of mine and Rick's mutual acquaintances had already reached out, asking 'isn't this your boyfriend?' I wasn't going to respond. This was only the beginning of Rick's nightmare because once I'd been to the police he'd have a lot more explaining to do.

32

As soon as I got to Jade's, she flung open the door, asking if I'd seen the photo of Rick. I was surprised it was still up.

He'd called me eight times on the way over, but I'd let each one go to voicemail. There was a lot I wanted to say to him, tell him what a despicable human being he was, but I couldn't engage. I didn't want to do anything to jeopardise a criminal investigation, it was better to let the police take it from here. No doubt he'd seen what Abbi456 had posted and assumed it was me getting my revenge, but I wasn't prepared to fight my corner, I didn't care what he thought, not after what he'd done, but I did send him one message.

> I want my key back!

Jade looked better, she was still a little pale, and the spark hadn't yet returned to her eyes, but she seemed on the mend. I told her I'd had nothing to do with the photo of Rick online; I didn't even tell her I knew it was a fake. Jade was gobsmacked, believing Rick might be into men too, and was more concerned about how I was taking this massive revelation, but any remorse I'd had about the way things ended between us had died last night. I couldn't forgive him for sleeping with and using my best friend for financial gain, and I wouldn't forgive him for the countless others either.

'Jade, I've got something I need to show you before I take it to the police.'

'That sounds ominous,' she said, her mouth twitching.

'It's not great,' I admitted, 'but I don't want you to freak out, okay.' I kept my tone matter-of-fact; still smarting at her betrayal. I did, however, care about her mental health, we'd been friends for a long time and the last thing I wanted was her to relapse because of the internet site. It was important she heard it from me, not some random police officer she'd never met before when she was eventually asked to make a statement. 'Why don't you make some tea while I set this up,' I said, pulling the laptop from my bag, adding, 'I'll need your Wi-Fi password too.'

A few minutes later, we were sat side by side on the sofa with my laptop balanced on my knees. Jade, who was wearing brown loungewear and fluffy slippers fidgeted, placing a cushion over her lap.

'You're making me nervous,' she said.

I grimaced, taking in a long breath before I spoke.

'There's a website,' I began, and Jade groaned. 'And your video is on there. You can watch it, or not, if you don't want to, but I need to show you the website.'

Jade's eyes were already damp, but she nodded, bringing the cushion up to her face.

I opened the website and scrolled down to Jade's video, hearing her gasp as it played on the screen. I averted my eyes, speaking loudly so their sounds of pleasure were muffled. 'This website, I believe, is owned or run by Rick and possibly Nathan too. They both appear on it, with different women. Some look so intoxicated I don't think they could have consented and I'm guessing, like you, they didn't know they were being filmed either.'

'Oh God, shut it off, it's awful. I'm so, so sorry, Abbi.' She buried her face in her hands and I clenched my jaw, forcing away the emotion that threatened to engulf me.

'I'm taking this to the police when I leave here.' I stopped the video and moved to the interactive category, watching Jade as she shook her head, muttering to herself.

'How many people have watched it, I just can't...'

'It gets worse,' I interrupted, a little coldly, but now wasn't the time for self-pity. I clicked on the single video in the interactive category, ready to endure Nathan grinning at the camera again like he'd won the lottery.

Jade squinted at the screen, trying to take in what was happening, reading the messages in the chat as they sprang up. 'Jesus fucking Christ, it's women to order, isn't it, get them online and pander to the crowd.'

I swallowed, bile rising up my throat. 'It appears so, yes, and it costs extra to view and be a part of the live streams. There's one tonight, which is why I'm going to the police now.'

'They'll have to arrest him, won't they? I mean, there's laws now. It's illegal to film someone without their knowledge,' Jade blurted, her tears replaced by clenched fists and white knuckles.

'Yes, and to profit from it too. I think it's where Rick's money has been coming from.'

'How did you find the website?'

'Something Nathan said and a bit of snooping on Rick's laptop. Hopefully, everything here will be enough for an arrest at least. You'll have to make a statement to say you had no idea you were being filmed.'

Jade nodded and my spirits lifted a little. She could explain to the police what I feared about so many women on that website; they'd never agreed to be filmed.

'So, who posted the video of me, and the photo of Rick today?'

'I honestly don't know, but I think that will stop now,' I said, trying to reassure her. 'I think they've got their pound of flesh.' It seemed the watcher's target was Rick and we were collateral damage, but I may never know why.

I drank my tea and told Jade I had to go.

'Do you think we could, maybe, meet up soon?' she asked hopefully, rising from the sofa as I packed the laptop away.

'I'm leaving Crawley,' I replied, my voice wavering. As much as it saddened me, how could I trust Jade again? If I got another boyfriend, I'd always be panicking there was something going on between them and I knew it would drive me mad.

Jade's bottom lip wobbled and my glacial exterior melted a little.

'Maybe,' I relented, 'in time. I hope you feel better soon, take some holiday, maybe a weekend in the sun somewhere. Hold your head up high, they'll soon get bored.'

'I will,' she managed. Her chin was shaking now, and she bit back tears.

'I'm sorry, I have to go.' I rushed towards the door, as though I couldn't catch my breath, like I would hyperventilate any moment.

Jade followed, her voice soft and calming. 'No, I'm sorry, Abs, I'm sorry I ruined everything.' I watched as tears poured onto her pale cheeks and her lip curled into a half smile. 'Make sure you nail that bastard's balls to the wall.'

When I got back to the car, I took a moment to compose myself – the last thing I wanted was to arrive at the police station and be dismissed as an irrational, overly emotional woman. I needed to present the evidence to Officer Barrett in a calm and dispassionate manner to ensure I was taken seriously.

At the front desk, I was asked to wait and sat on a hard plastic chair that had seen better days. Ten minutes later, Officer Barrett came through the entrance like he'd been out on patrol and they'd called him back in especially for me. His forehead crinkled when he saw me, not a frown exactly, more perplexed. Perhaps he was wondering why I was here, already conjuring up what he'd tell me if I demanded news from the Cyber Crime Unit.

'Miss Montgomery, how may I help you?'

'I need to show you something, it's urgent. There's been a development.' My nerve endings tingled with something resembling excitement. Rick's fun was about to be cut short.

'Debs, have you got any rooms free?' he called to the officer on reception.

'Five is, you can go in there, I'll block it out.'

Officer Barrett gestured towards a door to our left which led into a corridor. We entered another door marked with the number five, an interview room with cameras and a recording device on the table.

'Can I get you a tea or coffee maybe?'

'No thank you,' I said, already pulling my laptop out of the bag and booting it up. 'Do you have Wi-Fi here?' Adrenaline coursed around my bloodstream, but Officer Barrett looked genuinely confused. I willed myself to go slower, to not appear erratic.

'What is it you want to show me?'

I explained about the website I'd discovered, that Jade's recording of her having sex with Rick was on there and I suspected many others who didn't know they were being filmed.

'Some of the women look out of it too, I can't be sure it's all consensual. He's been recording himself having sex with multiple women, his brother too, and uploading them to this website.'

Officer Barrett's frown deepened, his eyes turning to slits. 'Have you found recordings of yourself on there?'

'No, but there's more...' I explained about the live streams and what they consisted of, that I didn't know who ran the website but you had to have a VPN to view the content, a way of controlling the traffic and making sure it wasn't from consumers in the UK. I guessed it was an easy way to avoid being caught. If none of the women could identify themselves, they wouldn't be able to report a crime having happened.

Officer Barrett's interest was piqued, and he got up from the table. 'Let me go and get the Wi-Fi password and I think we'd better record this.'

33

When Officer Barrett returned with a colleague, a lady in a suit who introduced herself as Detective Sergeant Gilchrist, he set the camera to record our interview and asked me to explain my findings again. Once I had, despite their poker faces, I could tell what I'd given them was sufficient for them to investigate further. Officer Barrett and I filled in the details of the initial complaint I made about Abbi321, partly for the recording, partly for the detective sergeant's benefit, to bring her up to speed. The account had been deleted or deactivated, but Officer Barrett stated he'd ensure the Cyber Crime Unit would stop it from ever being made live again, along with Abbi456, which had also mysteriously disappeared, taking Rick's fake homosexual photo with it. It was like chasing a ghost.

'I'll get them to freeze Rick's account too. You said you're not on Instagram anymore?'

'No, I only have one for my business, it's called Edgewater, but I've switched the settings to make sure no one can tag the account in any post.'

'That's good. Let me take down the details of the website and your log-in details. We should be able to get it taken offline today, but there's some legal hoops we have to jump through, proving the videos weren't consensual, et cetera.'

'My friend Jade is on there, she, um, slept with my boyfriend, Rick, that's how I found out. The video was sent to me.' I shifted awkwardly in my seat, neck flushing but they didn't bat an eyelid. 'She admitted having no idea she was being filmed.'

Detective Sergeant Gilchrist nodded, checking the notes she'd taken. 'Can you give me contact details for her please, we'll send someone around to take a statement straight away.'

She passed me her notepad and I wrote down Jade's address and phone number, warning the detective that Jade was fragile and recently discharged from the hospital. They needed to be gentle in their approach. There had to be so many women they'd need to trace, but at least I could supply one.

'What about the live stream? You can't let that go ahead. The last one is under the category Interactive. You can watch Rick's brother Nathan, he's doing what the people tell him to, to that woman.' Unable to hold the despair in any longer, I broke down and Detective Sergeant Gilchrist handed me a tissue.

'We'll take care of it, Abbi, you've done the right thing bringing this to us. We're here to make sure the exploitation of women stops.'

I held her gaze, silently imploring her to follow through on what she'd promised.

'And Rick doesn't have any idea you've found this site?' she added.

I shook my head.

'Good. Avoid all contact with him from now on.'

When I'd given the police everything, I left, sending a text to Jade to warn her she'd soon have an officer turning up at her door to take a statement. Rick had called over twelve times now and sent a barrage of abusive text messages, demanding to know where the hell I'd got that photo from and how I'd doctored it. He had no idea the storm that awaited him and I wished I could be a fly on the wall when the police knocked on his door. As long as that post couldn't be connected to me.

I quickly went into my camera roll and deleted the photos I'd taken of Rick the watcher had somehow managed to obtain. It worried me how easy it was for them to come in and out of my life, my flat, my car and my devices, leaving no trace behind. I hoped now they would disappear so I could get back to normal. With that in mind, I drove to the studio, despite having zero urge to paint today, I had to pack.

When I arrived, the door was wide open, but I knew I'd locked it when I left yesterday. I stuck my head in, reluctant to step fully inside without knowing what was waiting for me, but instantly saw that the caravan portrait on its easel had been slashed across the middle. Tiny threads of canvas stuck out and a scalpel had been tossed onto the floor.

'Fuck!' I shouted, letting out the frustration, pulling my hair at the roots until my scalp stung. The hours I'd put into that commission were now all for nothing. Linda wasn't around, so I couldn't ask her if she'd seen anything, but she must have been back this morning as her workshop was now locked. Maybe Rick had been here, trying to find me because of the Instagram post, losing his temper and lashing out, I wouldn't put it past him.

Trying to keep a lid on my anger, I set the portrait aside and immediately began another, making sure I locked myself in. Either way, the portrait would be coming home with me and I made the decision to pack the studio up as much as I could today. I was running slightly behind, but orders had slowed since YOLO264's comment on Instagram. Social media had catapulted my business and it could just as easily destroy it.

A couple of hours later, I'd recreated the caravan shell, which left the sky and grass to do, but wanted to call it a day.

Packing was easy, I'd had the foresight to flatten the boxes I'd used to bring my supplies in and kept empty ones when I'd ordered materials, stacking them in the corner so they were easy to rebuild. Most of the contents of the studio were packed in an hour, leaving a few select bits, so I could use the space if I wanted to until the date I had to hand the key back. Anything I was working on would now come home with me. I had a photo wall where I'd taken pictures of every completed commission and stuck them up with Blu Tack, a real-life Pinterest board for inspiration. Taking them down had created a profound emptiness in my chest, but it was amazing to see how far I'd come. It wasn't the end of the journey, just a blip along the road.

My phone rang with what I expected to be yet another call from Rick. I'd been checking periodically and the website was still up and running, but I imagined there was a lot of evidence collecting to be done. When I checked, it wasn't Rick calling, but a number I didn't recognise and I was apprehensive as I answered but figured it could be the police. The muscles in my back unclenched as Alfie's gentle voice came down the line.

'Hey, Abbi, did visiting the police go well?'

'It did, I think they will be paying Rick a visit today.'

'That's great! Listen, are you free this afternoon? I've finally got the keys to my friend's place he's renting out, I think it could be perfect for a studio.'

I frowned, the thought of staying in the area didn't appeal to me, not now. Instead, the pull to return closer to my parents, to have that level of security living near them would bring, was strong.

'I don't know, Alfie, I'm not sure about sticking around.'

'He'll do you a great deal, I'm sure of it. Come and take a look.' Alfie's hopeful voice sent a jolt of guilt through me. He'd been nothing but kind, I owed him to at least have a look at the place.

'Okay, I was packing up anyway. Where do you want me to meet you?'

'I'm in Horley, just finished work, it's not far from me actually.'

'I'll come and pick you up.'

'Or you could jump on the train, perhaps we could pop into the pub, you know, congratulatory drink. I think you earned it.'

'Ummm, sure,' I said, but I wasn't sure. I didn't want to give Alfie the wrong impression, but I did owe him for all his help. I said I'd drop my car at home, get changed and let him know when I got on the train.

I was getting ready to leave when Linda popped her head in, freezing when she saw the packed boxes.

'I'll be packed up by the end of the week,' I said, unable to keep the bitterness out of my voice.

'I'm so sorry, love, I didn't want it to end this way. I should never had let Alan put ideas into my head.'

'Alan?' I frowned – who was he?

'He's a regular, often does the Saturday morning class. Him and his big plans – too big, if you ask me – and I got swept along.'

'Why did you have my lease paperwork in your studio, Linda, that was private?'

'It was posted beneath the door. I assumed the landlord got the wrong studio, I meant to give it to you.'

I snorted, doubting that. I was sure the landlord didn't want to give away exactly what I'd been paying.

'I made you something.' From behind Linda's back, she pulled out a handmade trinket bowl with scalloped edges.

I smiled quizzically and took it, turning it around in my hand. I'd seen one before but couldn't place where, although Linda probably had hundreds of them. It was a nice gesture, but the bowl wasn't my style. 'Thank you, that's kind of you.'

'I thought you could paint it, seeing as you're so talented.' She beamed, her rosy cheeks glowing as though this made everything okay. There was no way the landlord had slipped the letter beneath her door, not when my copy had been posted to my home address. How had she got it? Linda made out she was all sweetness and light, but I wasn't so sure.

'Well, I better be off, I'm meeting my neighbour for a drink.' I put my bag on my shoulder and edged towards the door, laden with boxes and keen to get away.

'Tall, dark and handsome?' Linda winked.

'Not exactly: tall, pale with freckles and strawberry blond.' I laughed despite myself.

I stacked the boxes in the boot of my car and headed for home. I wasn't dressed to go out for a drink and couldn't be bothered either. Since the whole video thing, I'd barely made an effort with my appearance. Today my long red hair was tied up in a messy bun and the only make-up I'd bothered to apply was a dash of brown mascara, but it wasn't as if I was trying to entice Alfie, and it wasn't a date either. Other than a change of clothes, mainly to get rid of the smell of methylated spirits, he'd have to take me as I was.

34

Traffic was heavy getting out of the town centre and I parked around the corner from the flat, leaving the boxes in the boot. I hurried to the entrance, taking the stairs two at a time, worried I'd kept Alfie waiting long enough already. A woman's voice carried from above, followed by loud banging. Was someone at my door?

'For goodness' sake, Alfie, open up, you can't ignore me forever. You need to sign the divorce papers.'

When I reached the landing below, I looked up to see someone vaguely familiar leaning on the door to Alfie's flat, forehead resting against the wood as though gathering her thoughts. She turned to look as I climbed, the stairs creaking beneath my feet announcing my presence. I had my key already in my hand, intending to ignore her, but her expression changed to one of recognition.

We'd not met but seen each other before, the day I'd moved in. She'd been hurling insults at Alfie as she'd descended the stairs, nearly knocking the box I was carrying out of my hand.

'Do you know where he is?' She sighed, pursing her lips as if it was an effort to speak to me.

'At work, I guess?' I shrugged and she sneered at me, tucking a wayward strand of blonde hair behind her ear. She had a pointy nose and chin; one of those women who wore a perpetual look of disappointment on her face.

'Please tell me you're not going out with *him*?' She laughed, clutching her stomach, unable to control her mirth. I wasn't sure if she was insulting or ridiculing me.

'I'm not,' I said, mildly irritated. Poor Alfie being married to her, I bet she bullied him senseless.

'Good, because he's a pig!' she spat and I looked towards Alfie's door, searching for the camera he'd told me was there. I couldn't see anything but he'd have a lot to watch when he got home.

She went back to banging, still believing he was inside, and I lowered my head, sliding the key into the lock. Should I mention I was meeting him? Even though she was being a witch, I could offer to deliver the papers she was clutching. Alfie might need them.

I turned around, surprised by what came out of my mouth.

'Why is he a pig?' My curiosity had got the better of me and she gave me a hard stare, her nostrils flaring.

'Alfie is addicted to smut, or rather masturbating to disgusting videos, which is what he did instead of fulfilling his marital duties to me, his wife!' Words spewed from her mouth like acid, hatred for Alfie evident. He'd broken her heart, that was obvious, but porn? Alfie? The guy blushed at the mention of it; I'd seen his reaction when we'd had to watch it together and enjoyment wasn't the first thing that sprang to mind.

I didn't react, just nodded as if I believed what she'd said, although it made no sense to me. Every guy watched porn, that's what Nathan had said, wasn't it? Was it something wives and girlfriends were supposed to accept? And what was the difference between casual viewing and being addicted, watching every day, for hours a day? Was Rick addicted? No, he was addicted to creating content and the money it earned him. If anyone was a pig, it was him! Still, clearly there was bad blood between Alfie and his ex and I didn't want to get involved.

I left her banging on his door and hurried inside to get changed, not wanting to keep him hanging around waiting for me. When I came back out minutes later, she was gone and I jogged to the station.

Horley was only two stops away and a gale blew down the concourse. It was the middle of rush hour and some teenagers at the other end jostled each other for position as the train rolled down the track. I climbed on, staying by the door as there were no seats available. We pulled out of Crawley, rumbling along to Three Bridges, where more people piled on and a few got off. I could hear the teenagers two carriages away, singing, clearly intoxicated, and I imagined they were driving their surrounding passengers mad.

The next stop was Gatwick and the carriage was full, people standing astride suitcases ready to embark on a holiday, cheerful despite the lack of space. I was getting more claustrophobic by the second, squashed against the door with someone's elbow pressing into my arm. By the time we reached Horley, I was desperate for fresh air and, when the doors opened, had to fight my way onto the platform, where I bumped into one of the drunk lads, weaving his way through the crowd with a can of Stella.

'Sorry, love!'

'Jay, you've pulled, mate,' one of his friends behind chipped in and, buoyed by that, Jay slung his arm around my shoulders, keeping pace with me. I tried to shake him off, but he tightened his grip.

'Do you mind?' I asked, nudging him aside with enough force to separate us.

'No need to be a bitch – too fucking old for me anyway, Granny!'

'She's clapped, bruv.' One spat on the ground at my feet, but everyone ignored the commotion, hurrying to get through the barriers. Jay and his mate pushed ahead and jumped over while the others in the group tailgated people with tickets. I slowed my pace, scowling, then stalling when I saw they had grouped outside the exit and were staring back at me.

I fumbled for my phone to call Alfie and see where he was, but when I looked up again, I saw him waving at me on the other side of the barrier by the ticket machine. Relief engulfed me and I frantically waved back, tapping my phone to pay and joining him.

'You made it.' His eyes lit up, a broad smile stretching his cheeks.

'I'm so sorry, how long have you been waiting?' I glanced over his shoulder, the teenagers were still there, laughing at us. My palms began to sweat. Had I been with Rick, I would have felt safer, but Alfie was so mild-mannered, and he'd been mugged before, I wasn't sure how much protection he'd be.

'Only a couple of minutes, it's not far.' In a cowardly gesture, I linked my arm through his as we exited the station, turning away from the teenagers who sniggered.

'Oi, carrot top, you won't get far with her, mate, she's got a stick up her arse.' A shout came from behind us and Alfie froze.

'Let's go,' I said, trying to pull him forward, but he was rigid. Then he turned around, unfurled my fingers from his arm and walked slowly back towards the group. I wrung my hands together as I watched him approach, the breath catching in my throat. He was outnumbered and I was terrified I was about to witness a pile on. Alfie was unimposing by nature but when he reached the group, he leaned in close to say something. Whatever he said was so quiet I couldn't hear, but a second later they disappeared and he returned to my side.

'Onward, to the pub,' he announced.

'What did you say to them?' I gawped at how he'd seemingly defused the situation without it escalating, positive the rowdy bunch would have beaten him to a pulp despite their age.

'I told them they shouldn't speak to a lady like that.' Alfie grinned, but his eyes glinted. 'I also said I could see the police coming through the barriers and if they had contraband on them, they might want to move sharpish.'

I laughed, perhaps he was hardier than I'd thought.

* * *

'So how was your day?' Alfie asked once we were sat at the table of the Jack Fairman pub. He'd bought me a double gin and tonic and a pint of Guinness for himself.

'It's been, a lot,' I sighed, taking a sip and filling him in on my visit to Jade this morning to break the awful news she was on the website and my meeting with the police.

'Have they taken the site down yet?'

'I don't know, but what I found this morning was so much worse. Those live streams, they're interactive, people watch and give instructions via a chat box.'

Alfie swallowed and shook his head. 'That's awful.' He glugged his pint, as if trying to remove the bad taste it left in his mouth.

'I know, but they've got enough to start digging. The officer said they were going to interview Jade, she's the first witness, so to speak, before they can identify any others, especially if they weren't in a position to consent to sex or having it filmed.'

Alfie patted my hand, letting it linger a touch too long. 'It's over now, you did it, it'll be shut down and there'll be a criminal investigation, arrests will be made.'

'I hope so. I think Rick came to the studio this morning while I was at the police station; one of my portraits was slashed.'

'Really?' Alfie's eyes narrowed and I nodded. My anger had faded; in the grand scheme of all Rick had done, it was a drop in the ocean.

'The watcher put another post up this morning, one of him in a compromising position, shall we say, it had to have enraged him.'

Alfie frowned, clearly having no idea what I was on about.

'That's what I call my internet stalker – the watcher, but I don't know if they're friend or foe,' I admitted, picking at my cuticle, clearing the tiny specks of paint which clung to the skin.

Alfie shrugged, going back to his pint rather than voicing his opinion, but I guessed if he'd been attacked at the train station, the watcher was no friend to him either.

'I think a new studio would be a good thing, a fresh start.'

'I don't know, I still feel like I'm being followed. It's weird, the sensation of being watched all the time, like there's a presence around me.'

'Are you a ghost hunter now?' Alfie laughed and I nudged his shoulder.

'You know the police couldn't find the report you made, about your mugging.'

'I guess it's because I didn't make one.' Alfie grimaced, his cheeks blotching.

'Why on earth not?'

'I don't know, I was embarrassed, it was humiliating enough and the guy had a balaclava on anyway, they wouldn't have caught him.'

I shook my head, making my disapproval known. Perhaps Alfie didn't have any faith in the police or the judicial system, but Detective Sergeant Gilchrist's words rang in my ears: 'We're here to make sure the exploitation of women stops.' I hoped I could trust her.

35

'Earth to Abbi,' Alfie said, tapping my arm.

I smiled apologetically and picked up my gin and tonic, draining the glass. 'Sorry, I'm miles away.' He waved me away and I added, 'I forgot to tell you, your wife was looking for you earlier.'

Alfie's eyes turned to marble at the mention of his wife, his features twisting, making his face almost unrecognisable.

'My wife?'

I swallowed, unsure whether I should go any further. His abrupt change of mood unsettled me. I cleared my throat, knowing he was waiting for me to continue.

'Yes, when I popped back to the flat after work, she was knocking on your door, she had papers for you to sign.'

Alfie scowled. 'She can send them through the solicitors.' His knuckles turned white on his pint glass, the blood draining from them, and it seemed as though the temperature dropped by a few degrees despite being surrounded by a crowd of pubgoers. I shouldn't have said anything and words tripped from my mouth in a rush to fill the silence, wanting to get the evening back on track.

'Anyway, tell me about this space your friend is renting.'

Alfie's demeanour changed almost instantly and the mood lifted. 'I think it'll be perfect, Abbi. It was a welding workshop, a retirement hobby for my friend's father, but arthritis put paid to that. The place has been empty for ages.' As he spoke, he reverted back to the warm and friendly man I'd come to know, telling me about the space we were going to visit, and the tension evaporated from my shoulders.

As I listened to him, it struck me he seemed less awkward now, sat across the table, pint in his hand. His cheeks, usually prone to blushing, remained neutral and he didn't stumble over his words or seem shy. Perhaps I'd finally cracked through his introverted exterior and he felt more comfortable in my company. I beamed at the thought, he was the only friend I had left in Crawley.

'Shall we order some food? I'm getting a bit peckish.'

Alfie agreed, reaching for the menu. I wasn't in a rush to go home, knowing if I did, I'd spend hours on the internet, searching for my videos, hoping they hadn't hit YouTube. Had Rick already been arrested? I checked my phone, but he hadn't rung for hours, the fact he still had a key to the flat niggled me. At least I had the deadbolt. I could change the locks, but it seemed a waste of money, knowing I was planning on leaving within the week, or as soon as I'd given up the lease. Still, I'd feel safer knowing he was in a cell for the night, but without my laptop or VPN on my phone I couldn't look up the website and check it was live. Right now, I was safe with Alfie, who'd ordered some small plates for us to pick at from the Wetherspoons app, as well as another round.

Conversation flowed as we ate. Alfie told me he'd grown up in Billingshurst, a once sleepy village outside Horsham, but it had doubled in size in the past twenty years. His parents still lived there, and we briefly touched on him meeting his wife at college. The pair of them enrolled in a coding course and hit it off, but I didn't let the conversation linger there, not while his mood was so good. Eventually, after our third drink and a stack of empty plates left on our table, we headed out onto the street and Alfie guided me the short distance to the studio. It was a small unit in between a mechanic and the rear of a fast-food restaurant. Outside, it looked a bit grotty. The bricks were crumbling and the drainpipe hung limply outside of its fixing; the building clearly unloved for a while.

'It's got a parking space, here,' Alfie said, as I looked around at the patch of concrete overgrown with weeds and a pile of blown-in rubbish in one corner. 'Needs a bit of a tidy-up, but the rent is cheap.' He bobbed, fizzing with excitement I couldn't match. Perhaps he had a vision, but currently I couldn't see it. The door was rusted, secured with a large padlock, and in the dull glare of the streetlight, the building was uninviting. I shivered, wishing I'd worn a thicker coat.

'I'm not sure I'd feel safe coming in and out of here in the dark, it's not that well-lit, is it? What about in winter when there's barely any daylight?'

'We can always put up a security light and inside it's got fluorescents, it's really bright I promise, trust me.' Alfie was determined for me to see the positives and beckoned for us to go inside.

When he pulled open the door, the air was musty, a vague smell of damp that rang alarm bells. I loitered by the door while Alfie fumbled for the lights, which came on, blinding me momentarily.

'You weren't kidding about the fluorescents!' I laughed, squinting.

Despite my reservations, it was reasonably tidy. The concrete floor needed a sweep and with a bit of imagination I guessed it could be homely, but my mind was already calculating what I'd need to spend to bring it up to scratch. Not only that, but the major flaw was also no natural light, no windows at all.

'I know what you're thinking,' Alfie said, his hand on my back, 'it's a fixer-upper, but he'll do it for four hundred a month, electricity included. There's water too, at the back. We could get a sink plumbed in, some IKEA furniture, make the place somewhere inspiring.'

My brain got caught on Alfie's continued use of the word 'we'. This wasn't a joint venture, or was I overthinking it? Perhaps he was offering to help?

'I don't know, I need to think about it.' Alfie's hard sell was propelling me towards the exit.

'Linda said you wouldn't be interested, but I know it could be great for you, Abbi, and you get to stay local.'

My heart quickened its pace, and I turned to face Alfie, who stood with his hands on his hips, surveying the place like it was his prospective rental opportunity, not mine. 'Linda?' I frowned. 'You know Linda?'

It was Alfie's turn to frown, and he shrugged, scratching at the collar of his pale pink shirt. 'Well yes, I've been to a couple of her classes,' he finally admitted when the silence stretched out between us.

'That bowl, by your front door for your keys, you made it at one of her classes, didn't you?' It clicked into place, what I'd failed to see before. 'You're Alan,' I said flatly. 'You told her your name was Alan. You're the one who suggested she knock through into my studio.' I sucked in air, anger rippling beneath the surface, while Alfie stared at me, his expression impassive. I'd been expecting a denial, but none came, in fact he didn't say anything at all. 'Why did you lie about your name?'

'I didn't, I said my name was Alfie, she must have misheard me.' His excuse was weak, even he didn't sound convinced. 'I just want you to stay,' he added, stepping forward and gripping my upper arms. He planted a kiss on my lips before I could step back, lingering as though it was something he'd seen in a romance movie and thought he could replicate in real life. Initially, I froze, shocked at Alfie pressing his lips against mine and sweeping his tongue, seeking entry. Repulsion finally made me jolt backwards.

'Stop!'

When he released me, his body sagged like he'd misread the situation. My mind spiralled, had I led him on? Was this my fault?

'I can't do this, Alfie, we're friends but—'

'Friends can grow, can't they? I like you, Abbi, I always have and now you're not with Rick—'

'It's too soon. Jesus, after all that's happened, I thought you of all people would understand,' I snapped, waiting for Alfie to get out of the way, but he was blocking the door.

'You're upset,' he said, eyes searching my face like he couldn't make sense of the situation we'd found ourselves in.

'Of course I'm upset, if you wouldn't have suggested knocking through to Linda, she wouldn't have applied to take over my lease. You lost me my studio!'

'It was just in conversation, I didn't think she'd go for it.'

'Bullshit!' I shouted as the streetlamp blinked outside, the open door calling to me.

I wanted to leave, it had been a mistake to come here, a mistake to assume Alfie was any different. I couldn't trust him either.

'Move, Alfie, I want to go home.'

'Abbi, come on, this could be good.'

I wasn't sure if he was talking about the workshop or the two of us, but either way I wasn't interested.

He stood, filling the doorway, refusing to step aside, and for the first time in his company, fear pulled at me like a current.

'I want to leave.' My voice shook, coming out in rasps as I glared at Alfie, waiting for him to do the right thing. He was a good man, deep down, I was sure of it. He wasn't a predator like Rick. Alfie wouldn't hurt me, would he?

His wife's words from earlier thrummed in my ears, 'Alfie is addicted to smut, or rather masturbating to disgusting videos'. If he thought something was going to happen between us, did rejecting him make him dangerous?

My eyes cast around, searching for another exit or something I could use if I needed to defend myself. Alfie wasn't as tall as Rick, but he had weight behind him and my neck prickled with a cold sweat as I berated myself for agreeing to come here. I'd had no idea he wanted anything more, certain I'd never given him any signals that warranted his advances. But now here I was, in an empty workshop on a quiet back street in the dark with a man who clearly wanted more from me than I was willing to give.

I took a deep breath, perhaps I had to try a different tack.

'Alfie, thank you for showing me the property. I'll have a think about it, but I'm ready to go home now.' I was unable to stop my voice from shaking as I stood rooted to the spot, silently imploring Alfie to move. Perspiration formed beneath my arms as my body went into panic mode, I desperately wanted to get out of the workshop.

'Okay,' he said, letting his hands drop to his sides, sighing.

My eyes misted and my stomach began to unfurl from its tight coil.

'But let me finish the tour, there's another room in the back you have to see.'

36

As soon as Alfie moved past me towards the rear of the workshop, I took my chance and bolted out of the door onto the street. The whistling of the wind drowned out the shouts of my name behind me as I pumped my legs towards the train station. I knew it was an overreaction, something I'd feel silly about later, but better to go with my gut than regret ignoring it. What if I'd gone into the back with Alfie and he'd tried to kiss me again, got carried away in the moment and I couldn't fight him off. The thought kept my muscles working, I had to get back home, lock the door and hide out there. I could worry about being embarrassed later.

I reached the station in less than five minutes, panting and sweaty, eyeing the taxis that waited out front for commuters. Without hesitating, I jumped in the back of one, rousing the driver who was buried in his phone. It would be expensive but faster than the train, and with Alfie and I going back to the same place, I had to make sure I got there first to barricade myself in where I'd be safe.

He wouldn't hurt you, the voice in my head chided, telling me I was being silly, and perhaps I knew instinctively he wouldn't, not physically. But he had hurt me. Alfie had started the chain of events which had lost me my beloved studio in the first place. Was he trying to control the situation, did he have his friend's workshop in mind all along? But why – to keep me close? And why didn't he tell me he'd been to classes at Linda's? He knew where my studio was, I was sure I'd mentioned it, so why keep it a secret? If he was hiding that, what else was he hiding?

The post by his front door with the different last name than the one he gave me popped into my head and I wracked my brain as the taxi weaved through the traffic. The driver ignored me, playing with his radio to find the perfect station, but I was too anxious to make small talk anyway. I chewed my lip, the pop music jarring as I analysed mine and Alfie's every interaction, lingering on the awkwardness of scouring those videos on watchmefuck.com.

Just last night, in my kitchen I'd logged on to my laptop and he'd taken control as I squirmed at the erotic images I'd pulled up on screen. He'd scrolled right down to Jade's video without hesitating, with no direction from me. I gasped, catching the driver's eyes in the rear-view mirror as we got stuck at another red light.

'You're not going to be sick, are you?' he said, his voice gruff as if I'd been on an afternoon bender. It probably looked like I had, my reflection in the window was pale and my skin had a sheen to it, hands jittery as I rooted through my bag in search of a tissue to wipe my brow.

'No, no I promise, I'm fine.'

I was anything but fine. To my knowledge, Alfie had never met Jade, so how would he know what she looked like and why hadn't I picked up on it at the time? He must have seen my Instagram posts of the two of us or seen her at the flat. He'd also seen the photo of us on my bookcase. Or maybe he'd been on the website before and recognised her, his soon to be ex-wife said he watched smutty videos, had he found the site or was it worse. I'd been convinced Rick was the owner, but could Alfie be behind it all?

My head spun, an ache growing at my temples. For all I knew, Rick and Alfie might know each other, both into their tech, pulling the wool over my eyes.

Fifteen minutes later, the taxi pulled up outside my building and I tapped my card on the driver's handheld terminal to pay, eager to get inside.

'Thank you,' I said, getting out and staring up at the block, shivering at the temperature drop since I'd left home a couple of hours before. I was positive I'd got back before Alfie and even if he knocked on my door on his return to apologise or ask why I ran, I wouldn't open it. There were too many things about Alfie that didn't add up.

I climbed the stairs, for once comforted by the smells of various home-cooked dinners and the drone of televisions through the wall. It made me feel less alone. I should call Officer Barrett, get an update on what had happened today, surely, he should have contacted me. But when I checked my phone, the battery had died. Maybe Rick was being interviewed right now, sweating in his designer shirt because his empire was about to crumble around him. Some of those women hadn't been lucid enough to consent, it was statutory rape, plain and simple. The pain of it was a knife in my side. Two weeks ago, we'd been happy, I was going to move in, imagining the rest of my life like some Disney fairy tale. What a fool I'd been.

When I reached the top floor, all was quiet. I paused on the landing, blinking at my door which stood ajar, registering the small split in the wood of the frame. It had been kicked in and a tremor ran up from my toes. I let out an involuntary whimper, my bladder announcing the need to go. No sound came from inside my flat, but someone had been in there.

'Hello?' My voice was barely above a whisper, no one would hear me, but I couldn't muster another sound. I stood for a couple of minutes, rooted to the spot and listening intently. I should go downstairs, knock on another flat and call the police, but then I heard the door to the building squeak open below.

'Hey, Gloria, how are you?'

Sparks flew in my chest, it was Alfie. He was back already, chatting easily with the lady who lived on the ground floor.

'Alfie, good to see you, yeah we're all fine thanks, now the weekend is practically here.'

He must have got a taxi like I had, there was no way he'd have got back that fast by train.

I heard shuffling footsteps on the tiled floor and Gloria saying goodbye. Alfie would be climbing the stairs, up here in a matter of seconds, so I hurried inside my flat and eased the door closed, leaning my back against it. The deadbolt was hanging on by two screws, useless to me now. Sweat clung to the hair at the nape of my neck and the cool wood against my shoulder blades was an immediate relief. With my head turned, ear pressed to the door, I heard his footsteps approach and stop right outside.

A few inches of wood stood between us and I held my breath as Alfie cleared his throat and knocked. I winced, looking into the gloomy flat, waiting for whoever had ransacked the place to rush out, but no one came. Whoever they were, they were long gone now, and I wanted Alfie to leave, hoping he wouldn't notice the damaged door.

'Abbi?' Alfie's soft voice came through the wood, gentle as a bird, trying to coax me out, but I wasn't going to fall for it. 'I'm sorry, it's all a misunderstanding, please talk to me.'

I prayed he wouldn't try the handle. There'd be little I could do about it if he did. I heard his nails scratch the wood, a slight thump against the door as though Alfie had pressed his forehead against it, frustrated at how our evening had ended and my refusal to communicate.

'Abbi, I promise, I'd never hurt you,' he whispered, and I squeezed my eyes shut, willing him to leave, a tear slipping through my lashes. They all said that, but they ended up doing it anyway.

A minute later, the footsteps retreated and I heard Alfie go into his own flat, the door clicking shut. The low thrum of heavy rock music followed and I breathed a sigh of relief, pushing myself off the door and taking a step into the tiny hallway. From there, I could see into the lounge. Cushions were on the floor, the coffee table upturned, and the bunch of roses torn to bits. A bolt of fear took control of my limbs. The air was heavy and so were my legs as I struggled to make them move, terrified of what I'd discover if I ventured further inside.

It was a noise that made me shift, more of a sob than a whimper, and any reservations I had about investigating the damage were immediately dismissed. Someone was in pain and I rushed into the lounge to find a person curled up on the floor by the sofa in the foetal position, hands protecting their head.

'Jade!' I cried, dropping to my knees as soon as I registered it was her. 'Are you okay?'

She slowly raised her head, a red welt across her cheek, lashes wet with tears, but before she could speak, the air shifted behind me and I knew we weren't alone.

37

'I was wondering how long it would take you to get home.' Rick's deep voice cut through the silence and Jade sniffed, cowering where she lay.

'You hit her?' I screamed at him, clutching her against me.

'She hit me first, see?' Rick pulled the neck of his T-shirt away from his throat, showing bloody scratches that ran from his ear to his jaw.

'Bastard!' I hissed. 'Get out of my flat.' Why were they even here?

'You think you can trust her?' He thrust his arm out at Jade. 'She slept with your boyfriend.' Rick laughed, throwing his head back. Was he drunk, high on something or just manic? His erratic behaviour put me on edge, I needed him gone, now.

'Get out,' I repeated firmly, trying not to let my voice waver.

'Not without the camera, I know you took it, Abbi. Once I have it, I'll go?'

My head snapped up, eyes like slits as I looked past him at the devastation of my flat. 'So, you kicked my door in and tore the place apart looking for your filthy fucking camera? Why not use your key?'

He shrugged, chuckling, 'I lost it.' I looked from Rick to Jade, struggling to understand what was going on.

'I came here looking for you, but he was already inside.' Jade's voice was low and quiet, imploring me to believe her, but Rick sniggered.

'She's lying, you're both lying bitches. Give me the camera, Abbi, or—'

'Or what.' I got to my feet, pulling my arm away from Jade, who tried to keep me down. 'Or you'll post a video of me on social media, one where I don't know I'm being filmed?'

'Nah, I took your one off the website, wasn't that impressive, probably down to your tiny tits.'

It was a cheap shot but its strike wounded me and he relished the pain in my eyes, the tears that welled.

'I had some fun, though, those nights when you were *really tired*, couldn't keep your eyes open after a sweet, milky tea – remember those? A lot of us had fun.'

'You bastard!' I screamed, his words penetrated my skin like bullets, he'd drugged me. I'd been on the website too.

I hurled myself at Rick, clawing at his face, and he toppled backward, taking me with him. We hit the ground hard and I fell awkwardly, knocking the wind out of me, and had no time to recover. I was no match for his strength and, in a second, he had me pinned to the floor, his hands around my neck.

'Where's the camera?' Rick hissed through his teeth sending spittle raining onto me. He banged my head repeatedly on the floor until my vision blurred. Jade's screams came from above as she tried to pull him off me.

'I don't have it, I never did.' I wheezed as his fingers tightened. All this time, a part of me hadn't wanted to accept it was Rick's camera, that he'd knowingly filmed us, but I'd been living in fantasyland.

'Liar!' Rick shouted in my face before drawing his hand back.

I screwed my eyes shut instinctively and my cheek exploded, like I'd been struck by a scorching-hot poker branding my skin, spreading to my jaw and around my eye. My ears rang, sound suddenly muffled, and the metallic taste of blood filled my mouth.

I blinked slowly, trying to stay conscious, vaguely aware Rick had disappeared from sight, but I couldn't make my limbs move. All I could see was the white ceiling above, while a scuffle took place somewhere towards my feet. I registered the muted sound of more blows, whimpering, then terrifying silence.

A fuzzy Rick loomed over me, but I still couldn't focus. He kicked my side and I rolled over, shooting pains firing up my back. I was able to see Jade's leg, she was on the floor, not moving.

'Jade,' I croaked, trying to make contact with her, but my voice didn't sound like my own. Head pounding, I wanted to propel my mind elsewhere, somewhere safe.

'The camera, Abbi,' Rick persisted, 'do the police have it?' He kicked me again, at the base of my spine and I yelped, pleading with him to stop.

'I don't know,' I whined, 'please,' I sobbed.

Rick cursed, tearing the books from their shelves, pulling the television off the unit before moving into the kitchen, where the deafening noise of the kitchen cupboards being emptied onto the floor echoed around the flat. Someone would hear, the walls were thin. Someone would call for help.

Had Rick convinced Jade he'd had nothing to do with the website and got her onside to come around here and search for the camera? He'd expertly played the victim up to this point and I knew how convincing he could be when he put his mind to it. However Jade had ended here, the bastard had beaten her unconscious and she still wasn't moving. I tried to roll onto my front, dragging my elbows beneath me and pulling my knees up to a crawling position, while Rick moved from room to room, like a whirlwind. He banged and crashed around, destroying anything in the way of his search for the camera.

'Rick, man, what the fuck?'

I raised my head to see Nathan, a holdall on his shoulder, at the door to the lounge. His mouth hung open, pupils dilated as he took in the sight of me on all fours trying to stand. Blood dribbled from my lip and I could feel the swelling on the side of my face where Rick had struck. Nathan gawped at me, shocked at what his brother had done.

'I can't find it.' Rick's voice came from behind, the entrance to my bedroom.

'Leave it, let's go,' Nathan said, his chest rising and falling fast. I guessed the camera had to have its own memory card and what he'd recorded had to be more damaging than the website. 'We gotta go, Rick, come on. The police are at yours, I just drove past, there's cars everywhere. They'll come here next!'

So, they were running away, fleeing the authorities. How had they known the police were onto them, had the site been taken down or had someone tipped them off? Every second they waited was one second closer to them getting caught. Nathan knew it, his eyes were like orbs and he looked terrified.

'Last chance, Rick. I'm not going down for this.' Nathan was jittery, repositioning the holdall stuffed with his belongings. If they left here and hit the motorway, they'd be long gone before the authorities would catch up with them and I needed justice. Rick had to pay; he couldn't be allowed to get away with it.

I managed to pull myself up but was unable to straighten my back because of the pain from Rick putting the boot in.

'I will fucking kill you if you don't tell me where it is, Abbi.' Rick's words drifted over me, my attention drawn to Jade, who still hadn't stirred. I couldn't see if her chest was rising or falling, but as much as she needed my help, I had to stall for time.

'Why, Rick – why did you do it?'

He snorted, staring at me like I was the village idiot, pausing before emptying my cutlery drawer onto the floor. I cringed at the noise.

'Because it was an easy way to make money, and a fun one too, until that prick posted Jade's video.' He snarled, baring his teeth.

'I thought you loved me,' I wailed, hating myself. 'There were so many women.'

'Love is a strong word, Abbi, I'm not even sure I'm capable of it, but I had a soft spot for you, sure. It's why I took you off the website, I didn't want to share you. I thought we could make a go of things; I asked you to move in, didn't I? Nathan was going to take control of the content.' His tone was so matter-of-fact, I baulked.

'You raped those women.'

'I didn't rape anyone,' he shot back, delusional.

'Was it all about the money?' I sniffed, struggling to compose myself.

'Isn't everything. Listen, me and Nathan grew up with nothing, we used food banks, got given blankets instead of being able to put the heating on, barely any hot water! We had hand-me-down clothes and toys from the charity shop at Christmas.' He snorted, his lip curling back in disgust, pausing his search to stare at me. 'It made me a determined man, Abbi. Money is everything, it's how people judge you, what you wear, where you shop, what you drive. It's status and I was fed up being a bottom-feeder like my parents.'

'So instead you exploited women?' I blurted, not willing to excuse his story of poverty. Plenty of people grew up poor, it didn't turn them into monsters.

'I saw a gap in the market and I filled it. We were careful, our site was only visible in Europe and America, no possible chance of being found out here… until someone got hold of your video.'

It hurt to breathe, the pain in my back had moved to my ribs and was making me nauseas. I leant on the arm of the sofa for support, praying Rick hadn't ruptured my kidney or spleen.

He raised his eyes to the ceiling. 'It's probably some avenger, a fucking advocate of women's rights, the same tosser who bought you the flowers no doubt,' Rick continued, gesturing to the roses scattered across the rug, their petals wilting.

'I thought you bought me those.' The roses were left at the studio; I'd thought they'd been an apology.

'I didn't, trust me.' He sneered and I licked the mix of blood and saliva that dribbled from my swollen lip.

'Fuck this, I'm off, I'm not waiting any longer.' Nathan turned his back and hurried out, ignoring Rick's call of 'Pussy!'.

'Can't rely on him anyway, useless fucking freeloader.'

I guessed Rick had been behind the scheme and Nathan had come along for the ride, reaping the benefits and the profits of exploiting women. It made me flinch, had they no conscience? Couldn't they see the terrible things they'd done?

Rick seemed to second-guess himself, looking around the flat at the carnage. He'd left no stone unturned in the search for his precious camera. 'Have a nice life, Abbi,' he said, brushing his shoulder against mine as he stepped past me.

I shrank away from his touch, in too much pain to do anything but watch him follow Nathan out the door.

38

Rick made it as far as the hallway before he backtracked, palms out in surrender.

'Whoa, easy there, fella!'

My heart leapt, the police were here. I dropped to my knees and tried to rouse Jade, shaking her gently by the shoulder. She mumbled something incoherent and didn't open her eyes, but she was breathing, that was the main thing.

'Jesus, Abbi, are you okay?' I recognised his voice instantly but was still surprised to find Alfie at the entrance to the lounge. It wasn't the calvary come to rescue us, it was my neighbour summoned by the noise.

'She's fine, I'm leaving.' Rick was abrupt, but he didn't rush at Alfie, acutely aware of his size, blocking his exit.

'You're not going anywhere until the police get here,' Alfie hissed, narrowing his eyes at Rick before turning to me. 'They're on their way, Abbi, don't worry.'

My eyes misted as I stroked Jade's cheek, relaying the news even though she was barely conscious.

'Is this him then? The flower man? Bit of a downgrade.' Even in the face of his predicament, Rick couldn't control his tongue. He sneered at Alfie, the strawberry blond hair receding at the temples and pale freckled face that blotched pink with embarrassment at Rick's derogatory comment.

'Downgrade?' Alfie said indignantly. 'At least I look after her, I'm not pimping her and her friends out on a website for perverts to drool over.'

'Perverts? That's rich coming from you.' Rick threw his head back and laughed heartily as the blood in my veins slowed to a trickle.

'What do you mean?' I asked, my voice trembling.

Rick glared at me over his shoulder. 'You think I don't know who my subscribers are?' He turned back to Alfie. 'You may be able to hide your IP address, mate, but your credit card details – or rather the address connected to it – stood out a bit, seeing as you're my girlfriend's neighbour.' Rick snorted, shaking his head at Alfie's stupidity.

'You subscribe to his website?' I gasped, the air rushing into my lungs. Alfie had been my friend; I'd trusted him and all this time he'd been able to watch Rick do those awful things on those videos. He knew we were together, why hadn't he told me?

'Abbi, you don't understand...' he began, but it was the moment Rick had been waiting for, knocking him off balance and rugby tackling him to the floor. The bookcase with its empty shelves fell on top of them when they bashed into it.

I got up, staggering over, clutching my side, yelling at them to stop, but they continued fighting. Rick managed to get a punch in, but Alfie had more weight and quickly overpowered him. Sirens blared outside and I tried to step around them to get out of the flat, but they rolled again, catching my legs and knocking me to the ground with a thud. Rick sat atop Alfie and punched him in the face; blood streamed from a cut on his lip and while Rick prepared to strike again, he turned his face to look directly at me.

'It was all for you,' Alfie said before raising his arm from the carpet.

I glimpsed the panda paperweight clutched tightly in his hand for a second before he smashed it across the side of Rick's head. The man I'd once loved let out a groan, like a radio running out of batteries and a high-pitched scream filled the room. He toppled off Alfie, landing at my feet and it took a second to realise I was the one screaming, scooting backwards as a dark pool of blood spread out beneath Rick's head towards the toes of my trainers.

'What have you done?' I whimpered, my back pressed hard against the wall as Alfie got to his feet, wincing from the effort. Rick was unconscious, his face paling as the colour leaked out of him. 'Stay back,' I shrieked at Alfie, who took a step towards me, the paperweight still in his hand. His brows knitted together, eyes downcast as though he had the weight of the world on his shoulders.

Uniformed officers burst into the flat in a blur of fluorescent yellow and pointed what looked like a gun at Alfie, yelling for him to drop the weapon in his hand. Seconds later, he was on the ground, a man kneeling on his back, the bloody paperweight rolling away.

'We need paramedics in here,' an officer shouted above the din, his gloved hands examining Rick's head. 'Head wound but he's still breathing.'

I drew my legs towards me and buried my head in my knees. What had just happened?

Alfie was cuffed and the police officer now sitting on his back was radioing for backup. My body trembled and I shuddered as a chill folded itself around me. The flat was a hive of yellow uniforms, some were trying to speak to me but I was so light-headed, I couldn't communicate.

'She's going into shock; can you find her a blanket.'

I remembered little else after that, other than being vaguely aware of being led from the flat and down the stairs slowly. It was like an out-of-body experience and the only thing I could do was cry. Ambulances had been summoned: one for Rick which headed off with its blue lights flashing and one for Jade who they'd managed to bring round. I was checked over by a paramedic and made to drink a cup of hot sweet tea that Gloria from flat number one provided when she'd emerged to see what all the sirens were about.

They recommended I go to hospital, but I refused, still trying to make sense of what had happened. I wasn't much help to the police, mumbling something about Officer Barrett and it being his investigation, that Rick had broken in looking for a camera. Several of the neighbours had dialled 999 because of the noise, they'd assumed a domestic was taking place. Perhaps Officer Barrett or Detective Sergeant Gilchrist were at Rick's, searching the penthouse and I had no idea where Nathan had gone. For an hour I sat shell-shocked on Gloria's sofa, a buxom woman who I'd only interacted with a handful of times. She stayed with me, attempting to soothe her crying toddler who'd been woken up by the banging.

'Can I call someone for you, lovey?'

I shook my head; fingers wrapped around the mug. It was getting late and I didn't want to call my parents and ask them to drive down the motorway to pick me up, but at the same time my flat was a crime scene and I couldn't stay there. I was in no state to drive that distance either, my hands wouldn't stop shaking.

I finished my tea, clutching my coat and bag one of the officers had retrieved for me. I'd asked for my keys and my phone, which they'd found, the battery was still dead, but at least I had it. Maybe Rick's penthouse wouldn't be cordoned off, or they could have searched it already. Hell, I didn't even know if they had a warrant for Rick's arrest over the website because I'd not spoken to Officer Barrett, I was only going on what Nathan had said before he'd fled.

I stood on wobbly legs, handing Gloria back her empty mug. 'Thank you so much for taking me in and for the tea. I'll let you put your boy to bed.' I smiled, gesturing to the toddler whose legs were wrapped around his mum's waist, sniffling into her shoulder as she rocked him gently. 'I'm really sorry about all the noise,' I added, glancing upwards as if I could see through Gloria's ceiling through all the other flats into mine.

'Don't be silly. Are you sure you don't want to stay – the sofa is quite comfy.'

'No, but thank you, Gloria, you've been so kind.' I didn't want to take up any more of her time or hospitality and saw myself out.

Only one empty police car remained outside, and I guessed someone was still upstairs in my flat or maybe Alfie's. I huddled lower into my coat, glad to get in the car and whack the heating on. It was only a short drive to the penthouse and I still had Rick's key. Although it was the last place I wanted to be, it was cheaper than a hotel. Nathan had to be long gone, halfway around the M25 by now in his supercharged Focus, I didn't have to worry about him turning up unannounced.

As though my head was full of cotton wool, I drove ridiculously slowly, still jittery but thankfully the roads were quiet due to the late hour, and the warm glow of reception welcomed me at Harper Court. Rick's Audi was gone, his visitor space free as well.

By the time I approached the automatic doors, Todd was already on his feet rushing around the counter.

'Thank God,' he said, coming over to envelope me in an embrace. 'I've been worried about you.'

'I didn't think you'd still be here,' I said, leaning into him; he smelt like

Old Spice and cough candy, and I breathed in the comfort that reminded me of my dad.

'I swapped shifts, it's my granddaughter's fifth birthday tomorrow.'

'Why were you worried about me?' I asked, following him to the plush seating area, where he lowered me onto the sofa as though I was a fragile doll.

'The police came earlier looking for Rick. I had to let them into the penthouse. He wasn't here but they stayed to search the premises.'

'He's in hospital, but I think the police are with him.' I sighed, overcome with exhaustion. 'Are they still here?'

'No, they left around twenty minutes ago, seized his laptop, some other bits in bags. What has he been up to?' Todd asked.

I gave him the short version, Rick was going to be arrested for filming women without their consent, potentially drugging and preying on them. He'd posted them on the internet and likely generated hundreds of thousands of pounds from the scheme.

'Nathan brought a few ladies up, but I didn't see Rick with anyone, unless they came back after ten when the day shift ends.' That made sense, the pair of them likely hunted these women at bars, plying them with drink first before inviting them back for late-night debauchery. 'What happened to your face?'

I couldn't stop the tears from falling when I told Todd he'd attacked me, and my neighbour had knocked him unconscious.

'Honestly, Abbi, you look like you've gone ten rounds with Mike Tyson. I can't believe he'd hit a woman; it's disgusting.'

'I'm okay, bruised and sore. I'm so tired and I can't get into my flat. Do you think I can stay here? At Rick's?'

'I don't see why not, I won't tell anyone.'

39

Rick's penthouse felt strangely different since the last time I'd visited, almost like there was a presence. The ghosts of all the women he'd filmed, knowing they'd trod the same path and consumed the same space I was standing in. At first, it was eerie, but then I felt weirdly at ease, perhaps it was being here alone, knowing no cameras were watching me or that nobody but Todd knew I was there. I expected it to be a mess as the police had searched, but it was relatively tidy, only some drawers left open and paperwork on the side. I didn't waste time looking for the camera, hopefully the police had already found it. Exhausted, I made a tea, grabbed some painkillers and went to bed. Determined never to set foot in Rick's bedroom or the en suite again. Instead I chose to settle in the guest bedroom, a room I hadn't seen on the website. I plugged my phone in to charge, but without my laptop I couldn't check if the website had been taken down, or whether a live stream had gone ahead. I assumed it hadn't, if the police had been here to arrest Rick and secure his laptop. Where was Officer Barrett now? Was he at the hospital with Rick, or chasing Nathan down the motorway in a high-speed pursuit? Or interviewing Alfie, as they'd taken him into custody. Even if he had been a subscriber to that abomination of a website, he'd been the hero of the hour, stopping Rick from fleeing.

I laid in bed staring at the ceiling, mind whirring, trying to unpack the events of the past couple of hours. I hoped Jade was okay – at least she was conscious when she was taken to hospital. I sent her a text once my phone came to life but it was too late to call her mum. I didn't want to create a panic despite a ball of it slowly building in my chest. It would all be out in the open now, the grooming and sexual exploitation of women, there would be nowhere for me or Jade to hide. The amount of people who would have to watch those videos for the criminal investigation made me feel dirty and selfishly I hoped Rick had been telling the truth that he'd taken my video down. Although not before the watcher had found it.

Had I been on one of Rick's interactive live streams? There'd been nights I'd fallen asleep quickly, the evening a blur, but I'd assumed I'd been exhausted, not that Rick had drugged me. I hoped it was lies, spat from Rick's mouth to hurt me, a parting shot, because the memories I had of the night the clip was taken of us were still fresh. We'd gone out for dinner, a fancy French restaurant. I'd had a few glasses of wine, but I'd been lucid and consented to sex, believing I was making love with my boyfriend, not performing in front of an audience.

Tears fell, unbidden, and I howled into the pillow, unable to move past the betrayal. I'd believed Rick loved me when he asked me to move in, convinced I'd won the lottery, but I'd never seen his mask slip. Beneath he was a monster, motivated by greed and a lifestyle he'd do anything to maintain.

Eventually, I fell into a fitful sleep, waking at dawn to take more painkillers. My side hurt more than my face, Rick hadn't held back, and it was lucky Alfie arrived when he did. I had mixed emotions, unable to comprehend Alfie being a subscriber to the site, but he didn't deny Rick's accusation. Would Rick have really left if Alfie hadn't have stopped him, or could my injuries have been much worse?

When I woke again to run a hot bath, the sight of my face in the mirror made me shudder. My cheek was purple, as was my torso, and no amount of make-up would make it look like I hadn't been punched in the face. I'd charged my phone all night, but no messages waited for me except for a voicemail from Officer Barrett. He'd called in the early evening, but my battery had already been flat, letting me know a warrant had been issued for Rick and Nathan's arrest and the website had been removed from the internet; no live stream would be going ahead. That gave the brothers all the heads-up they'd needed to know time was running out. Officer Barrett said Jade's statement had been helpful in making both possible and I guessed she had been telling the truth, coming to my flat to check on me and let me know the police had visited. I felt sick for doubting her, but the watcher had made me doubt everyone and Rick's gaslighting hadn't helped. At least now it was over.

My phone rang, making me jolt in the bath, and pain radiated across my back causing my breath to hitch.

'Abbi, it's Officer Barrett, where are you?'

'At a hotel,' I lied, not wanting to tell him I was at Rick's when I probably shouldn't be.

'We need you to come down to the station and give us a statement about last night's events.'

'Okay, I'll be there soon. How's Rick and Jade?'

'Jade's fine, she's been discharged, but Rick is still in hospital, I have officers with him. He's been in overnight for observation, but he was lucky, no bleeding on the brain or swelling.'

I exhaled slowly, panic rising in my chest. I was relieved he'd survived but felt unnerved at the news. *It's okay, Abbi, you're safe.*

'He's already been cautioned and we'll bring him in as soon as he gets signed off. As I said in my voicemail, the website has been taken offline and we're trying to locate the women on the footage retrieved.'

'And Nathan, Rick's brother?'

Officer Barrett let out a dry chuckle. 'He was picked up at Dover early this morning trying to board a ferry to France.' Relief washed over me, I no longer had to look over my shoulder.

'Thank God.'

'I had the landlord out last night to fix your door too.'

'That's brilliant, thank you,' I replied, not caring it would mean my deposit had gone up in smoke.

'I'll see you soon, Abbi.' Officer Barrett hung up and I sank beneath the water, enjoying the loss of all my senses until I had to come up for air.

Once I was ready, I took a final look around the penthouse, it would be the last time I was there and I was grateful to Todd for allowing me to stay. Potentially he could have risked his position for the infraction, but I had nowhere else locally to go.

Knowing Rick and Nathan couldn't harm anyone else and their vile website had been taken down made me a little lighter, but there would be other women whose dignity would be in tatters. Numerous other victims who'd be getting a knock on the door and delivered the horrendous news their casual hook-up had been filmed and shown to thousands, maybe more. Some might have little memory of that night, most I'd seen had looked out of it and maybe those sleeping pills in Rick's bathroom cabinet had been the reason why.

Every time it came unbidden into my head, a part of me died inside. The only way through would be to try to put it out of my mind, to move back home and start again. It could have been so much worse. Yes, my video had been shared with friends and family, but I was lucky it hadn't gone viral or lost me my business. Jade had suffered more than me, and I'd always hate the watcher for their methods. I still didn't know who they were and there were so many questions I needed answers to, I knew I wouldn't be able to move on until I had them.

When I opened the front door to leave, a pink gift box had been placed on the tiled floor, an envelope on top with my name on. I picked it up and took it back inside, my stomach lurching. I'd had enough of surprises and wasn't fooled by the sparkly white bow; who knew what it contained?

I sat at Rick's breakfast bar and opened the card first.

Dearest Abbi,

I thought about giving this to you last night, but you were traumatised and too exhausted for me to explain. I'm sure you'll know how I came by this, without me having to put it into words. I don't know what's on it, but it's your choice what you do with it now.

Take care of yourself and don't be a stranger.

Todd

I pulled at the bow, intrigued as to what Todd had gifted me with a cryptic message like that. Inside, wrapped in tissue paper, was a small white camera, no bigger than the palm of my hand. It had a memory card slotted in the side. I remembered my conversation with Todd, telling him I wanted time in the penthouse by myself to delete a video on Rick's laptop. That he had a camera hidden somewhere. Perhaps he felt sorry for me, a lovesick puppy with no idea her boyfriend was an arsehole, maybe Todd had let himself in while Rick was at work and found the camera.

I could take the memory card and destroy it, so whatever was recorded on it would never come to light. Deep in my gut, I knew I was on there. I wasn't sure I could stomach watching myself again but how could I let anyone else watch it? What if there was a trial and my video put up on screen, how would I bear the humiliation? Still, I had no choice, it would be critical evidence, and I had to hand it over to Officer Barrett.

I put the camera in my bag and headed to the police station, nodding to the security guard who'd replaced Todd on shift. I owed that man a whole case of expensive red wine and at least it proved there was one man on earth, besides my immediate family, that I could trust.

40

When I arrived at the station, Officer Barrett had an interview room ready and waiting. Despite his outward patience, I could tell he was harassed and, at his request, I relayed the events of last night, coming home to find my door had been kicked in and Rick and Jade inside the flat. I picked at my cuticles, at points choked by emotion that bubbled in my throat reliving the violence I'd been a victim of and that I'd witnessed, but Officer Barrett didn't try to rush me.

'So, your neighbour, Alfie Stockton, was summoned by the noise?'

I tried not to twitch at the use of Alfie's last name, the one on his mail and not the one he'd given me. I still didn't know why he'd lied, but I imagined it had something to do with him being a subscriber to the website. He'd gone to the lengths of changing his name at Linda's pottery class too and I guessed he didn't want me connecting any of the dots.

'I guess so, yes.'

'And the item that was used to hit Rick, he brought that with him?'

'No, it was mine, a paperweight of a panda. It was lying on the floor, knocked off my bookcase. They were fighting, but Rick had already hit me.'

'I see.' Officer Barrett frowned and looked at his blank pad. 'You witnessed the altercation?'

I leant back in my seat, trying not to let my frustration mount. It was a process and I was an eyewitness; Officer Barrett was only doing his job.

'Yes! Rick started it, he launched at Alfie, trying to get out of the flat and make a run for it. Alfie was blocking the door, he said the police were on their way.'

'So, Rick hit Alfie first?'

'Yes, they were rolling around on the carpet, Rick was attacking him.' Officer Barrett nodded and I maintained eye contact, pushing away the image of Alfie lifting his arm to strike Rick. *It was all for you, Abbi.* 'Is Alfie being charged?' I asked.

'Do you believe he shouldn't be charged with a crime?' Officer Barrett steepled his fingers, resting his chin on top.

'It was self-defence,' I mumbled, guilt gnawing at me for leaving part of the story out. Could Alfie have restrained Rick without whacking him with the paperweight? Probably. He could have easily killed him, but maybe that's what he intended.

'Funny, that's exactly what his solicitor is saying.'

'He was protecting himself, Rick was sitting on top of him, hitting him.' My voice was weak as if my words had little conviction.

'Okay, any idea why Rick came to your flat?' Officer Barrett said, moving on. 'Why didn't he run if he knew we were looking for him?'

'He was searching for this.' I rummaged inside my bag and pulled the camera out, placing it on the desk, stomach lurching at handing it over.

'What's on it?'

'I don't know, but I think it's the camera that filmed the videos, it has an SD card and...' I paused, shrinking into my seat, 'I think I might be on there.' I trailed off. Rick and Nathan had to go down for what they'd done and if the evidence on the SD card meant they would, I had no choice but to surrender it.

'How did you come into possession of this?'

'I took it, from Rick's penthouse. I was going to see what was on it before I gave it to you, but I didn't get a chance,' I lied. There was no way I was going to drag Todd into it and thankfully Officer Barrett didn't probe any further.

'Thank you, Abbi, I'll pass it to the tech team. As I've already said, video evidence has been downloaded from the website, it's going to take a while to get through, but it's no longer live.'

'What about the subscribers?' I had a lump in my throat, knowing Alfie was among them. 'Because one of them was me, in my brother's name, so you can't go after him.'

'Technically, the subscribers haven't done anything illegal, they paid for a membership to a pornographic website. If any of the women were under the influence and unaware they were being filmed, the subscribers have plausible deniability. It would be extremely hard to convict.' My back stiffened. 'However, we've also downloaded the chats embedded in the recorded live streams, there may be incitement there. It's too early to tell, but I promise you, Detective Sergeant Gilchrist and I will leave no stone unturned in bringing charges.'

I chewed my thumbnail, eyes prickling with forthcoming tears.

'Can I go back to my flat now?'

'Yes, it's all clear,' he said, 'although it's a bit of a mess.'

A bit like my life.

* * *

I didn't head to the flat straight away, I sat in my car and called Jade. Her mum answered and told me Jade was in bed, sleeping off a concussion. She was abrupt and stand-offish, saying she'd pass the message on that I'd called. There was no point in trying to defend myself, to give Claire some home truths about her daughter and how she'd got tangled up in this mess to begin with. She was simply a mother trying to protect her daughter. I understood and was glad to hear Jade was back home, bruised and battered like I was, but, ultimately, she'd be okay.

The last job I had to do before I went home was collect the last bits from the studio. Thanks to Rick, I was behind on a couple of projects and it would take about a week to catch up, but pouring myself into my work seemed like it would be a good distraction from the fallout I knew was coming. If he and Nathan didn't plead guilty to any charges, there would be a trial, which would mean standing up in a witness box and defending my character against the prosecution. It wouldn't be pretty and could last for months, but I'd do what I needed to, to make sure those bastards got prison time. I knew Jade would too, she'd stand up and be counted to be certain justice was served.

For the first time ever, I managed to get a parking spot right outside. I could see Linda had a class going and was hoping to be in and out before it finished. Most of my things were still in the boot of my car, but I had at least one more box to pack.

Barely inside for ten minutes, I was only on my way out when she came to say goodbye.

'Jesus, Abbi, what happened to you?'

'It's a long story,' I said. 'I've got the last of my stuff, so I guess I might as well hand my keys over to you.'

'There's no need to be like that, I've said I'm sorry.' Linda was getting exasperated with me, but I didn't care, I had nothing to lose now, I wasn't coming back to the studio again.

'Sorry for what? For stealing the lease, for painting the word slut on my door?' I snapped.

Linda took a step back, her hand flying to her chest. 'I'm so sorry, I felt awful, but Alan said you might dig your heels in and make trouble for me, that you might need a little push. It's why I bought you those roses, and made you that bowl, I felt so bad,' she said, trying to defend herself.

'So, you did paint my door, what else did you do? Slash my portrait? Turn off the electricity and try to frighten me to death?' Linda bit her lip, her face pucer than I'd ever seen it. 'I bet you shared around that video too, didn't you, anything to ruin my reputation, my business, so you could take the studio. You know you really are a piece of work, Linda!' I spat, shoving past her and back into the building, rage propelling me along the corridor to my studio. She scurried behind me like a rat. 'Oh, and Alan doesn't exist. His name is Alfie; he's my neighbour and, clearly, he's as trustworthy as you are!'

'What?'

'You've been duped, Linda, as have I it seems, by everyone.' I threw the remaining items in my bag and checked the barren space before thrusting the keys at Linda's chest. 'Here you go, you're welcome to the place.'

I wanted to say more, but instead I held my head up high and marched out to my car. I wasn't about to lower myself to her level, scheming and manipulating to get what she wanted. This weekend I'd move back to my parents' permanently. The sooner I was away from here, the better.

My mood was still sour when I got back to the flat and wood chips were scattered on the carpet where Rick had split the door frame to get in. At least the frame had been fixed, the lock worked and the door was secure. Across the hall, no noise came from Alfie's flat. How long would it take them to release him? I didn't want to be around to find out, have some awkward confrontation outside my door, unsure whether to hug him or hit him.

I let myself in, freezing at the entrance to the lounge where Rick's blood had soaked into the carpet. The flat had been ransacked by him and rage poured through my veins like molten lava. It spurred me on, and I got busy, righting the furniture, scrubbing the bloodstains. I bleached the flat like it had been exposed to some contagious disease and didn't stop until my hands were red raw – a psychiatrist would have had a field day.

If I'd had any sage to light and waft around, I would have done that too. Once the entire place had been disinfected of Rick and Nathan's presence, I put things into a couple of boxes I had spare, the rest into piles ready for packing. I emptied the cupboards, throwing away anything I didn't want to take with me until three full bin bags sat by the front door. There was little point unloading what I had in the car, only to load it up again tomorrow, so I slumped on the sofa and called Mum.

41

Mum wanted me to FaceTime halfway through our call as I was telling her what happened last night, and once I explained how to get her to accept the video call, she gasped when she saw the state of my bruised face. The colour drained from her usually rosy cheeks; lips stretched to a thin line.

'I'll send Dad to come and pick you up. You need to come home, Abbi, where we can protect you.'

'Mum, it's fine, Rick is in hospital and as soon as he's discharged, he'll be taken to the police station, I'm safe. I'll come tomorrow, there's no point in leaving my car here.' I tried to reassure her and after fifteen minutes of convincing, she relented but still wasn't happy about me staying alone. It had been agreed Dad would come tomorrow morning because hopefully we could get most of my belongings in two cars and for the small amount of furniture I wanted to salvage, I'd have to hire a van.

I made do with beans on toast for dinner. The bread was past its best, but I didn't want to go out again. I had no idea when I'd bought the beans, but they were a welcome surprise when I'd emptied the cupboards. Outside, the afternoon was getting late and I'd intended to curl up in front of the television until I saw the giant crack down the middle of the screen, where Rick had knocked it onto the floor. There were scuffs on the paintwork too where he'd torn the place apart last night. With that and the door being fixed, there was no way I was getting my deposit back and I still had another two months on the lease, but I'd forgo the rent. Better to be happy and secure back with my parents than lonely and miserable here.

Without the TV, I had a soak in the bath instead, listening to calming music. Jade messaged checking I was okay and apologising about her mum being so offhand. I replied to say I was fine, moving back home tomorrow and left it at that. Our friendship was at a crossroads and I wasn't sure if things would be the same again, but I was glad she was safe.

When I got into bed, I slid my phone under the pillow and tried to sleep, but I kept hearing noises, hyperaware of sounds coming from elsewhere in the building. It was Friday night, which was always lively, being the start of the weekend. Usually, the activity didn't bother me, but every thump or bang sounded ominous and had me spooked.

It was a flash of light that woke me, the room illuminating for a split second as though a storm raged outside. I blinked through the gloom of my bedroom to see a figure sat at the end of the bed. I jerked upright, instinctively pulling the duvet up to my neck.

'It's okay, Abbi, it's me,' Alfie said, his phone in his hand. Had he just taken a picture of me sleeping? My tongue glued to the roof of my mouth, unable to speak, breath solid in my chest. 'Do you want to turn the lamp on?' His voice was soft and calm as though this was a normal situation.

I willed myself to move but was rigid beneath the covers, backed against the headboard.

'It's okay, I'll do it.' Alfie rose from the end of the bed and I slid my hand under the pillow for my phone. I keyed in the code to unlock it, trying to navigate to the keypad so I could dial 999.

After a click, the bedside lamp came on and I squinted as the room was suddenly bathed in a warm glow. Alfie smiled, thankfully moving back to the end of the bed. Like mine, his pale face was bruised, a scab forming where Rick had split his lip.

'You look a fright.' He frowned. 'Are you in pain?'

I nodded, trying to stay calm, although inside I was freaking out. What on earth was he doing here, in my bedroom. How had he got in?

'Let me get you some more painkillers, I saw some in the kitchen.' Alfie got up and I quickly keyed my code to open my phone again, pulling up my recent calls. I was about to move to the keypad to dial the police, but Officer Barrett's mobile phone number was the second one down, below Mum. I tapped it, turning the volume off, snapping my head up as Alfie returned with a glass of water and packet of ibuprofen. He set it on the table and perched on the edge of the bed, closer this time, and it took all my strength not to shrivel away from him. A citrus scent wafted around him and I could see his hair was damp, he must have recently showered.

'It's okay, Abbi, I mean you no harm. I just wanted to make sure you were okay.' He patted my knee, and I flinched beneath the duvet.

'When did they let you out?' When I finally spoke, my voice was scratchy.

'Late yesterday afternoon. I had to go to a court hearing; they charged me with ABH, if you can believe it. My solicitor thinks it'll be dismissed, but at least I was given bail.'

'But how did you get in here?' I swallowed the lump in my throat.

'Ah, I'm sorry about that,' he grimaced. 'I've had Rick's key for a while, he left it in the door the day you ran up to the roof. Lucky for me, they fixed the frame and didn't replace the lock, but we probably should still get them changed.'

My head got stuck on the word 'we' and I glanced at the door, knowing there was no way I'd get to it before him.

'Alfie, I'm leaving, I'm moving back to my parents.'

'I saw the boxes, but there's no need to do that. I'm here.' He was delusional, talking to me like I was some fragile bird who'd broken its wing. One he was intent on nursing back to health. Seemingly having no idea how unsettling his behaviour was.

'You helped Linda, you forced me out of the studio!' I blurted, the cortisol rocketing around my system, spurring me to life. He pursed his lips, shoulders climbing up around his ears as the mood shifted.

'How can you be so ungrateful, Abbi? Linda used to badmouth you all the time, you needed to get out of there and I found you somewhere perfect, close to where I work. I just want to be with you all the time.'

I stared at Alfie, open-mouthed.

'I did it all for you. I got rid of Rick and your cheating friend; I exposed them. Without me, you'd still be with that arsehole. He's brazenly slept with so many women behind your back, he has no morals, Abbi! When I recognised you on that website, I couldn't believe he could put you on there. Admittedly, it wasn't for long, but I watched that video time and again.'

I choked back a sob, praying Officer Barrett was listening to this, that he'd send help because Alfie was mad, obsessed even. He'd admitted his part in the whole thing. He was the watcher but instead of relief at his unmasking, I pressed my knees together, pulsing with revulsion as I imagined him watching me and Rick, planning to have me for himself.

'You can move in with me, we'll look for somewhere new. A new flat and a new studio, a fresh start. I love you, Abbi, I knew that from the first moment I saw you.'

'How can you love me? You humiliated me, you sent that video to all my followers, you created the fake Abbi accounts.'

'It was a barely a ten-second clip and it was necessary. You needed to hate him; you were blinkered to what sort of man he was.' The muscles in his jaw throbbed with agitation and he curled his fingers around the duvet, squeezing it until the blood left his knuckles.

'So why didn't you just tell me, point me to the website and let me go to the police?'

'I had to take them down first, use the website against them.' He ran a hand through his hair. 'I guess I thought you might see me as a knight in shining armour, someone you could rely on. I'm the only one you can trust, not Rick, not your best friend.' He paused to sigh, shaking his head. 'I wanted to ask you out, yet you never seemed to notice me, not really. You were polite, stopping to speak when we bumped into each other, but you didn't want to be friends.'

I blinked, remembering the innocent chats we'd had, the occasions we'd come out of our flats at the same time, talking about the weather or work. Had those been staged? Had he fitted a door camera so he could watch me come and go, timing him leaving to make sure we interacted?

'I asked you for a coffee or a drink three times, but you always had an excuse, you were too busy for me. I had to do something,' Alfie continued, making me squirm.

'Have you been in the flat before?' Realisation hit, I knew the answer before Alfie uttered a word.

He became animated, frustration leaking out of every pore. 'I've done nothing wrong. I've taken care of you, left you gifts, bought you shopping, even filled your car up with petrol.'

My mouth gaped, all the times I'd thought I was losing the plot and it was

Alfie sneaking in and out as though he lived here too. Knowing he'd been in the flat while I'd been sleeping made my skin crawl.

'Even now you don't appreciate it.' He scowled at my horrified expression, flexing his fingers of the arm that had supposedly been broken.

'You didn't get mugged either, did you?'

Alfie's face lifted and he smiled knowingly. 'You're one smart cookie, Abbi. No, my arm is fine, but I wanted you to grasp the severity of the situation, you had to take those emails seriously.'

'You wanted me to think my life was in danger?' I swallowed the incredulity like a bitter pill.

'I wanted you to dump Rick. We all got hurt in this, some more than others.' He pointed to the skin around his eye which was now a dull yellow. It chilled my core that he was crazy enough to bash his own face in, pretending he'd been mugged, and for what – so I'd feel sorry for him?

With each of the pieces slowly coming together, more questions popped into my mind. 'How did you get the photo off my phone, the one you posted of Rick?'

'You sat in front of me and logged into your laptop, all your photos are on the cloud. When you were viewing the website on my machine, in my flat, I had yours remember, to put the VPN on. I saw the photo you'd taken, and I took it, made a little addition I knew would be the nail in the coffin for his employers, and posted it. I thought you'd be happy. You told me to destroy him! He's going to prison, Abbi; he can't hurt you or anyone else anymore.'

'*You* hurt me! You stalked me, Alfie, can't you see that? You sent me threatening messages, texts, I thought I was being followed, that someone was out to get me.'

'Maybe I went too far, but I wanted you to come to me and ask for help, and you did, so it worked.' He really was off his rocker, gazing at me like some love-struck teenager.

The silence grew thick and I tried a different tack, softening my tone, hoping to talk some sense into him.

'Alfie, you can't force someone to fall in love with you, that's not how it works.'

'Well, I tried the normal route, but it's all in the past now, Abbi, don't you see, they're gone. Rick and Nathan will go to prison, Jade was never a friend to you and Linda, well, she was only ever interested in herself. You have me, we can build something together. Let me take care of you.' Alfie reached over and grasped my hand before I could snatch it away. His palm was clammy, eyes wide boring into mine, his touch causing bolts of repulsion around my body.

He'd had access to everything, my flat, my car, my social media, emails and photos, smearing himself all over my life without me knowing, infecting everything.

'So, you were a subscriber to the website, that's how you knew I was on there, how you recognised Rick and Jade.'

'You've got photos of Jade on your bookshelf and I'd seen you with Rick, I hadn't expected to watch a video of the pair of them together.'

'And the website, is that why you lied about your name, to me, to Linda?'

He shrugged. 'I didn't want you to find out I was on there, or that I'd been to the pottery class, it was just an excuse to get closer to you.'

'But that website, Alfie,' I said, a tear rolling down my cheek, 'it's awful.'

'It's just porn, everyone watches it.'

There it was again; the same excuse Nathan had given me, as if it was a prerequisite to being a man. Something he'd probably told his wife, only she'd had the foresight to run for the hills before his madness could escape.

Alfie wouldn't meet my eye and my stomach rolled.

I'd been on that site, maybe when Rick and I first got together. Perhaps Rick was telling the truth, that when his feelings for me had grown, he'd taken the video down, not wanting to share me. I glared at Alfie with as much disgust as I could muster yet was glued to the bed. He was unpredictable and I had to be careful with my words. The depths of his infatuation terrified me, it had led him down some dark paths already, but how much further was he willing to go to get what he wanted?

42

I inhaled deeply through my nose, trying to keep my voice level.

'I'm sorry, Alfie, but I'm leaving Crawley. You need to give me the key back and go home, you can't come in and out of my space when you feel like it. It's not okay.'

Alfie laughed, as if I was being silly or overreacting and it was like the spark to a rocket. Making sure the phone was hidden beneath the pillow, I swung the covers over my legs and stood to walk out of the bedroom. He caught me by the wrist, yanking me towards him, and I stumbled, half on the bed, half on his lap. 'You're beautiful when you're angry.' He brushed my hair away from my face. 'I know we haven't had the most conventional start, but it'll be so good, trust me.'

I tried to resist as he cupped my head and pulled me in for a kiss, squashing his moist lips against mine. His erection poked my thigh and I struggled to wriggle out from his grip as he manoeuvred his weight on top of me, forcing me down on the mattress.

'Alfie, stop!' I whimpered as he kissed my neck after turning my face away.

'I love you, Abbi,' he breathed into my hair.

My nightdress was flimsy and I shuddered as his hand gently grazed the fabric. His breath was laboured, too carried away in the moment he thought we were enjoying together. I needed to reach him, make him understand I didn't want this, that he wasn't like Rick or Nathan.

'Alfie, don't do this, you're better than them.'

He froze, as though I'd finally penetrated him with my words, his weight crushing me, and the seconds stretched out. My body was rigid as I waited for him to do the right thing. Eventually, he lifted himself up and I slid out beneath him, rushing out of the bedroom, straight into the chest of Officer Barrett.

'Where is he?'

I didn't have time to respond because he moved me aside, whipped out his baton and confronted Alfie.

'Alfie Stockton, you're under arrest for sexual assault.'

My head whipped around, sexual assault?

'Wait, what?' Alfie raised his palms. 'There must be a mistake.'

Officer Barrett handcuffed and read him his rights. Alfie looked at me, eyes pleading his innocence, before another man in uniform led him away.

'What's going on?' I asked.

'Thank God you called me – although you should have dialled 999,' Officer Barrett berated. He looked tired, the shadows stretched out beneath his eyes.

'You're arresting him for sexual assault? I mean, if you'd been any longer, he might have but—'

'Did he hurt you?' Officer Barrett interrupted.

I wrapped my arms around myself, exposed in the nightdress. 'No, not really, he got a bit amorous and I'm glad you're here, but sexual assault?'

'Not you. Footage on that camera has him assaulting an unconscious female.'

Officer Barrett's words made me double over and I crouched to the floor, palms flat to the carpet as though I'd taken a blow to the stomach. Alfie wasn't just a stalker; he was a rapist? I let the words sink in, bile rising in my throat.

'Do you have someone I can call for you?'

'No, no, I'll be fine, just give me a minute,' I replied weakly. I was anything but fine. How could I have got it wrong both times? How could Rick, Alfie and Nathan all be monsters? I wasn't sure I'd be able to trust another man again.

I looked up at Officer Barrett, his somewhat haggard face and the stubble protruding from his chin. They weren't all predators, some were protectors, I had to remember that. He held out his rough hand and I took it, allowing myself to be pulled upright.

'Thank you,' I said and he shrugged, like it was a normal day on the job. 'I mean it, thank you for following it up, for coming out tonight.'

I saw a splash of pink bloom on his cheeks, but he simply nodded.

'If you recorded that phone call, then you'll have heard Alfie admit he posted the video, he's been stalking me all this time.'

'I heard, it'll make for an interesting interview when we get to the station. I'd say his solicitor is going to be pretty upset to get his call tonight.'

Despite all that had happened, I laughed, welcoming Officer Barrett's injection of humour.

'I better get back, but I'll be in touch,' he said before giving me a salute and walking out of the flat. 'And you'll need to get that door fixed again!' his voice boomed as he descended the stairs. My door had been kicked in for the second time in two days, but I didn't have the energy to leave. I dragged a chair and propped it beneath the door handle. It wasn't perfect, but by the time I'd stacked all my saucepans on top like a game of cookware Jenga, if I had another visitor in the middle of the night at least I'd be alerted. It wasn't like I was going to sleep anyway. After tonight I might never sleep again.

EPILOGUE
FOUR MONTHS LATER

I wrapped up another commission, securing the bubble wrap with Sellotape before stacking what I'd have to post this afternoon on my desk. A trickle of sweat descended my spine and my hair, wisps of it stuck to my neck. The new studio was like a sweatbox in the mid-July heatwave, and I propped open the door to allow the breeze in.

Summer had well and truly arrived after what had seemed like weeks of grey skies, and I was here for it. The studio, found by my mum, was perfect with plenty of natural light and, after some negotiation on rent, I'd signed a six-month rolling lease. With a bit of help from my dad, a few tins of paint and new flooring, it became homely, somewhere I could be inspired, and new orders were coming in every day. If it carried on, I'd have to set up a waiting list as I wouldn't be able to keep up with the demand, but it was a wonderful problem to have.

The press coverage of the 'Brothers Grim', as they'd been dubbed, had thankfully been minimal and I was still relatively anonymous. One magazine had published an article, portraying me as a pseudo-Miss Marple, who'd discovered my boyfriend's dark scheme to make money. There had been a lot of backlash since towards the police and demand to raise awareness on women for sale, human trafficking and revenge porn where my name was sometimes tagged in the outrage on social media. Eventually after a few weeks, it had blown over and surprisingly, instead of Edgewater sinking, the commissions of my portraits steadily rose.

A week after the incident, Officer Barrett had visited me at my parents', where I'd been taking sanctuary, grateful to be out of Crawley and all the gossip doing the rounds. I'd braced myself as we'd sat at the table, each with a cup of tea, expecting to be delivered awful news, but, as it turned out, the videos recovered directly from the camera weren't of me. One night while Rick was out Nathan had used his flat for an impromptu live stream before Todd had crept in and taken the camera he'd left on display. He'd sent a mailshot to all the members of www.watchmefuck.com and Alfie had paid his fee to watch Nathan have sex with a drugged Elena.

Officer Barrett had told me that when the cyber team had downloaded the chats attached to the live stream, Alfie had offered more money to come to the flat so he could have his turn, knowing Rick lived close by. It had been more money than Nathan was willing to turn down and with Rick out, he'd figured why not make a little cash on the side just for him.

What Alfie hadn't realised was, even though the live stream had finished, the camera, which worked on motion, had still been recording. Elena was unconscious when Alfie had his two minutes of fun, the money exchanged hands and Rick on his return was none the wiser. Elena had woken up with what she'd thought was the mother of all hangovers after Nathan took her home. Officer Barrett's discovery sickened me and the saliva turned to acid in my mouth, the only comfort being that Nathan and Alfie were going to go down for a long time. With the evidence mounting against them, both had pleaded guilty, and Nathan had already turned on his brother, citing him as the mastermind behind the scheme in the hope of a lesser sentence.

Rick was as slippery as a snake. The police had so far managed to identify only one of the women he'd been with and, in interview, she'd admitted to consenting to sex, but, like Jade, was unaware she was being filmed. So far, Rick had been charged with voyeurism, revenge pornography and sharing intimate films on a public platform. It wasn't illegal to own a pornographic website, but because it did not have a robust age verification in place to prevent access by children, his assets had been seized and he would likely be bankrupted by a hefty fine. Nathan and Alfie would go on the sex offenders register and Rick could too, if any of the victims in Officer Barrett's search denied consent. He'd told me, in confidence, he suspected that they'd each get around ten years inside for the multitude of crimes but he was seeking the maximum penalty on all current charges.

Due to the nature of the case and the extreme distress caused to the women Rick filmed, he had been remanded in custody after a short stint in hospital. He'd written me a long letter apologising for his behaviour, citing me as the reason he'd wanted to stop making content for the website and hand the reins over to his brother. His words and actions, when we'd last seen each other, were those of a desperate man, he'd written, and he really had wanted to settle down. Ultimately, his downfall was how motivated he was by money and, again, he referenced his poor upbringing, using that as his excuse for chasing wealth. Once the money from the website had started pouring in, with thousands of subscribers paying thirty-seven pounds each, converted from dollars, in individual subscription fees, he couldn't stop. He wrote that whatever happened, he was sorry and that I had no reason to fear him, and if I could find it in my heart to visit so he could tell me that face to face, it would bring him hope.

I'd burnt the letter, sickened he hadn't bothered to mention any of the women he'd groomed, filmed and potentially raped. Rick was the most self-involved man I'd ever met, hiding beneath the exterior of a loving, kind boyfriend. He'd certainly pulled the wool over my eyes and it seemed, after speculation from those that knew him, he'd done the same with them too. I'd been assigned a family liaison officer initially, who'd suggested therapy to help me work through some of the many conflicting emotions I had about Rick, and Alfie, as well as the guilt I carried for not seeing behind their masks. So far it was helping.

Officer Barrett had wished me well, letting me know I could get in touch whenever I needed to. I shook his calloused hand and walked him to the door, knowing I wouldn't have closure until Alfie, Nathan and Rick were sentenced. Despite that, my parents had been amazing in helping me heal, telling me I could stay with them as long as I liked. I'd paid the remaining rent on my flat in Crawley and was looking for somewhere of my own, in Wallington. All of us were excited at the prospect of a week in Turkey next month to visit Ben. A holiday would be just what I needed because even being in a different county, I'd struggled to shake the sensation of eyes on me wherever I went; Alfie's stalking had affected me more than I realised.

But I felt safe being back where Ben and I grew up and I'd even reconnected with one of my old school friends, Leila, who taught art at the local college. She'd been pestering me to run an evening portrait class for some of her existing students and I was considering it. I missed Jade's wild personality and was slower to trust now, but Leila and I had been out a few times and I was enjoying our blossoming friendship. She was different, more spiritual and calmer than Jade, but it was nice to have someone my own age to socialise with.

Jade and I had exchanged a few messages, mainly about the investigation, but she was doing well, having transferred to Brighton ambulance centre, where she found her reputation hadn't followed. She'd suggested meeting up and I was considering it once the whole thing wasn't so raw. I was surprised to learn Elena had been in touch with her, trying to get her to speak out, like she had on Nathan, being another victim of the 'Brothers Grim', but Jade had declined. Elena was campaigning for longer sentences on voyeurism and sexual assault and I wished her luck. She was happy being in the public eye, whereas Jade and I wanted to remain as anonymous as possible.

I'd stopped using all social media except for the Instagram Edgewater account and was better for it. My world was more secure, I had no online hate or sleezy messages, no journalists trying to get in touch to tell my story. Life was private again, just as I liked it, and despite Leila's protests, the wall I'd since built around myself was impenetrable. I'd never let anyone hurt me again, and as for men, I wasn't in a rush to find someone new. If it was going to happen, I wanted it to be natural and real. It would be hard to trust, so whoever he was, he'd have to be patient, but that was okay. I was concentrating on my business and making myself happy and that meant staying out of the limelight because I'd learnt the hard way, you never really knew who was watching.

* * *

MORE FROM GEMMA ROGERS

Another book from Gemma Rogers is available to order now here:
https://mybook.to/NewRogersBackAd

ACKNOWLEDGEMENTS

As always, thank you to Caroline Ridding, my brilliant editor, and the entire Boldwood Team who have made my publishing journey a fantastic experience. I can't believe I've been on this ride, coming into my seventh year. I hope it never ends.

A massive thank you to Adam and Kayleigh Kick, who were on standby to help me out with some legality fine-tuning, I really appreciate you responding to my random messages sometimes without context of 'what would happen if...'

For Mum, my first reader, because 'this one wasn't scary', it's so nice to have you demanding more chapters. It means I know I'm on the right track.

Jade Craddock, my excellent copyeditor, who never fails to elevate my book into something quite magical, I applaud your meticulous eye for detail; thank you so much. Same to Shirley, my lovely proofreader, who always spots something I've missed!

To my lovely husband who is so supportive and always cheering for me from the sidelines. I wouldn't want to do this with anyone else. Bethany and Lucy, thanks for explaining all the slang that kids use these days and for making me smile when I'm deep in editing hell. I'm so lucky to be your mum.

Lastly, and most importantly, an enormous thank you to my readers. Without you coming back time and again to pick up my latest book, pre-ordering and leaving reviews, I'd be lost. Thank you for continuing to spread the word, it still amazes me that people read what I write. If I'd have told fifteen-year-old me, who loved my English GCSE lessons (but found Thomas Hardy boring), that one day I'd be published, she'd have been ecstatic. Thanks for making my dreams come true.

ABOUT THE AUTHOR

Gemma Rogers was inspired to write gritty thrillers by a traumatic event in her past. Her debut novel *Stalker*, released in 2019, marked the beginning of her writing career. Gemma lives in West Sussex with her husband and two daughters.

Download your exclusive bonus content from Gemma Rogers here:

Follow Gemma on social media:

facebook.com/GemmaRogersAuthor
x.com/gemmarogers79
bookbub.com/authors/gemma-rogers
instagram.com/gemmarogersauthor
tiktok.com/@gemmarogersauthor

ALSO BY GEMMA ROGERS

Stalker

The Secret

The Teacher

The Mistake

The Babysitter

The Feud

The Neighbour

The Flatmate

The Good Wife

The Honeymoon

The Night Shift

The Stranger at No.6

The Girlfriend

THE Murder LIST

THE MURDER LIST IS A NEWSLETTER DEDICATED TO SPINE-CHILLING FICTION AND GRIPPING PAGE-TURNERS!

SIGN UP TO MAKE SURE YOU'RE ON OUR HIT LIST FOR EXCLUSIVE DEALS, AUTHOR CONTENT, AND COMPETITIONS.

SIGN UP TO OUR NEWSLETTER

BIT.LY/THEMURDERLISTNEWS

Boldwood

Boldwood Books is an award-winning fiction publishing company seeking out the best stories from around the world.

Find out more at www.boldwoodbooks.com

Join our reader community for brilliant books, competitions and offers!

Follow us
@BoldwoodBooks
@TheBoldBookClub

Sign up to our weekly deals newsletter

https://bit.ly/BoldwoodBNewsletter

www.ingramcontent.com/pod-product-compliance
Lightning Source LLC
Chambersburg PA
CBHW011949150426
43194CB00018B/2849